FAIRY TALE RAILROAD

The Mohawk and Malone.
From the Mohawk, through the Adirondacks
to the St. Lawrence

By
HENRY A. HARTER

North Country Books, Inc.
Utica, New York

ISBN 0-932052-97-5

FIRST EDITION 1979
FIRST PAPERBACK EDITION 1992

North Country Books, Inc.
18 Irving Place
Utica, New York 13501

Dedicated to my wife
Grace

PREFACE

This history of the Mohawk and Malone Railway is the outgrowth of my collecting information about the railroad for my own enjoyment. As the material accumulated, it was easy for the idea to form that there might be others who would like to read about Dr. W. Seward Webb's "Fairy Tale Railroad" or as some folks like to call it the "Golden Chariot Route."

The search for material led to many gracious persons whom I can now call friends and that in itself is very rewarding. I extend my thanks to everyone who assisted me in my research and I hope that I have not overlooked anyone.

In particular, I must pay special tribute to my sister, Mrs. Ernest Blue, to F. Ray McKnight and to Edward P. Baumgardner.

Mildred Blue was able to supply many unique items pertaining to the history of the Adirondack & St. Lawrence Railway and its successors and, at the same time, lend a great deal of support to me in my research.

F. Ray McKnight, the son of an Adirondack Division railroader, spent his youth near the railroad and worked on the division for several years before transferring to a downstate branch of the New York Central.

His familiarity with the physical aspects of the Adirondack Division, along with his knowledge of operating procedures, were called upon many times and his answers were always lucid and based on fact.

I am also grateful for the many photos that Ray McKnight provided. The pictures were well dated and much pertinent information accompanied each one.

Edward Baumgardner has been a student of railroad history for a number of years and he was able to supply several documents that would have otherwise been unattainable.

During the research period, Ed Baumgardner made many valuable suggestions and posed some very interesting questions that received their deserved attention.

I should also like to acknowledge the assistance and counsel given to me by Richard F. Palmer, William F. Helmer and Michael Kudish. There is a list in one of the appendices of those who have been of great help to me. There are many others who contributed in some degree to the overall research and to them, also, I extend my appreciation.

Believing that notes and footnotes can be as distracting as they are valuable, I have endeavored to indicate the source of my information as it is used and I hope that the readers will enjoy this method.

Henry A. Harter
Hamilton, New York
August 1979

CREDITS

It is through the cooperation and assistance of the following that this book was made possible. Heartfelt thanks is extended to each and every one of them.

Edward P. Baumgardner
Mrs. Ethel Belknap
Mrs. Mildred H. Blue
Bruce M. Brown
Clifford Butterfield*
Edward Comstock
R. Brownell Dana
Mrs. Margaret P. Davis
Mr. and Mrs. Ellis Denio
Frank G. Dugan
William D. Edson
John A. Fitch
Linus Ford
Eugene Gadway
Michael D. Gieryic
William F. Helmer
Albert A. Hess
Mrs. Lucy Howe
David M. Hunt
Mrs. Floy S. Hyde
Robert B. Igoe
Leon Johnson
Sheldon S. King

Michael Kudish
Gordon R. Lyons
Mrs. Mary MacKenzie
David Mahler
Edward L. May
F. Ray McKnight
Joseph Mercier
Timothy O'Connor
Richard F. Palmer
Douglas Preston
Eugene Rando
Miss Helen Schermerhorn
Miss Marcia Smith*
Mrs. Jane Spellman
William Szymko
Edward S. Tattershall
Richard Tucker
J. Watson Webb, Jr.
Frank H. Weber
Kenneth E. Wheeling
Sumner Wickwire
Luke Wood

*To their memory

MUSEUMS

    Adirondack — Blue Mountain Lake, N.Y.

    Franklin County Historical and Museum Society — Malone, N.Y.

    Herkimer County Historical Society — Herkimer, N.Y.

    Oneida Historical Society — Utica, N.Y.

    Railway Historical Society of Northern New York — Brownsville, N.Y.

    Shelburne — Shelburne, Vt.

LIBRARIES

    Adirondack Museum — Blue Mountain Lake, N.Y.

    Burke — Hamilton College — Clinton, N.Y.

    Case — Colgate University — Hamilton, N.Y.

    Hamilton Public — Hamilton, N.Y.

    Herkimer County Historical Society — Herkimer, N.Y.

    Morrisville Agricultural and Technical College, SUNY — Morrisville, N.Y.

    Shelburne Museum — Shelburne, Vt.

    Goff-Nelson Memorial — Tupper Lake, N.Y.

    Gannett — Utica College — Utica, N.Y.

    Utica Public — Utica, N.Y.

CONTENTS

CHAPTER I
The Hopeful Years

From the time of the first settlement in what is now the Mohawk Valley of New York State, the vast area to the north became a matter of deep concern to those living near the river. In early years the northland was the avenue of the Indian raiders who caused death and desolation throughout the settled area. Particularly violent were the raids during the French and Indian Wars and the American Revolution and it was only in the last decades of the 18th century that peace of any duration came to the Mohawk Valley area.

With the fear of war behind them, it was not long before the inhabitants began to look to the north country with ideas of transportation and travel through to the St. Lawrence River basin. Relatively few years later, in 1817, construction of the Erie Canal was started in the area where it was possible to utilize the Mohawk River. Hardly had this project been completed in 1825 before thoughts were directed to the opening of the north country by means of lateral canals.

However, the opening of the Liverpool and Manchester Railway in England in 1829 gave tremendous impetus to the planning and building of railroads throughout the world. In 1826 the Mohawk & Hudson Railroad Company was chartered by the New York State Legislature and it was organized to build a railroad from Albany to Schenectady, a distance of approximately 17 miles. The construction was completed in 1831 and the railroad was opened for use. Just what this engendered is indicated in the chartering of the "Black River Company" by an act of the legislature on April 17, 1832. This company was created to build a railroad or canal from the Erie Canal at Rome or Herkimer or at any intermediate point to the St. Lawrence River. Nothing tangible resulted in this undertaking.

Speaking before the Herkimer County Historical Society on November 10, 1900, Robert Earl of Herkimer said:

> For many years after 1830, repeated efforts were made to penetrate the Adirondack region with canals or railroads and to connect the St. Lawrence River with the Mohawk Valley. These efforts seem to have

1

been made by men who had no adequate knowledge of the difficulties to be surmounted and hence their schemes were generally impractical and abortive. It is only in recent years, that with better knowledge and more ample means the early schemes, which were then little more than dreams, have been carried to practical success.

In 1836 an act was passed to provide for the construction of a railroad from Herkimer to Trenton and in 1837 a company was chartered to build a railroad from Trenton to Sacketts Harbor. No construction followed in either case but the Herkimer-Trenton endeavor will be discussed later. Several attempts were made to penetrate the mountains from the southeastern fringe and also from Lake Champlain. The only one of these that resulted in construction was the Adirondack Company which reached North Creek in 1871 and what eventually became the Chateaugay Railroad which reached Saranac Lake in 1887.

Towards the end of 1852 and in early 1853 there was a determined effort put forth to build a railroad from French Creek (Clayton) to the Mohawk Valley. Although the proponents from Herkimer made a valiant effort to locate the southern terminal in their community, the railroad was eventually built north from Utica as the Utica and Black River Railroad. This, of course, was later extended northwards but skirted the west side of the Adirondacks.

The New York, Utica & Ogdensburg Railroad Company was organized in 1870 to build north through the West Canada Creek valley eventually reaching the St. Lawrence River at Ogdensburg. Very little work was done on this projected road before the project was abandoned.

As mentioned earlier The Herkimer and Trenton Rail Road was formed in 1836 to construct a railroad from The Erie Canal at Herkimer to Trenton. Timothy B. Jervis, Civil Engineer, made a survey of the route and on February 1, 1837 submitted his report to the Commissioners of the Herkimer and Trenton Rail Road.

CHAPTER II
The Narrow Gauge

The route surveyed by Timothy B. Jervis for the Herkimer and Trenton Rail Road followed the valley of the West Canada Creek through its whole length, from Herkimer to Trenton. The line surveyed commenced on the Erie Canal at the old Mohawk bridge, a short distance east of the village of Mohawk. It followed the common road to its intersection with the Utica and Schenectady railroad near the center of the village of Herkimer. It was then proposed to build the railroad on Main Street in Herkimer, turning north at Trenton Road (presently German Street) and follow the west side of the West Canada Creek to Middleville. At that point the creek was to be crossed and the road laid on the east side through Newport and Poland to the Russia-Trenton bridge where the creek was to be crossed again. The road was to follow the west bank until Steuben Creek was reached and there it crossed the latter near its mouth and followed it along to the village of Trenton where the railroad was to terminate near Case's tavern. The projected length was 26.9 miles and it ascended 388 feet. The estimated cost was $175,151.92.

Engineer Jervis concluded his report by saying:

> Permit me to state that the fertility of the valley of the West Canada Creek, and almost unlimited extent of water power, and the facility of using the same which it presents; together with the increased means of access to the beautiful and romantic scenery in the vicinity of Trenton Village, which the construction of the proposed railroad would offer, present inducements for investment in the stock of your road, which, should not, and doubtless will not be overlooked by capitalists.

Even if Jervis was taken by the beauty of Trenton Falls and correctly assessed its romantic loveliness and attraction it apparently was not enough to cause the Herkimer and Trenton Rail Road Commissioners to be convinced that the rail road should be built. The project simmered for more than forty years before it underwent revivification.

Thomas W. Spencer of Utica, an engineer, was instrumental in the resurgence of the proposition to build a railroad north from Herkimer. In 1879 he interested many residents of the villages of Herkimer, Middleville, Newport and Poland in the possibilities of building a narrow gauge railroad. One of those particularly enthused over the idea was Major Edward M. Burns of Middleville.

The project came near to abandonment in June 1880. Difficulty was encountered in the lack of subscriptions in Poland so it was decided to have the terminus at Newport. This did not produce the desired result and for a while it looked like the "people living along the West Canada Creek, between Herkimer and Poland had failed to avail themselves of one of the grandest opportunities they have ever had to secure a railroad up this beautiful and thriving valley." This newspaper report proved to be premature and someone persisted in his efforts to persuade the inhabitants of the area that too much was at stake to completely give up the idea, because construction work was started within the next month and Poland was to be the northern terminus.

The route laid out and followed by the Herkimer, Newport and Poland Narrow Gauge Railway was to start from the eastern end of the Village of Herkimer in proximity to the New York Central and Hudson River Railroad and proceed north from that point. It roughly followed the line of Jervis' survey of 1836–37 until it reached Middleville and north of there it crossed the West Canada Creek and recrossed it so that it came into Newport on the west side of the West Canada. It was therefore necessary that it again cross the creek to reach Poland and it did so at the southern boundary of the village.

The NEWPORT WEEKLY ADVERTISER on January 7, 1882 reprinted an article which it attributed to the UTICA HERALD:

> The route is a most picturesque one. Right here might be mentioned the difficult engineering that was required in surveying, locating and building the road. The West Canada Creek valley is a very narrow and exceedingly tortuous one. The stream is the most rapid and difficult to cross and contend with, of any in this section of the state. It has long been a very leviathan to railroad engineers. It was the first intention to cross this creek four times before reaching Newport. But at the suggestion of Judge Earl, the line was altered to run around what is known as the lower dugway, a beautiful and precipitous bank around which the creek runs. The view from the cars at this point is fine, and furnishes a splendid opportunity for the genius of a Church or a Bierstadt. By the adoption of the suggestion of Judge Earl, two bridges were avoided, thus cheapening greatly the cost of construction and maintenance. The next engineering exploit was in the dugway just above. Here tons of

hard pan were taken away, a substantial stone wall was constructed and the railroad built on this wall between the creek and the road. A long, high, board fence separates the ordinary road from the railroad. Thousands of dollars have been expended on these dugways and the road bed is now considered strong and firm.

This routing of the railroad via two dugways, one between Kast's Bridge and Dempster's Bridge and the other between Dempster's Bridge and Countryman's may have saved two bridges but it would appear that the fallacy of having a lawyer select a railroad route was never more evident than in this case. For nearly all of the years of the railroad's existence, the dugways presented problems. There were many mud and rock slides, some of a serious nature such as the one on March 27, 1893 in which the engineer, Charles Bassett, was severely injured. In fact, it was this interruption of service which caused the permanent shifting of the southern terminal of the Mohawk and Malone Railway passenger trains from Herkimer to Utica, the trains being switched over at Remsen.

The hazardous conditon persisted until the later 1960's when the creek bed, the highway and the railroad were all relocated and the dangers permanently eliminated. Unfortunately the railroad service was abandoned just a few years later and at the present time (1978) this section of relocated roadbed is probably the best section of line on the whole Mohawk and Malone right-of-way. Now it awaits the dismantlers who were reported to have started working north from Herkimer in 1977.

There were two certificates of incorporation of the Herkimer, Newport and Poland Narrow Gauge Railway Company filed with the Secretary of State. One was dated on December 18th, 1879 and the other on July 8th, 1880. According to the report for 1880 by the State Engineers and Surveyors, the road was chartered on June 29, 1880. It was projected to run from Herkimer to Poland, a distance of sixteen and one half miles. The original amount of capital stock authorized by the charter was $88,000.00.

The first directors were: Thomas W. Spencer of Utica; John W. Vrooman, Warner Miller and William Smith of Herkimer; Edward M. Burns, George H. Thomas and Wallace W. Mosher of Middleville; Henry R. Burlingame, Henry W. Dexter and Newell Morey of Newport; Stephen R. Millington, Warren A. Brayton and John Hemstreet of Poland. The president was Thomas W. Spencer and he was also the chief engineer. George H. Thomas was the secretary and treasurer.

Edward M. Burns was a businessman who had served in the Civil

War and in 1867 went to Middleville. Henry W. Dexter was a farmer and later a dealer in livestock and produce. He resided in Newport and during construction of the railroad he was referred to as the superintendent. William Smith was a Herkimer banker. The three locomotives of the Herkimer, Newport and Poland Narrow Gauge Railway were named for Messrs. Burns (No. 1), Dexter (No. 2) and Smith (No. 3).

The "Newport Advertiser" on July 2, 1881 gave the following account of the first annual meeting of the railway company:

> President Spencer reported in part as follows: That the Engineers began work July 7, 1880, and that the work of grading was commenced August 8, 1880; that the right of way has been secured in every instance save two; that about one mile of the road has been graded from Poland south; that from Newport to the point where the road crosses the West Canada Creek, the road is mostly completed and that the work at the Fishing Rocks near Middleville, which is quite difficult is progressing favorably; that between Middleville and Herkimer the grading is substantially complete, and the track laid to Kast's Bridge; that one locomotive, eight freight cars, and two service cars have been delivered, and an engine house and water tank built at Herkimer; that connection has been made with the New York Central and Hudson River Railroad.

The railway was completed to Middleville on September 6, 1881. Certainly this was an amazing amount of construction for the first year of work considering that all of the work was done by manual labor and the use of horses for grading. Later mention is made of the use of "steam drills" particularly at the Fishing Rocks area near Middleville.

The Herkimer-Middleville road was put into operation immediately following its opening on September 6, 1881, with two trains each way daily. The schedule called for 40 minutes for the nearly nine miles and the fare was set at 45 cents.

George A. Hardin in his HISTORY OF HERKIMER COUNTY stated that the railroad shops were located in Middleville. He also said that Frank M. Molineaux of Middleville did all of the painting for the railroad.

Edward M. Burns was associated with the railroad from its inception and he continued to hold various positions for many years as the railroad grew. He was born in Albany and served in the Civil War. In 1867 he married Miss Mary Thomas and came to Middleville. There he joined partnership with his brother-in-law, George H. Thomas, and continued the business of tanning calf skins which had been carried on by his wife's grandfather, father and brother.

Middleville had a population of about 750 at the time the railroad reached there. The main industries were the tannery and the W. W. Montgomery Cotton Mills.

On October 4, 1881 it was announced that Thomas W. Spencer had resigned as President and Chief Engineer. Edward M. Burns was chosen president and it was understood that he had purchased Mr. Spencer's stock at the rate of seventy-five cents on the dollar. Albert Wilber became the chief engineer.

Sadness filled the Kuyahoora Valley on November 23rd, 1881 because the first fatal accident on the railroad occurred at Middleville. Irving H. Griswold, the conductor, suffered injuries which caused his death in a short time. At the time he was coupling cars and was crushed between them. He was an extremely well known man. Prior to his employment by the railroad he had the contract for carrying mail by stage from Herkimer to Gray, via Middleville, Newport, Poland and Cold Brook.

Mr. Griswold was also an active volunteer fireman and nearly 100 members of the Herkimer fire companies attended his funeral. They along with other friends were passengers on a special train provided by President Burns of the H. N. & P. N. G. Ry. who also attended, along with all of the railroad company officers.

Life was not entirely humdrum even in the vale of the West Canada for on the last day of 1881 the first passenger train entered Newport. One must assume that it was a rather lively affair if one reads between the lines of a then contemporary news item:

> The first regular train on the narrow gauge railroad ran through to Newport on Monday, January 2nd (1882) but a "make-up" train ran to that village the Saturday previous, the last afternoon of the last day, of the last week, of the last month of 1881, some fifteen passengers who were aboard when the train reached Middleville, entered a petition to President Burns, to let the train hands run on through to Newport, a petition that genial gentleman granted on condition that the passengers should first pay their regular stage fare to the stage driver who was on hand and waiting for his share of the patronage, and, in addition they shall remunerate the train men for their extra trouble. This the passengers did, and went sailing away to Newport, leaving the happy stage driver to plod on alone, but well paid for drawing an empty stage coach. Thus the first iron horse ever seen at that village went snorting in, Saturday evening, Dec. 31, amid the shouts and uproar of the "numerous" populace who had assembled to witness the advent of the "elephant."

In its annual report for 1881, the company reported that it had carried 1635 passengers and 1400 ton miles of freight and had lost $144.82 in the process.

HERKIMER, NEWPORT & POLAND RAILWAY.

Open to Newport.

Daily Stages from Middleville for Fairfield, and from Newport for Norway, Poland, Cold Brook and Gray.

TIME TABLE NO. 5.

In Effect January 2 1882.

Trains Going North.			STATIONS.				Trains Going South.		
1	3	5					2	4	6
A. M.	P. M.	P. M.					A. M.	P. M.	P. M.
7.20	12.15	5.15	Leave	Herkimer.	Arrive		10.05	3.40	7.40
7.27	12.22	5.22	"	*North Herkimer,	Leave		9.58	3.33	7.33
7.32	12.27	5.27	"	*Kast Bridge,	"		9.50	3.25	7.25
7.40	12.35	5.35	"	*Countryman's,	"		9.40	3.15	7.15
7.50	12.45	5.45	"	*County House,	"		9.30	3.05	7.05
8.00	12.55	5.55	"	Middleville,	"		9.20	2.55	6.55
8.10	1.05	6.05	"	*Jones' Crossing,	"		9.10	2.45	6.45
8 25	1.20	6.20	Arrive	Newport,	"		8.55	2.30	6.30

*Denote stations at which trains do not stop except on signal or to leave passengers.

ALBERT WILBER, Supt.

Dated Herkimer, N. Y., January 5, 1882.

Issued at the time the railroad was completed to Newport, January 2, 1882. (Linus Ford collection)

Time Table No. 5 was published, effective January 2nd, 1882 with three trains each way daily between Herkimer and Newport. Fifty-five minutes was the scheduled time for the thirteen miles but it must be remembered that there was station work to be done along the line.

At a meeting of the stockholders held in Newport in March 1882, President Burns reported that with the railroad in operation for four months to Middleville only, and for two months through to Newport, the receipts were $7,700 with operation expense of $4,200. He forecast a very rosy future.

The ILION CITIZEN reported as a "Newport Item" that on Friday, June 9, 1882:

> The new coach that we have been waiting to see passed over the road for the first time Wednesday last. You could hardly call it a drawing room car, but it is far ahead of many of those so-called passenger coaches run by the N. Y. C. R. R. As fast as the road settles, it is re-ballasted, and every effort is being put forth to put it in first-class order and keep it so. We heard a man say last winter that he could drive his horse to Herkimer quicker than the railroad could run a train there. Would like to see him try it now.

In the 1882 REPORT OF THE STATE ENGINEER AND SURVEYOR OF THE RAILROADS the H. N. & P. reported that it now had 2 locomotive engines, 1 passenger car, 1 combination car and 18 box, flat and coal cars, plus 2 freight cars which were leased by the company. 9,129 tons of freight at the average rate of 11.66 cents per mile was carried. 33,840 passengers were transported at the rate of 5¢ per mile. $27,076.77 was earned and $18,902.19 was charged against earnings leaving a surplus of $8,174.58.

In February 1882, Rand McNally's OFFICAL RAILWAY GUIDE was listing three trains each day from Herkimer to Newport. The first train left Herkimer at 7:18 A. M. and the last train arrived from the north at 7:10 P. M. which represented three turn around trips.

leave Herkimer	arrive Newport	leave Newport	arrive Herkimer
7:18 A. M.	8:20 A. M.	8:35 A. M.	9:40 A. M.
12:15 P. M.	1:30 P. M.	2:30 P. M.	3:40 P. M.
4:50 P. M.	5:55 P. M.	6:05 P. M.	7:10 P. M.

In all probability all of the trips were made by the same crew as this would be in keeping with the working hours of the period. This would result in at least twelve hour days and probably quite a lot more if and when the weather was not clear.

Up to September 1884 it was reported that $182,518 had been used for grading, masonry, bridges, rails, etc. $13,613 had been spent on the building of stations and engine houses including fixtures while $27,709 was charged to locomotives and rolling stock. The grand total was $223,840. The rolling stock for passenger service consisted of two cars, one a first class passenger car and the other a combination passenger and baggage car. Seven box cars, ten platform or flat cars and two gondola cars for coal made up the freight equipment.

The main line was 40 lb. steel rails and 30 lb. iron rails laid at the 3 foot 6 inch gauge. About 40,000 passengers were carried this year. The freight ton-mile figure was 191,442. An $8,000 profit was realized for the year's operation. There were only the two locomotives in service on the line and they certainly could not have had very much idle time.

In March 1888, a much needed third locomotive was purchased. This was a Baldwin engine built in 1878 and was formerly the *J.C. ANDERSON* of the Georgia Land & Lumber Company. This was a 2-6-0 or "Mogul" type and was numbered #3 by the HN & PNG Ry and named the *WILLIAM SMITH*.

Also in 1888, a Ramsey hoist for transferring trucks under car bodies as located at Herkimer. Standard gauge cars of large capacity were then transported over the road. A standard gauge track from the "Central-Hudson" was laid into the narrow gauge yard to facilitate the transfer of car-load freight.

In the report to the Railroad Commissioners for 1890, the HN & PNG Ry reported that $225,236 had been spent on the road for construction and improvements. Together with $34,666, the cost of rolling stock and locomotives, the total investment in the railroad was now $259,902. Passenger, mail and express earnings were $19,087, while the freight earnings were $23,539, or a total operating revenue of $42,626. The year's operating expenses were $28,638, interest and taxes cost $5,356, which resulted in a surplus of $8,632. It is interesting to note that 21% of the freight hauled was lumber, 17% was coal and coke, agricultural products was 21% while the remaining 41% was made up of manufactured goods and general merchandise.

No dividends were ever paid on the stock of the HN & PNG Ry and 1890 was to be the last year of operation of the road under its original name and management.

The report of the inspector to the railroad commissioners showed that the line was in fairly good condition. The bridges were carefully examined and some repairs were recommended. The use of 60 lb. steel rails, previously used by the New York Central was noted.

Also the use of used ties from the New York Central was approved. In Herkimer, the "Central-Hudson" depot was used while in Newport and Poland there were good frame depots but at that time the Middleville depot was a house used for that purpose.

All in all it would appear that the narrow gauge was well managed and it was also apparent that if it was not going to be a great financial successs, it certainly was a means of increasing the general welfare and economy of the West Canada Creek valley and its environs. This was one of the natural outlets from the Mohawk Valley to the north country. Once in operation, the residents of the area served by the "Narrow-Gauge" would have been highly adverse to returning to the days of stages and freight wagons to and from the Mohawk Valley and the New York Central and Hudson River Railroad.

Despite a diligent search, photographs of the HN & PNG Ry were not to be found with the exception of the pictures of engines: No. 1, *EDWARD M. BURNS* type 4-4-0; No. 2, *HENRY W. DEXTER* type 2-4-4T; No. 3, *WILLIAM SMITH* type 2-6-0. It was a constant hope that a photo of a narrow gauge train would come to light but sorry to say, none was discovered.

A cloud began to appear over the horizon in the spring of 1890. Whether it was the black, storm laden type or the kind that has a silver lining is hard to say. However, great changes were now in store for the approximately 44 persons employed with the aggregate amount of $20,362 paid to them during the year for their services. None was to be more affected than the president, Edward M. Burns, by the reports that there was to be a change in the ownership and that the road was to be lengthened.

Stock Certificate, Herkimer, Newport and Poland Narrow Gauge Railway Company.

Herkimer, Newport and Poland Narrow Gauge Railway No. 1, the EDWARD M. BURNS. It appears that this engine was purchased from the Baldwin Locomotive Works in 1881. It was later rebuilt to standard guage for use on the Adirondack & St. Lawrence Railway and eventually was transferred to the Central Vermont Railroad. Picture taken in Herkimer probably about 1885. (Herkimer County Historical Society)

Herkimer, Newport and Poland Narrow Gauge Railway engine No. 2, the HENRY W. DEXTER was purchased second hand. It was used for construction and maintenance on the narrow gauge road but after the road was widened the disposition of No. 2 is obscure. The location of the picture and date is not known but it would have to be in the 1880's. (Timothy J. O'Connor)

HN & PNG No. 3, the WILLIAM SMITH, was purchased second hand in 1888. This engine was rebuilt to standard gauge for use on the A&StL and it was eventually transferred to the Central Vermont. William Smith was one of the directors of the company. (Herkimer County Historical Society)

CHAPTER III
Eyes to the North

In 1890 the New York Central and Hudson River Railroad did not control any rail lines north of the Mohawk Valley. This in itself was not easy for the Vanderbilt interests to contemplate for it meant in effect that there was no direct entry into Montreal or any Canadian city east of Niagara Falls.

The Adirondacks region had so far successfully repulsed any efforts to make its great central area reasonably accessible for visitors or commercial interests.

The Rome, Watertown and Ogdensburg Railroad Company was under the control of Charles Parsons and (in 1886), he added the Utica and Black River Railroad Company to his holdings. Parsons had extended the RW & O from Norwood to Massena Springs where it made connections with the Grand Trunk Railroad which led straight into Montreal. The RW & O along with the U & BR skirted the west side of the Adirondacks and made connections on the north side with the Ogdensburg and Lake Champlain Railroad.

The Delaware and Hudson ran north through the Champlain Valley on the east side of the Adirondacks. The Adirondack Railroad reached from Saratoga into the mountains as far as North Creek near the headwaters of the Hudson River. The Chateaugay Railroad ran from Plattsburgh to Saranac Lake. Both the Chateaugay and Adirondack were under D & H control. The Sacketts Harbor and Saratoga Railroad was incorporated in 1848. In 1853 a route was surveyed from Jessup's Landing (now Corinth) and construction was started. Only about 30 miles of right of way had been graded when funds were exhausted. Several changes of name were made but in 1863 the property came under the control of Dr. Thomas C. Durant and some of his associates. The name was changed to the Adirondack Company and the terminus was to be Ogdensburg. By 1870 Dr. Durant had succeeded in building a railroad for sixty miles from Saratoga to North Creek. The final change of name was to the Adirondack Railway Company and in 1889 it was sold by William West Durant to the

14

Delaware and Hudson. The Chateaugay Railroad was the first railroad to cross the "Blue Line" and enter the mountains. It was a three foot gauge line running from Plattsburgh to Saranac Lake. It had started its life as a narrow gauge railroad built and owned by the State of New York to serve New York State's Clinton Prison at Dannemora, N. Y. It was leased by the Chateaugay Company in later years and was gradually extended to Saranac Lake, reaching there in 1887. The D & H controlled this line for many years before actually taking it under a 500 year lease in 1903.

John Hurd of Bridgeport, Connecticut was the instigator of the second railroad to penetrate the so called "Blue Line" of the Adirondack Park. This railroad was the Northern Adirondack and was built from Moira, N. Y. on the Northern Railroad, later the Rutland, southeast to St. Regis Falls. By degrees it was extended until it reached the present village of Tupper Lake in 1889. This was a very hilly and curved line and was built for one purpose, to harvest timber, lumber and any other forest products.

It was a hard and tedious trip to get to Old Forge on the Fulton Chain of lakes and the only way was via the Brown Tract road from Port Leyden or Boonville. This wagon trip from Moose River to Old Forge was only for the most hardy souls. The worst part of the trip was from Moose River to Old Forge. To ease the rough and trying trip a railroad was proposed in May 1888 to run from the Moose River Settlement in Lewis County to Old Forge in Herkimer County. While it was being constructed it was decided to terminate the railroad at the hamlet of Minnehaha on the north branch of the Moose River, making it just under 8 miles long. Following the construction of a dam on the Moose River in 1888 it was possible for a small steamboat to make the trip from Minnehaha to Old Forge. Put in operation in June 1889 the Fulton Chain Railroad more popularly called the "Peg-Leg" Railroad operated during the summer seasons of 1889, 1890, 1891 and 1892. With the coming of Webb's Adirondack & St. Lawrence the little railroad which operated on wooden rails was used to haul supplies into the construction area of the new railroad and in so doing sealed its own doom. Richard F. Palmer wrote an interesting history of the Fulton Chain Railroad and this is published as part of RAILS IN THE NORTH WOODS.

Articles began to appear in the newspapers calling attention to the danger of destruction of the Adirondack forests. On June 22, 1890 the NEW YORK TIMES carried the following letter:

Utica, June 15 — A movement is on foot among capitalists of northern Herkimer County and elsewhere, of which C. V. B. Barse of Olean,

N. Y. is one of the principal leaders for the purchase of the Herkimer, Newport and Poland Narrow Gauge Railroad. A considerable portion of the stock has already been secured at 50 cents on the dollar, and it is believed by the date of the annual meeting for the election of officers on June 24 a sufficient amount will have been obtained to give the new stockholders a controlling interest. It is their intention, should they get control, to change the road from a narrow gauge to standard gauge, and extend it into the heart of the Adirondacks.

Now that the attempt to purchase the Herkimer, Newport and Poland Narrow Gauge Railway Company was out in the open and the purpose for which the ownership was desired became known, events moved along rapidly. The participants in the purchase were identified in the newspapers as Ex-Governors Waller and Loomis of Connecticut; Henry S. Ives, F. S. Phillips, R. H. Leonard and others of New York City; Mills W. Barse of Olean; Henry Patten of Albany; Thomas H. Degraw of Poughkeepsie and Ex-Senator Warner Miller of Herkimer. On July 1, 1890, The NEW YORK TIMES said that the combination of some of the members who were reaching for the timber and iron deposits of the Adirondacks, hand in hand with men whose publicly avowed purpose was the preservation of that region from assaults and depredations of selfish persons, presented a curious spectacle. Members of the syndicate were reported to have acquired up to 400,000 acres of well-timbered forest lands in the vicinity of Jock's Lake and Moose Lake.

The formal contract for the sale of the property and franchises of the Herkimer, Newport and Poland Narrow Gauge Railway to a new company had been formally executed, it was announced, on September 16th, 1890. At that time it was revealed that the existing railroad would be widened to standard gauge and extended thirty miles to Jock's Lake and would be named the Herkimer, Poland and Jock's Lake Railroad Company. This later name does not seem to have been used at any other time. The purpose of the extension was to furnish facilities for transporting lumber to the outside markets. The railroad company also expected to build hotels and cottages to aid in the popularization of the Jock's Lake region as a summer resort, particularly for hunters and fishermen. The reported price paid was fifty dollars for each one hundred dollar share of stock and at that time 1,785 shares were outstanding.

What might be termed the "Jock's Lake Syndicate" had little more to do with the railroad for in the fall of 1890 Dr. William Seward Webb acquired control of the Herkimer, Newport and Poland Narrow Gauge Railway from Mills W. Barse and agreed with Barse to widen the gauge and extend it to Hinckley.

On October 31, 1890, the Mohawk Valley and Northern Railway Company filed Articles of Association under the laws of the State of New York with its termini at the Village of Poland and at a place called Noblesborough also in Herkimer County.

CHAPTER IV
Doctor Webb Arrives

Now that Dr. William Seward Webb had made his entrance as the purchaser of the Herkimer, Newport and Poland Narrow Gauge Railway Company and as he is about to set forth on the construction of his "Golden Chariot Route" through the North Woods let us become a little acquainted with him.

William Seward Webb was born in New York City on January 31, 1851, the son of General James Watson Webb and Laura Virginia (Cram) Webb. He took a medical course at Columbia College from 1868 to 1871 and then studied in Europe for two years in the hospitals of Paris and Vienna. In 1873 he returned to New York where he entered the College of Physicians and Surgeons of Columbia College. He was graduated in 1875 with the degree of Medicine. He was on the staff of St. Luke's Hospital, New York City, as an intern for two and one half years following which he went into private practice. He practiced only a few years and then abandoned his profession and joined the Wall Street firm of Worden and Company which in 1888 became the W. S. Webb Company.

In 1881 William Seward Webb and Lila Osgood Vanderbilt were married. She was the youngest daughter of William H. Vanderbilt and Maria Louisa (Kissam) Vanderbilt.

In 1885 he was elected president of the Wagner Palace Car Company and remained in charge of that corporation until it was merged with the Pullman Company in 1899. During his presidency of the Wagner Palace Car Company he greatly improved its condition, physically and financially. He set a high standard of service and efficiency and increased the rolling stock from 170 to 800 cars, all built in the company shops. By his executive ability and talent for organization he transformed a decadent enterprise into a highly profitable one, with a reputation second to none.

Now he was set to begin the most ambitious enterprise of his career, the construction of a railroad through the North Woods from Remsen to Malone and at the same time complete the rail route north from Malone into Montreal by construction, leasing and trackage rights. It would demand every bit of every ability that he possessed. For one man to be able to drive through the planning, legalities, engineering, construction and financial problems of building a railroad consisting of nearly 200 miles of track, within a period of less than twenty months is almost unbelievable. Charles Burnett said it all:

> On October 24, 1892, trains were running through on schedule time from New York to Montreal. A railroad of one hundred and ninety-miles through a wilderness had been constructed and placed in operation within eighteen months from the time the surveys were started. It is doubtful if this record, which was truly phenomenal in view of the difficulties involved, has ever been equalled under similar conditions. The wilderness had at last met a man whom it could not conquer.

The author was told by one of the present day family members that William Seward Webb was named after a close friend of his father, William Henry Seward, who was Secretary of State when the Territory of Alaska was purchased. The author was also told that it was considered as a little joke within the family that as William Henry Seward had as his folly the "Alaskan purchase" so had his namesake as his folly the "Adirondack Railroad."

The New York Central and Hudson River Railroad had decided in late 1890 that the time had come to build its own line into the north country of New York State and the Mohawk and St. Lawrence Railroad Company was formed. On February 17, 1891 the NEW YORK TIMES reported:

> The route of the New York Central's new line has definitely been determined and the work of construction will begin in two or three weeks. . . . H. Walter Webb is the president. The city of Rome is the southern terminus and the single track road will run along the bank of the old Black River Canal to the Town of Northwestern. . . . The Black River will then be followed to Carthage where one branch will extend to Gouverneur and another branch to Watertown, Chaumont and Clayton.

According to the HERKIMER CITIZEN of March 10, 1891 work was started on the Mohawk & St. Lawrence on March 3rd, the same day that Dr. W. Seward Webb and Edward M. Burns were installed as president and vice president of the Herkimer, Newport and Poland Narrow Gauge Railway.

The BOONVILLE HERALD on March 5 also reported much activity and that all contracts had been awarded for construction.

However, on March 14, 1891 the Rome, Watertown & Ogdensburg Railroad announced that the entire road and property of the company had been leased to the New York Central and Hudson River Railroad. The Mohawk and St. Lawrence was discontinued following this announcement and the Railroad Commissioners in later years reported that this company had never made a report to the commission.

Edward Hungerford in his MEN AND IRON said that Dr. W. Seward Webb's plan was to unite the Herkimer, Newport and Poland road with the Mohawk & St. Lawrence and when the latter road remained in an inchoate state, Dr. Webb was forced to change his plans and build north from Remsen to Malone. Be this as it may, it is again difficult to see how the Mohawk & St. Lawrence projection could have been much more than a direct threat to the Rome, Watertown and Ogdensburg and it certainly brought the latter road into the New York Central system very quickly. Dr. Webb's intention to build through the Adirondacks to Malone was to all intents a separate endeavor to open the North Woods to the public for recreation and commercial purposes. It hardly seems plausible that the Doctor would have wanted to merely involve himself in the construction of a little short feeder line to the Mohawk & St. Lawrence.

Chapter 78 of the laws enacted in 1891 authorized the Herkimer, Newport and Poland Narrow Gauge Railway Company to change its gauge and authorized the company to reincorporate as a standard gauge railroad under the name of the Herkimer, Newport and Poland Railway Company. W. Seward Webb was president of the new company and Edward M. Burns was vice-president. On April 30, 1891 the Mohawk Valley and Northern Railway Company and the Herkimer, Newport and Poland Narrow Gauge Railway Company filed a certificate to consolidate under the name of the Mohawk Valley and Northern Railway Company. Edward M. Burns was the general manager of this railroad.

In changing from the three and one half foot gauge to standard gauge, the permission of the various villages and towns had to be obtained. The applications for this authorization were filed under the name of the Mohawk Valley and Northern Railway Company. There was no apparent difficulty in obtaining the necessary permission to make the change. It was reported that by June 8, 1891 standard gauge trains were running on the railroad and that the fare had been reduced to three cents per mile.

On September 11, 1891 the NEW YORK TIMES reported that Dr. Webb had the Herkimer, Newport and Poland Extension Railroad incorporated. The TIMES said:

> The company will operate a standard gauge line from the point of
> intersection with the Herkimer, Newport and Poland Narrow Gauge

Adirondack & St. Lawrence R'y

TIME TABLE NO. 1.

Daily Stages From Middleville for Fairfield; From Newport for Norway; From Poland for North Gage, Cold Brook and Gray.

To Take Effect at 12:01 a. m., Monday, Aug. 31, 1891.

FOR THE INFORMATION AND GOVERNMENT OF EMPLOYEES ONLY.

All trains on this line may be required to do both freight and passenger service.

TRAINS MOVING NORTH.					STATIONS.			TRAINS MOVING SOUTH.		
5 MAIL.	3 MAIL.	1 MAIL.	Miles				Miles	2 MAIL.	4 MAIL.	6 MAIL.
P. M.	P. M.	A. M.						A. M.	P. M.	P. M.
5.10	12.25	7.10	0	Lv	HERKIMER.	Ar.	17	9.20	3.40	7.25
5.17	12.32	7.16	2	"	*NORTH HERKIMER.	"	15	9.11	3.32	7.16
5.21	12.35	7.19	3	"	*KAST BRIDGE.	"	14	9.08	3.27	7.13
5.26	12.40	7.21	4	"	*DEMPSTER'S.	"	13	9.05	3.22	7.08
5.30	12.45	7.24	5	"	*COUNTRYMAN'S.	"	12	9.02	3.17	7.04
5.37	12.52	7.29	7	"	*COUNTY HOUSE.	"	10	8.56	3.10	6.57
5.45	1.00	7.35	9	"	MIDDLEVILLE.	"	8	8.50	3.00	6.50
5.50	1.05	7.39	10	"	*JONES' CROSSING.	"	7	8.40	2.50	6.45
5.55	1.10	7.42	11	"	*FENNER'S GROVE.	"	6	8.36	2.47	6.42
6.05	1.20	7.50	13	"	NEWPORT.	"	4	8.30	2.40	6.35
6.10	1.25	7.56	15	"	*SHERMAN QUARRY.	"	2	8.23	2.32	6.32
6.20	1.35	8.05	17	Ar.	POLAND.	Lv.	0	8.15	2.25	6.25

All trains moving south have the absolute right of track over trains of the same class, moving in the opposite direction.

Trains must run carefully through Herkimer yard, speed not to exceed eight miles an hour.

All trains run daily except Sunday.

*Denotes stations at which trains do not stop, except on signal.

EDWARD M. BURNS,
GENERAL MANAGER.

JAMES MACBETH,
ACTING SUPERINTENDENT.

The first time table issued after the HN&PNG was changed over to standard gauge. (Railway Hist. Soc. of Northern New York)

1888 pass issued to Superintendent E. A. Bond of the Carthage & Adirondack Railway Company. (Edward Baumgardner collection)

Railway, at or near the Village of Poland, in Herkimer County, northerly to the Village of Remsen, in Oneida County, with a branch running from the main line from the Village of Prospect, Oneida County, to a point at or near the Village or Town of Northwood, in Herkimer County. The total length of the road will be twenty miles.

The Mohawk Valley and Northern Railway had petitioned the Supreme Court for an order to permit it to construct a railroad north from Poland. This was apparently the same railroad that the Herkimer, Newport and Poland Extension Railway was to operate. Just why it was found necessary to organize all of the various companies to complete the railroad to Remsen as a standard guage line is a little difficult to understand. Perhaps it was because the MV & N was originally intended to terminate at Noblesborough.

CHAPTER V
Opposition to the Railroads

In the last quarter of the twentieth century we often are hearing the phrase, "If they tried to it now, it couldn't be done." This, of course, refers to the present day opposition by environmentalists to the impact on our natural resources of such proposals as that of building a railroad through the center of the Adirondack Park.

During the last decades of the nineteenth century forces were just getting organized for the same purpose. The NEW YORK TIMES on June 22, 1890 reported on the incorporation of the Saranac Lake and Lake Placid Railroad Company. At the same time it reported that the Herkimer, Newport and Poland Narrow Gauge Railway was being sold to a group who intended to widen it to standard gauge and extend it into the Adirondacks. On July 1, the TIMES reported:

> The appearance of Henry S. Ives in connection with the operations of the syndicate that recently bought the valuable Blake track of 100,000 acres in the Adirondacks will be a surprise to many persons who were favorably impressed with the avowed purposes of the syndicate because of ex-Senator Warner Miller's connection with the project.
>
> Henry S. Ives, reaching out for the timber and the iron deposits of the Adirondacks, hand in hand with men whose publicly avowed purpose is to preserve that region from the assaults and depredations of selfish persons, presents a curious spectacle.

From that date on many of the newspapers carried items on the destruction and waste of the Adirondacks using such headings as:

The Adirondack Vandals
Nature's Treasures Despoiled by the Relentless Axe
Miles of Barren Land
Railroad and Lumbermen Ruining the Adirondacks
Adirondack Railways Creeping in from Every Quarter
Save the Adirondacks
Railroad Schemes to Ruin the State Preserve
The Adirondacks Threatened
Adirondack Invasion
The Big Forest in Danger

The ARGUS on September 2, 1890 stated that the Adirondack Park Association had been quietly formed in New York City in April of 1890. The specific purpose of this organization had as its objective the preservation of the Adirondack forests and by practical means the establishment of a state forest park. Many prominent men were listed as subscribers to the purposes of the organization.

The New York Forest Commission had been established in 1884 and 1885. The New York State Land Board was set up earlier. The jurisdiction of both groups was the subject of much debate as Dr. Webb and his Adirondack and St. Lawrence sought permission to build across certain state lands. On May 27, 1891 the NEW YORK TIMES reported that the Adirondack Park Association had passed a resolution in favor of the building of railroads in the Adirondacks with certain provisions. Obtaining the support of the Adirondack Park Association for the Adirondack and St. Lawrence was viewed by some as a major accomplishment towards the eventual completion of the railroad. According to the TIME'S May 27th article, Dr. Webb had promised the Adirondack Park Association:

> That he had no intention whatever of injuring the Adirondack re-
> gion. On the other hand he, as a large property holder there, was
> deeply interested in protecting it from destruction. He proposed to in-
> stitute a system of forestry on his own property. . . . He was willing to
> pledge himself that his road should not convey any timber out of the
> region that had been cut from logs less than twelve inches in diameter,
> and furthermore he would promise that his road would not carry any
> lumber of charcoal made from green timber.

Running through the articles is the idea that the Adirondack and St. Lawrence as originally projected was only an attempt by the New York Central to threaten the Delaware and Hudson and force it to sell its Montreal branch. This would be reminiscent of the method taken by the New York Central to obtain the Rome, Watertown and Ogdensburg. The TIMES said on May 16, 1891:

> It was stated that the (Forest) Commission had not moved sooner to
> stop the proposed building of the Adirondack and St. Lawrence Rail
> Road because it was generally supposed, until very recently that the
> charter for the road was to be used merely to "bear" the stock of the
> Delaware and Hudson Canal Company's Montreal Branch in order to
> enable the Central to force the sale of that branch to the Central road.
> As soon, however, as the actual intention of Dr. Webb to build became
> definitely known, the commission prepared to act.

Charles H. Burnett in CONQUERING THE WILDERNESS indicates that the Delaware and Hudson had much to do with the oppo-

sition to the building of the Adirondack and St. Lawrence. Some reports say that the reference to the horrible destruction of the forests etc., was actually devastation that was permitted along the Delaware and Hudson controlled Chateaugay Railroad, so it had a first hand source of ammunition for its fight against the Adirondack and St. Lawrence's possible ruining of the forest land.

Controversy continued about the right to build on State lands but the solution came according to Burnett:

> At length a way was found out of the difficulty. A ruling was obtained that although the State could not sell lands in the Forest Preserve it could exchange them for lands of equal or greater area and value. Such lands were immediately offered in exchange and the fight was won.

It is interesting to note that the Delaware and Hudson secured permission from the State Forest Commission in the last week of December 1894 to extend its Adirondack Railroad from North Creek to Long Lake. The State Land Board declared it had no jurisdiction in the matter. An injunction was obtained which restrained the railroad company from acting until a hearing was held. A constitutional amendment absolutely prohibiting the use of State lands by railroad companies for any private purpose went into effect on January 1, 1895 and the Delaware and Hudson did not build the extension.

CHAPTER VI
Doctor Webb
Builds His Railroad

Having secured control of the Herkimer, Newport and Poland Narrow Gauge Railway in February 1891, Dr. Webb became the president on March 3rd. Immediate action towards widening the narrow to standard gauge was undertaken and by June 8, 1891 the standard gauge trains were operating to Poland.

On May 7, 1891 the BOONVILLE HERALD published an article of some length on the consolidation of the Herkimer, Newport and Poland Railway Company and the Mohawk Valley and Northern Railway Company. The country through which these railroads passed on their way to Remsen was described:

> No where in this vicinity is the landscape as attractive as that in the valley of the West Canada Creek, from Herkimer northward. Here are the steep inclines, reaching up from the creek, along the banks of which winds in serpentine curves the narrow gauge track. The road bed is in many places cut from the rock, and is supported on the side next to the creek by walls of huge stone. This, together with the tumbling creek and the pretty hills, makes the scene one of great beauty, and forms a Rocky Mountain view in miniature. Above Poland there are also many pretty sights including Trenton Falls, the falls at Prospect and others. Above Hinckley's the country gradually becomes more sparsely settled, until there is nothing but wilderness.

At the same time the HERALD reported that work on the road north of Poland was being rapidly pushed along by experienced contractors. Just north of Poland the course of the West Canada Creek was changed and a new channel 1600 feet in length was dug, thereby eliminating the necessity of constructing two long bridges. After leaving Poland the grade of the road gradually ascended. At Gravesville a bridge 280 feet long crossed the Mill Creek at considerable height and the railroad passed directly over the settlement. Above Gravesville was one of the worst obstacles encountered in the building of the

Preliminary construction for the bridge at Gravesville, 1891. (Helen Schermerhorn)

Deep cut near Gravesville. Although primitive means for loading cars is shown, The HERKIMER CITIZEN reported that a steam shovel was in use at this site that loaded 40 cars an hour each carrying 2 cubic feet. (Helen Schermerhorn)

road. This was the "Gravesville Cut" which was three-quarters of a mile in length and varied from 15 to 75 feet in depth.

The West Canada Creek was crossed by a bridge above the Mill Dam Falls of the Trenton Falls Cascades. This bridge was 350 feet long and about 75 feet above the stream. About two miles north of the bridge, Prospect Junction was established. From here a branch line a little less than three miles long was built into Hinckley or Gang Mills as it was then known.

At Remsen, about two miles from Prospect Junction, the connection was made with the former, New York Central controlled, Utica and Black River Railroad, later part of the Rome, Watertown and Ogdensburg. The "Herkimer" road coming in from the east and south paralleled the older road for a short distance. The same depot was used and an interchange was laid out.

A short distance above Remsen the new road diverged to the northeast towards the general direction of Forestport. It should be noted that the mileposts on the railroad all indicated the distance from Herkimer. This continued to be true as the railroad was built northward and to this day the existing mileposts south of Malone all show the indicator "H" and the distance. The distance from Herkimer to Remsen is about 6.3 miles longer than from Utica to Remsen. The public timetables usually showed the distance from Utica but the employee timetables showed the distance from Herkimer until the 1940's when the latter were changed to show the distance from Remsen. This, of course, makes little difference except to the researcher or rail-fan who, on occasion might like to locate a specific area by reference to the mile posts.

Up until the late spring of 1891 the definite route all the way northward had apparently not been fully decided. It was generally thought that the railroad would be built as far as Tupper Lake and there would be connected with John Hurd's Northern Adirondack Railroad which had been built by degrees from 1883 to 1889 from Moira to Tupper Lake. By connections with the Grand Trunk Railway north of Moira and Bombay, Dr. Webb's road would gain access to Montreal. This would leave Malone and Saranac Lake off the route. Charles Burnett reported that John Hurd had been offered six hundred thousand dollars for his poorly built and money losing railroad but he declined the offer. Later John Hurd reconsidered and made a deal with Dr. Webb, but, the night before the papers were to be signed, Hurd agreed to sell his railroad to Mr. Paine of the Pope-Paine Lumber Company for fifty thousand dollars more than Dr. Webb had agreed to pay. The next day when Dr. Webb was notified that the deal was off he naturally became very irate. Later Paine came in and offered to sell his option at an increase in price but the offer was declined and Dr. Webb made his decision to build north from Tupper Lake to Malone. Following his failure to sell the Northern Adirondack to Dr. Webb, John Hurd's fortunes seemed to steadily decline. The Northern Adirondack Railroad Company was sold at a foreclosure sale on May 25, 1894 to the Northern New York Railroad Company. The latter in turn became the New York and Ottawa Railway which in turn was taken over by the New York Central in 1904.

Dr. Webb spent the summer of 1891 at Saranac Lake so that he might be as near as possible to the construction work which was underway at several points, once the northern terminus had been firmly established as Malone. Edward M. Burns, who was president of the Herkimer, Newport and Poland became the general manager of Adirondack and St. Lawrence, W. N. Roberts was appointed chief engineer and W. J. Curtis was made assistant chief engineer. Herschel Roberts was named the division engineer of the south end and W. J. Curtis was the division engineer for the north end. George C. Ward acted as resident engineer for the section from Forestport to Big Moose Summit. Mr. Curtis was injured in an accident and W. N. Roberts took personal charge of the north end leaving Herschel Roberts in full control of the southern end with the title of assistant chief engineer. Burnett reported that W. N. Roberts never saw portions of the southern part of the road until he rode over them on a train.

To give an idea of the speed with which the enterprise was being carried out is the account of Herschel Roberts, as reported in the BOONVILLE HERALD of June 18, 1891:

> Long Lake (near White Lake Corners). Engineer Roberts and his assistant Sullivan left White Lake Corners Thursday morning by way of Moose River for Old Forge. The wind was high and the water poured from the sky. They were bewildered and they lost their way, walked all day and were out all night. The first welcome sound that they heard was a rooster crowing. Following the sound, they reached Long Lake at nine o'clock Friday morning, wet, tattered, and hungry.

In a letter of September 8, 1915, Herschel Roberts wrote about this event and also gave an insight of the terrific speed and pressure under which he was working:

> I would say that the surveys were started from Poland early in March 1891 but I think it was early in the following May before anything was done north of Remsen . . . I remember that I personally rushed the location as far as Remsen and on the Hinckley branch and that work

was begun on the latter as soon as the frost was out of the ground. The contract for the work from Poland to Fulton Chain was let to Westbrook before that time and subcontracts were let by him before the location was ready, for the entire distance . . .

I do not think any construction work was done near Otter Lake until about July 1st, 1891 for I recall trying to go with Maurice Sullivan, Westbrook's superintendent, over the line from White Lake to Moose River and getting lost. After floundering around the shores of Otter Lake all the afternoon we came to the outlet about dark and slept there in the rain and followed the outlet out to Long Lake the next morning. Though we were soaking wet for hours and I fell into Long Lake in trying to build a raft to ferry us across, I remember that we did not suffer from the cold and I would therefore put that date at about the end of June. At that time the preliminary line had only progressed to within about a mile of Otter Lake. Not having a line to follow was why we got lost.

At this time Walker and his party were in camp at Minnehaha pushing the line from Moose River to Fulton Chain and Patton was rushing the location across the DeCamp lands south of Township 8 to get that condemnation suit started at the earliest possible moment. . . . I remember hustling around via Boonville and Moose River Village to Minnehaha that night. There I got in telephone communication with one of Patton's party and after finding out what men and tools they lacked I took these from Walker's party, sent them by small boat to Old Forge and thence up to Second Lake and had the party at work again. These circumstances all lead me to think it was at least July first before construction work was done at Otter Lake but recalling the speed with which everything was rushed, I doubt if it was much later than that.

If a map of this part of the line was filed before work started I would say it was more from accident than design for the contractors were on the work the minute the stakes were ready.

The only data I have left are the "letter" books. Everything else was turned over to the New York Central and was later burned up in the fire which destroyed the American Express building in New York . . . I doubt if the books would throw much light on the early stages of the work for at that time my headquarters were "in the saddle" and there was neither time nor necessity for much correspondence.

I saw every foot of my division at least twice every week and through an arrangement with the telephone company, I had every one of my assistants on the line at seven o'clock each night so we could all talk to each other and in that way we all kept in touch without much correspondence.

As stated earlier, construction was started at various points along the proposed route. From Poland north; from Remsen; sections near the Moose and Black River crossings, with supplies and materials teamed in from Boonville or Lowville; from the vicinity of Fulton Chain; from Tupper Lake because materials could be brought in over the Northern Adirondack Railroad; in the Loon Lake area because materials could be brought in over the adjacent Chateaugay Railroad operated by the Delaware and Hudson; and from Malone because of the Rutland facilities.

Due to the remoteness of some of the areas where work was begun, it had to be carried out by hard manual labor. It was impossible at this stage to bring in modern equipment and machinery.

As Herschell Roberts stated in his letter, the contractors started working as soon as the stakes were in which indicates that much of the railroad was under construction before the final location of other parts of the road had been decided.

Before we temporarily leave the construction story of the southern division we can look at a few contemporary newspaper accounts of progress in building the railroad.

May 5, 1891 — Work is being rapidly pushed by experienced contractors. On the main line, from Poland to Remsen, the work is being done by Brady Brothers. The spur to Gang Mills (Hinckley) is being graded by Captain Sullivan. Both of these parties have just finished work on the Harlem branch of the Central. They have large forces of Italians at work.

June 11, 1891 — Locomotive No. 1 of the Adirondack and St. Lawrence has arrived and is in the yards at Herkimer. The tender bears the inscription ADIRONDACK & ST. LAWRENCE RAILWAY COMPANY No. 1.

The narrow gauge track has been completely replaced with standard gauge.

June 13, 1891 — Dr. Webb arrived in Remsen Tuesday morning in his private car. With him were Edward Burns and Engineer Roberts. They drove to White Lake Corners where a large section toward the Moose River has been graded. Dr. Webb inspected the line from Remsen and drove to Poland where his private car met him.

June 11, 1891 — The headquarters of the Enterprise Construction company is at Boonville. All of the work will be sublet by Enterprise. Twenty-five miles are to be finished in five months.

June 18, 1891 — A large quantity of tools and machinery has been taken to the woods and a boat load of dynamite and powder is on the way.

Nov. 26, 1891 — The Adirondack and St. Lawrence is nearing completion on many parts of the line. Monday morning a special train consisting of a new Adirondack and St. Lawrence combination car and private car "Ellsmere" left Utica and arrived Remsen at 11:50, Dr. Webb's party arrived overland from Herkimer on tour of inspection. Dr. Webb, Engineers Robert and Herschel Roberts, General Manager Burns, Private Secretary McKeever of the Adirondack and St. Lawrence and C. D. Flagg, superintendent of the Wagner Palace Car Company were in attendance. The train was switched to the Adirondack and St. Lawrence tracks at Remsen and proceeded to inspect operations at the Black River.

The combination car was vestibuled, three apartments, one for mail, one for baggage and the other for passengers. At each end of the car was lettered "Adirondack Limited."

January 21, 1892 — We went on an inspection trip last Friday to Black River. The bridge is 240 feet long, center span 100 feet, 49 feet above the water. The bridge proper is 25 feet high and balance of the piers are granite. Dr. Webb was present on this trip. There are 4,000 men employed on the construction of the railroad. The heavier work at Gravesville is done. The bridge at Trenton Falls is nearly completed. It will be the largest solid floor bridge in the world — 350 feet long, middle span 200 feet and will be 75 feet above the water.

The construction of the railroad has put a lot of money in circulation.

The rails are 75 pounds to the yard and are wider and heavier than those in common use. There are ten locomotives used in construction and a large number of steam shovels.

February 4, 1892 — Sixteen loads of dynamite hauled to the railroad from Lowville.

March 10, 1892 — Enterprise sent 61 loads of supplies from Lowville. This is a total of 125,000 pounds An average of 25 teams leave daily with supplies, beef, pork, flour, groceries, hay and coal. It takes two days to make a trip. The men receive 50 cents per hundred for hauling to Stillwater, twenty-eight miles from Lowville. An additional 20 cents per hundred when goods are delivered at camps from nine to fourteen miles above Stillwater. D. B. Sperry of Watson has charge of the teams.

CHAPTER VII
South from Malone

At the same time as the construction from Poland north proceeded, great things were happening in and near Malone. The NEW YORK TIMES of May 18, 1891 said:

> The unanimity and vigor with which all of the great journals of the metropolis have suddenly awakened to the fact that a railroad is to be built through the Adirondacks, is a little amusing here, where the enterprise has been the one absorbing topic of conversation and newspaper comment for more than a month. Everything now ascertainable has been known in Malone for weeks, and the three newspapers of the town have weekly published from one to two columns regarding the project. On the first of April one of Malone's citizens received a telegram from Henry Patton, the Albany millionaire lumber merchant, saying that Dr. W. Seward Webb would be in Malone the next day, and at once arrange for the building of a railroad from the village southward, past the Saranacs, and extending to a connection with the New York Central. No one in Malone had theretofore heard even a suggestion of such an undertaking. The dispatch was regarded for a time as an April Fool joke. But Dr. Webb came as announced, a great public meeting was held, and a proposition was submitted. Dr. Webb said: "Raise $30,000, secure its payment to me when the road is finished and in operation, and I will build a railroad from your village through the Adirondacks to Herkimer or Schenectady, skirting the Saranacs, the first fifty miles to be completed within four months and the entire line within two years." He gave only one week in which to raise the bonds, but it was in hand at the appointed hour.
>
> Without waiting for the expiration of the week Dr. Webb set his surveyors at work, laying out a line and getting ready for the contractors. They have been continuously at work ever since, and the line is now located through almost to Paul Smith's while for six or eight miles south from this village all the cross section and detail work is completed
>
> Still greater progress would have been made but for the fact that after starting the work and finding that the road from Malone to the Saranacs could not be finished in time to handle the Central's Adirondack business this season, it was determined to effect a trackage ar-

rangement with Hurd's Northern Adirondack Railroad from Moira to Tupper Lake, and from the latter point build a spur to Saranac Lake, which should be in operation by the 1st of July. This new undertaking compelled a division of the engineer corps recruited for Malone, which has somewhat delayed operations here.

The spur referred to will have a length of fifteen or twenty miles, and will pass near the Saranac Inn and Corey's Carry on the Upper Saranac, and terminate at the Village of Saranac Lake. Work is now being crowded upon it with great energy. Two hundred Italians have begun the work of grading and their number will be increased as fast as the surveyors can make ready for them. A part of this spur may be utilized as a link in the main line, but otherwise so much of it lies to the westward of the trunk line will amount, after this season, to hardly more than a side track. It is counted upon to serve as a great aid in expediting work upon the permanent line, by affording the means of carrying rails and other materials of construction. (The part that might be utilized as the main line is the Tupper Lake to Lake Clear Junction segment of the later day main line.)

Work at Malone has not yet reached considerable proportions. Mr. Westbrook of New York has the contract for grading the first forty miles south from Malone. He has sublet the work to Sullivan and Hawkes, I. A. Hodge, and McLane & Co. — the last firm beginning ten miles to the south and engaging to do all of the grading through to Paul Smith's. The only one of these firms that has as yet broken ground is Sullivan & Hawkes, and they are working only forty or fifty men. McLane & Co.'s contract covers a territory whose beginning lies at the entrance of the forest. They have not cut a tree nor lifted a shovel of dirt.

The specifications under which the new road is to be built are precisely the same as those used in the construction of the West Shore Railroad. The rails are to weigh 75 pounds to the yard, the fishplates are for 6 spikes, and the ties to be 3,000 to the mile instead of the usual 2600. The equipment of the road is to be the best money can buy.

In the June 1, 1891 issue of the NEW YORK HERALD, correspondent Thomas G. Alvord made a long report on Dr. Webb's Adirondack Railroad. The Franklin County Historical and Museum Society reprinted excerpts from Alvord's article and among these we find:

> The work of building the railroad from near Tupper Lake, where it crosses the Northern Adirondack road (over which cars can come from New York via the Rome, Watertown and Ogdensburg road) to Paul Smith's is being pressed with great vigor. Already Messrs. Ellsworth, Chapman & Lathrop, who have a contract for building that section of the railroad, have pushed their choppers six miles into the forest, and

the bed is ready for a mile and a half of rail. Mr. Ellsworth asked Dr. Webb for rails enough to lay a mile and a half, and Webb sent nearly enough rails to build the whole road. Ellsworth asked for a light locomotive for construction work, and Webb sent No. 207, an old Central road engine weighing thirty tons. That is a sample of the way the Doctor is pushing things. He is driving the contractors nearly crazy with his impetuosity and impatience. Construction Superintendent Whalen, who weighed 320 pounds when he left Whitehall two weeks ago, now wears a 14½ collar.

Whalen is at work near Saranac Inn, pressing toward Tupper Lake about eleven miles away, while Ellsworth is pushing from Tupper Lake toward Whalen. They have about five hundred men at work on this eleven mile section, and if it is possible they intend to have it done so that those wonderful vestibuled, mahogany, buffet, club special trains can arrive at Saranac Inn before July 4th.

While the work is progressing on this Tupper Lake to Paul Smith's section J. W. Westbrook, a contractor, is pushing down from Malone. Construction Superintendent Miles Carroll, who has worn out four teams of horses traveling up and down the line, tells me that he has about 250 men at work. He has plain sailing for twenty miles of the thirty-five to Paul Smith's. After that the line runs through State lands, and work will have to be stopped until the right of way is obtained. A detour of fifteen miles through a very rough country can be made to get around the State land, but at great expense. (It should be noted that the Paul Smith's referred to is the Paul Smith's Station, later changed to Gabriels.)

On the whole, contrary to general supposition, the building of this road through the mountains presents no engineering difficulties, and the contractors, who have had great experience in such work, tell me that it is a very easy undertaking. The ground is mostly light sand and there are but few rocks. It would be a more profitable undertaking if Dr. Webb was not in such a hurry. He cannot understand when he wants it done why the road cannot be built in a few weeks. His hurry will add much to the cost of the road. One of the contractors remarked to me, "When Dr. Webb gets through he will know more about railroad building than he does now. He comes up here one day and sees the forest standing, is back again within a week and is mad because the rails are not laid. We are pushing ahead more rapidly than any road we have built in this country and in order to keep the Doctor half satisfied we have sublet our contracts in small sections in order to get a large force of men here and the largest possible plant."

None of the railroad men to whom I have talked put the cost at less than $4,000,000 and some estimate it as high as $5,840,000.

It is interesting to watch the construction of a railroad in the forests. First the wood choppers are sent in along the line run by the engineers. As soon as they have felled all the standing timber for a short distance up the one hundred foot wide lane a second gang goes in and the tops and branches of the trees are chopped away, the whole mass being piled high in the center of the cut. Then it is fired. Hardly are the embers cold before another gang appears with stump pullers, grubhooks and block and tackle. The stumps are rapidly cleared away and then come Italians with shovel and pick to cut into the sand banks and throw up the grade. After that the sleepers are put down and the rails laid. Each of these six gangs follows close behind the other.

When I arrived at Malone it was necessary, in order to save my life, to indicate that my intentions were not hostile to the proposed railroad. I never saw a community more thoroughly in accord on one subject. Its enthusiasm approaches hysteria. It did not take long to convince me that there was a good and sufficient cause for this state of feeling. Malone is the most isolated village in the state, but in spite of its isolation and the fact that it has been for years at the mercy of a branch railroad, it would be hard to find a more bustling, prosperous and enterprising community. The people have felt that it was necessary for them to work out their own salvation, and their beautiful public buildings, their almost palatial homes, their clean and attractive streets, their splendid schools and their general air of thrift and progress show how well they have done it.

Solving the difficulty of getting through the State lands continued to be the prime objective of Dr. Webb and his lawyers. At one time it appeared as though the most feasible route was to cross the tracks of the Chateaugay Railroad just south of the Loon Lake station and then for seven miles run parallel to that road on the east of it before recrossing just south of Rainbow Lake. The crossings were, naturally, opposed by the Chateaugay and the matter dragged on until on January 14, 1892 the NEW YORK TIMES reported:

Dr. W. Seward Webb has at last been successful in his attempts to get the four miles of State Land in Township 20, Franklin County, which was all that was necessary in order to insure a direct and feasible route through the Adirondack wilderness from Malone to Herkimer. It will be remembered that on May 29 last, the State Commissioners of the Land Office refused either to grant or sell this land to Dr. Webb, on the advise of Attorney General Tabor that jurisdiction over these lands was confined to the Legislature.

Another method, however, was adopted and carried to a successful conclusion through the person of Dr. Samuel B. Ward of Albany who acquired the original title to the township after the lands in this township, comprising some 30,000 acres, had been sold for taxes at the State tax sales in 1881 and 1885, this land having been bid by the State. Back in the years 1887–89 Dr. Ward had the sale of the lands for taxes set aside on the grounds that the township was assessed as a whole instead of by lots: that the lands were all assessed as non-resident land, when, in fact, some of the land was resident, and such distinction should have been made in the assessment, and that the Board of Supervisors of Franklin County failed to extend the taxes on the assessment rolls of the town. These reasons for having made the sale set aside were sustained by the Controller, and the sale of one-third of the township, the southeastern portion, was cancelled and a clear title given to Dr. Ward on his payment of some $10,000 in back taxes. This is the portion in which is embraced the Upper Saranac, on which stands the famous Saranac Inn.

A few months ago Controller Wemple was asked by Dr. Ward to cancel the sale of the remainder of the township, some twenty thousand acres, on the same grounds that the former cancellation was based. This Controller Wemple did before the expiration of his term of office on December 31, last, and Dr. Ward paid the back taxes on the same, amounting to some $22,000. The land desired by Dr. Webb for his roadway comprises about four miles, 100 feet wide, running through Lots 4, 27, 28, 34, 37, 38 and 39, in all about 141 (sic) acres. Dr. Ward says that he will sell Dr. Webb the land which he needs for the construction of the railroad, as he thinks the interests of the northern section of the State demand the construction of this railroad.

Township Twenty is certainly one of the best watered townships in the Adirondacks, where unusually good hunting and fishing abound.

Before granting Dr. Ward's cancellation application Controller Wemple sent word to the State Forest Commissioners asking if they could see any objection to the granting of the application. The Forest Commissioners sent word back that as no proofs in the matter were presented to them they could see no objection if the application were regular.

The contractors on Dr. Webb's railroad are already working on this land and have the construction of their roadway at that point well under way.

It must have given Dr. Webb and his associates a considerable amount of satisfaction and relief when the construction crews finally started through these four miles needed so badly to complete the right-of-way. Now the necessary attention could be given to other details.

It is time that we learned what progress was being made from Malone northward in the matter of building a railroad towards Montreal.

CHAPTER VIII

North from Malone

The residents of Malone had been trying for many years to gain more ample railroad facilities and successive failures had brought them almost to despair. Then hope was revived because cooperation came from Canada. Valleyfield was a thriving little city on the St. Lawrence River with unrivaled water power and boundless energy among its people. Some of its citizens conceived the idea of building a railroad to the Adirondacks in order to secure ore so that iron could be manufactured in Valleyfield. They prospected for a route and then obtained from the Dominion Parliament, a charter for a railroad, with subscription almost sufficient to meet the cost of construction. This was the St. Lawrence and Adirondack Railway Company, a corporation of the Dominion of Canada formed in 1888 to build from Valleyfield to the New York State line. Its final destination and exact direction were not exactly stated but it was understood it was to reach Lyon Mountain but whether it would go through Malone or Chateaugay was undecided.

However, this charter extended only to the international boundary where the line could connect with nothing nor command enough business to defray the cost of operating.

Two years more of agitation and negotiation followed and then Edson J. Chamberlin, manager of the Canada and Atlantic Railway, interested himself in the matter with the result that he guaranteed to extend the road from the border to Malone, a distance of eleven miles, if Malone would pay him a cash bonus upon the completion of the work amounting to about $37,000. This money was raised by the people who were confident that if they could get a railroad to the St. Lawrence that link would be an attraction which would in time bring one from the Hudson or the Mohawk. As a part of the scheme there was organized at Malone, the Adirondack and St. Lawrence Railroad Company, with a capital of $2,000,000, and the articles recited the object of the company to build a railroad from the Canadian border through to Schenectady. That part of the road lying in Canada was to be styled the St. Lawrence and Adirondack Railroad.

On April 2, 1891 when he visited Malone, Dr. W. S. Webb entered into a contract with Mr. Chamberlin, by the terms of which he was to become the owner or perpetual leasee of the St. Lawrence and Adirondack Railroad, which began at the Canadian line, at the terminus of the Adirondack and St. Lawrence and extended north twenty miles to Valleyfield, where connection was to be made with the Canada and Atlantic Railway, leading directly to Ottawa, and also with the Grand Trunk and the Canadian Pacific. Construction work from Valleyfield toward Malone was then underway. The connection between Malone and the Adirondack & St. Lawrence, at the boundary line, was to be made by the Malone and St. Lawrence Railway, incorporated on September 11, 1891.

To review this let us turn to HERALD correspondent Thomas G. Alvord's report of June 1, 1891:

> From Malone the Webb line runs almost due north to the Canadian boundary. There the St. Lawrence and Adirondack road which is the same corporation with the name reversed as the Webb Road, runs to Valleyfield on the St. Lawrence River. There is a new railroad bridge from Valleyfield to Coteau connecting with the Grand Trunk Railroad for Montreal and the Atlantic Road for western Canada and the Canadian Pacific. It is about thirty miles from Malone to Valleyfield and about forty from there to Montreal. This would make the distance from New York City to Montreal by this line about 450 miles. The distance now over the Delaware and Hudson road is 384 miles. Dr. Webb expects with fewer curves to make up the difference of seventy miles by greater speed.
>
> It will thus be seen that there may be considerable method in Dr. Webb's alleged madness. There are no sharp curves, the greatest being four degrees. Malone is about 800 feet below the Adirondack Plateau, the top of which the road must reach within ten miles. The average grade for this stretch will be about eighty feet to the mile, but there are places where it will reach as much as ninety feet. Northward from Malone there is a 585 foot decrease in elevation to Valleyfield and in particular the drop from Malone to Constable is 314 feet in 5.3 miles. It is already said that Dr. Webb intends to locate his railroad shops and main roundhouse at Malone so that heavy engines can be kept here to be used as pushers over the heavy grades. About sixteen acres of land have been bought here by the Doctor for railroad purposes.

Construction proceeded rapidly on the line from Valleyfield south and the first train reached there from Malone on January 11, 1892.

Meanwhile the main line construction was being carried out from Malone south and from Remsen north. However, before the two divisions could be connected a dire situation came up particularly in connection with the southern division contractors.

CHAPTER IX
Labor Troubles

The darkest and most dismal part of the construction period of the Adirondack and St. Lawrence began to be apparent in March 1892. Many hundreds of workers had been hired as laborers on the railroad by the various contractors and sub-contractors. Many different ethnic groups were employed but those who lived in northern New York and Canada were most acclimated to the Adirondack area. Among these were many St. Regis Indians as well as residents of the area.

Some of the sub-contractors hired many black people in Tennessee. It was claimed that false premises were made to them as to the rigors of the winter weather in northern New York State. It was also charged that it was not made clear to them that transportation costs would have to be paid for by the individual and that clothing of more substantial nature would be required. As a result the unfortunate men found themselves rather deeply in debt before they even started to work. Hundreds of these southern workers arrived in Utica and were, as explained, ill prepared to endure the weather conditions in February and March in the North Woods. Many went no further than Utica and the authorities in Utica found themselves caring for these men until they could be sent in a homeward direction.

Many Italian and Polish laborers were hired in New York City and they too did not find the Adirondack winter weather to their liking.

Certain newspapers began to print stories of cruelty and oppression in the greatest of "yellow journalism" style. Many reports of cruelty were made in the newspapers and claims for non-payment of wages were also heard. Some of the workers attempted to walk off the job before they had earned sufficient amounts to pay off transportation and clothing charges advanced to them. This resulted in some cases in which the employers attempting to force some of the workers back into the camps so that they could resume work and square their company account. As might be expected, justifiably so or not, the subject of poor food was always brought to the front. There seems to be no question that some of the sub-contractors were more than overzealous in their efforts to force men back to work and serious confrontations occurred. It also must be pointed out that in many of the cases it was the most unsatisfactory type of worker who found themselves most involved. One of the contractors told the labor commissioners later that he had lost $25,000 on transportation alone.

During the last half of March 1892 many news stories were printed on the subject. Also a number of letters to the editors also appeared covering both sides of the problem. Many were rehashed stories or at least very similar to each other. They all carried the same general theme that the workers of some of the camps were generally mistreated. It is very difficult to assess what were the actual conditions. Undoubtedly some camps were better managed and some camps had better workmen. It looks like most of the complaints came from two or three of the contractors' camps.

It was inevitable that Dr. Webb would be very upset by these sinister reports. He decided to make a personal inspection and here is the report as carried in the Utica OBSERVER:

> Dr. Webb, Major Burns and Others on a Tour of Investigation! The stream of stories of abuse by contractors of employees of the Adirondack & St. Lawrence Railroad Company continue to be poured into the ears of sympathetic people by workmen coming from the Woods, and these stories finding their way into the newspapers decided the officials of the road to make another tour of the route to investigate. With this object in view, and without apprising anyone of their intentions, a party composed of Dr. Webb, President of the Company, Major Burns, General Manager, Superintendent Flagg, of the Wagner Palace Car Company, the Chief and Resident Engineers, and two friends of Dr. Webb went to Remsen last Wednesday, and from that point started over the route of the A. & St. L. Road, going its entire length. Major Burns was seen by the OBSERVER representative in Herkimer this forenoon, to whom he said emphatically that the stories of abuse were not true. Dr. Webb himself and the rest of the party came upon the contractors and men absolutely without warning and unexpectedly, and ate and slept with the men. He asserts that the men, and animals, too, were being better cared for than he had anticipated, much better cared for than is generally the case under similar conditions. The men were well and hearty, and were frequently heard laughing and singing at their work, and among them some of the southern workers were ready to dance for a dime.
>
> Major Burns said, as has been stated before, that there were a few cases of desertion, where lazy men had had their transportation paid to their destination, and then refused to refund the amount in work. The contractors he said, have a great deal to contend with on their side. They are doing their best to fill their contracts within the given time

and are losing money in the attempt. They therefore cannot pay the men money until they have worked out the amount advanced in paying their fares. He also states that the men leaving the work are few in number, and that most of the stories of abuse told to the poor authorities and others are told by the men who have never been in the woods at all — tramps who are roaming from place to place and working the "Adirondack" dodge, as it is called among them, for all it is worth. As to food, Major Burns says there is at the present time $40,000 worth of flour and other supplies along the line in the woods. The cost of transportation forty miles or more into the wilderness is of course considerable, and must be added to the price at which the supplies are sold. There may be exceptional cases of extortion in charges, but the party did not see or learn of any on the trip. Major Burns expressed himself as perfectly satisfied with what he saw, and said that Dr. Webb and himself were more than ever satisfied that the work was progressing under circumstances as favorable to the workmen as they could be made. There had been some thought of having Deputy Sheriffs appointed, to be paid for by the Company, whose duty it should be to watch for any abuse and make arrests for the same, but nothing was found to call for such a step.

At the end of March, Commissioner Florence Donovan of the State Board of Arbitration and Mediation, Board Members William Purcell and Gilbert Robertson and Assistant Secretary Everson held hearings at Utica, Lowville and Boonville and on ensuing days visited seven labor camps. Many employees or former employees were interviewed and again they reported that there were serious abuses but the usual number of hearsay stories seemed to be repeated. On April 2, 1892 the NEW YORK DAILY TRIBUNE reported:

> Utica, N. Y. — April 1, 1892 — State Commissioner Donovan and party spent yesterday visiting the camps of the railroad laborers in the Adirondacks. They visited seven camps. By telephone to the OBSERVER from Stillwater, it is learned that little foundation was found for the stories of cruelty and abuse that was sworn to by witnesses in Utica and Lowville.

The report of the Board of Abritration and Mediation appeared late in April. The members had found the chief complaints to be against the sub-contractors for the Enterprise Contract Company, which was building the road for about seventy miles between Moose River and Tupper Lake. . . . The evidence showed that agents made false pretenses about the climate in the Adirondacks and also in reference to the cost of living and the payment of transportation. Enterprise evidently did not authorize agents in making false pretenses. The camps were properly constructed and well-heated. The charge of the sub-contractors about armed guards proved true in only one case and that man has since abandoned his contract.

It was hoped that this report would put an end to the complaints of disgruntled workers but that view was overoptimistic for discontented workers still came out from the camps but did not necessarily complain of physical mistreatment.

Charles H. Burnett in CONQUERING THE WILDERNESS summed up the situation as follows:

> It developed that an employee of the State Labor Bureau was supplying the newspapers with their sensational material. He offered to discontinue his activitites for a round sum. He was invited to a meeting with a representative of the railroad at Boonville, and induced to repeat his demands while Major Burns and others listened through stove-pipe hole in the ceiling. This was a very primitive dictograph, but it served the purpose. When threatened with exposure he was never heard from again.

Complaints eventually subsided but great damage had been done to mar the reputation of the railroad builders and permitted the superstition to develop that many men were buried along the right-of-way. That everyone who was employed in the camps did not suffer and enjoyed his work was best told in the Albany ARGUS on January 22, 1892:

> Whitehall, Jan. 22 — John R. Anderson, foreman for Brady Brothers, contractors for section grading and construction on Dr. Webb's Adirondack and St. Lawrence Railway, passed through town this noon on conductor Thayer's train with a party of Hungarian laborers from Poland, Herkimer County. They had finished their contract work on the line between Poland and Trenton Falls, and are now going to strike in on the section embraced in the lands recently acquired by Dr. Webb from Dr. S. B. Ward, of Albany.
>
> The party appeared well fed and jolly, and as many of them have acquired sufficient of the English vernacular to enable them to converse intelligently, the ARGUS correspondent inquired of them as to the truth of current stories of abuses by the contractors. All who could speak English said that they had been well treated, both in pay and accommodations, and as to board, they provided that for themselves, and had had abundance for the wants of working men. They had been paid in full up to yesterday, and were cheerfully accompanying Foreman Anderson to the new section.
>
> The party consisted of thirty-nine men, two women and a young girl. The women are the cooks of the party and one of the men is steward of the camp. The others wrestle with the pick, bar and shovel. They have been at work in the Town of Poland since last April and a happier and

more contented lot of workingmen never passed through this place. One young fellow had a unique musical instrument of the fiddle family. It was of his own construction and from which he was sawing out music of an evidently Wagnerian order, to the delectation of his companions and the amusement of the passengers who went into the car to hear him. It was carved out of a basswood log and had a body of about thirty by eighteen inches in dimensions, with a sounding board, bridge and keys of the same material. The instrument had but two strings — linen wrapping twines, the larger of whipcord size. The bow was improvised by a crooked birch twig and black horse hair, and when the artist touched it to the strings and sounded a waltz the Hungarian feet would beat time to its harmony (?) in a unison that proved that everything goes in the line of music when the listener is soul happy and free from care. This party certainly did not bear any evidence of contractors' niggardliness and cruelty.

It is noted that this group said that they provided its own board so it must be the group that while in Poland, perpetrated a great hoax on one of the local residents. Miss Helen Schermerhorn told the author that a work camp was adjacent to her father's garden. When it came time to harvest his potatoes that fall he found that every hill had been skillfully dug into from the side and every potato in the patch had been removed leaving only the dried vine sticking out of the top of the ground.

CHAPTER X
Putting it all Together

Considerable difficulty was also experienced in getting the railroad through lands variously described as the Lyon estate or DeCamp lands in the Moose River area south of Old Forge. Herschel Moore in his letter referred to getting the DeCamp condemnation suit started and the matter was in the hands of the courts for some time. It was in the spring of 1892 before anything could be done to get the railroad through that area.

It almost seems incredible that work could be carried on during the winter months but we know that it was because of the difficulties reported in some of the contractors' camps. The RAILROAD GAZETTE reported in March 1892 that the line had been graded north of Poland to the Moose River and that the tracks would probably reach White Lake Corners by April 15th. The longest continuous section was from Malone south toward Tupper Lake. The other track that had been laid so far was in small pieces at various points. By May 27th the GAZETTE reported that the track was laid thirty-three miles north of Poland except for the bridge at Trenton Falls which was not completed at that time.

The name of the Adirondack and St. Lawrence Railway had been used since the great enterprise was first started and it was going to last through till the end but on June 23, 1892 Dr. Webb consolidated the different railroads that made up his Adirondack system into one corporation. The joint agreement of consolidation of the Herkimer, Newport and Poland Railway Company, the Herkimer, Newport and Poland Extension Railway Company and the St. Lawrence and Adirondack Railway Company forming the Mohawk and Malone Railway Company was filed in Albany. However, the appelation "The Adirondack and St. Lawrence Line" was used on timetables and on some accounting forms with "Mohawk and Malone Railway Company" also appearing in smaller letters. There seems to be considerable question as to whether the Mohawk and Malone name ever appeared on any rolling stock of the company. Certainly it did not appear on any locomotives.

Despite the change in name, the use of Adirondack and St. Lawrence Railway continued in so far as the newspapers and advertisements were concerned. On June 26, 1892 the NEW YORK TIMES was able to report that the southern division from Herkimer to Fulton Chain Station would be opened Friday, July 1st. There is a little conflict about this date and the RAILROAD GAZETTE said the date was July 2nd. This confusion may have resulted from the fact that the first train was scheduled to leave New York City at 9:15 P. M. on July first but would be running north from Herkimer and arriving at Fulton Chain on July second.

As of the first of July 1892, the unfinished portion of the track laying was on the section between Old Forge and Lake Lila, 31 miles, and between Rainbow and Loon Lake, 14 miles, on the section north of Tupper Lake. The work had been considerably delayed by very unfavorable weather. The heavy and continuous rains retarded the ballasting on the northern division so that it was necessary to postpone the opening of the road from Malone to Tupper Lake and Childwold until July 16th.

The first timetable showed both the Southern and Northern Divisions of the Adirondack & St. Lawrence Railway. The Southern Division had been considered open since the first scheduled train left New York on July 1st via Herkimer arriving at Fulton Chain on July 2nd. The Northern Division's first train left New York on July 15th and arrived on the Northern Division on the 16th. These trains were routed via the Rome, Watertown and Ogdensburg to Norwood, from there to Malone on the Central Vermont Railroad and from Malone south to Childwold on the main line and to Saranac Lake Village via the branch line.

On August 12th, 1892 the RAILROAD GAZETTE stated:

> About 25 miles of road remains to be constructed between Raynor's Pond to the north, 16 miles from Childwold, N. Y., and from three miles, north of Old Forge, on the Fulton Chain of lakes, on the south. Between these points the roadbed is about completed and the rails will be laid in a few weeks. A large section of the roadbed now in use was laid in frosty weather and when the ground thawed the roadbed settled under the weight of the heavy rolling stock in use on the road. These portions of the road will thus have to be reballasted. Nearly 2,000 men are now employed in pushing forward the work on the road, which will be completed toward the last of September.

The gap was narrowing rapidly and by September 21, 1892 only sixteen miles of track was needed and the grading had already been done.

OPEN FOR PASSENGER TRAFFIC.

SOUTHERN DIVISION,
HERKIMER TO HINCKLEY AND FULTON CHAIN. } **NOW OPEN.**

NORTHERN DIVISION,
MALONE TO SARANAC VILLAGE AND CHILDWOLD. } **JULY 16TH, 1892.**
(From New York & Albany
July 15th, 1892.

--- THE ---

ADIRONDACK & St. LAWRENCE

·R·A·I·L·W·A·Y·

WILL BE OPENED FOR THE REGULAR HANDLING OF PASSENGER TRAFFIC ON THE
DATES SPECIFIED ABOVE.

To The Adirondacks.

MAGNIFICENTLY APPOINTED COACHES AND WAGNER PALACE SLEEPING CARS IN

VESTIBULED TRAINS, WILL BE RUN SOLID, DAILY,

FROM NEW YORK CITY (Grand Central Station
N.Y.C. & H. R.R.)

(Commencing Friday Evening, July 15th 1892.)

— LEAVING —	— TO —	— ARRIVING —
NEW YORK, 7.30 P. M.	Mountain View,	9.03 A. M.
	Loon Lake, (Station)	9.35 "
	Paul Smith's, (Station)	10.02 "
ALBANY, 11.35 P. M.	Saranac Junction,	10.15 "
	Saranac Village,	10.40 "
	Saranac Inn, (Station)	10.25 "
UTICA, 2.10 A. M.	Tupper Lake Junction,	11.15 "
	Childwold, (Station)	11.30 "

CONNECTING

At LOON LAKE,	Stage	For LOON LAKE HOUSE,
" PAUL SMITH'S,	"	" PAUL SMITH'S HOTEL, MEACHAM LAKE AND BLOOMINGDALE.
" SARANAC VILLAGE,	"	" MIRROR LAKE AND LAKE PLACID.
" SARANAC INN,	"	" SARANAC INN (HOTEL),
" " " (HOTEL),	Steamer	HOTEL WAWBEEK, RUSTIC LODGE, Etc.
" TUPPER LAKE JUNCTION,	"	" BIG TUPPER LAKE.
" CHILDWOLD,	Stage	" CHILDWOLD PARK HOUSE.

WAGNER PALACE SLEEPING CARS

Will leave New York daily at 8:00 P. M., Reaching **Trenton Falls** at 6:30 A. M.; Remsen, 6:40 A. M.;
White Lake, 7:14 A. M.; **Fulton Chain,** 8:00 A. M., Connecting at Fulton Chain for Fulton Chain
of Lakes, Raquette Lake, Etc.

Intending Visitors to the Adirondacks should engage space in Wagner Cars Promptly.

*Issued for the opening of the Northern and Southern Divisions of the
Adirondack & St. Lawrence the time table shows trains scheduled from
Grand Central Station in New York on the evening of July 15, 1892
reaching the A&StL on the morning of July 16th. The line between
Fulton Chain Station and Childwold was still uncompleted so trains for*

SOLID VESTIBULED TRAINS,

CONSISTING OF THE FINEST PASSENGER EQUIPMENT EXTANT.

RAPID AND SAFE TRAIN SERVICE.

TO ALL THE RESORTS OF THE

NORTHERN AND SOUTHWESTERN

ADIRONDACKS.

-:- CONDENSED TRAIN SCHEDULE. -:-

SUBJECT TO CHANGE WITHOUT NOTICE.

⟶ NORTHERN DIVISION. ⟶

TO THE NORTHERN ADIRONDACKS.		FROM THE NORTHERN ADIRONDACKS.	
	Daily.		Daily
L've New York, (N. Y. C. & H. R. R. R.)	7.30 P. M.	L've Childwold Park House, (Stage.)	2.00 P. M
" Albany, " "	11.35 "	" Childwold, (A. & St. L. R'y.)	3.05 "
" Utica, (R., W. & O. R. R.)	2.10 A. M.	" Tupper Lake Junc. " "	3.30 "
L've Chicago, (Mich.Cent.) daily except Fri.	10.10 P. M.	" Hotel Wawbeek, (Steamer.)	11.00 A. M.
" Detroit, " "	9.50 A. M.	" Saranac Inn (Hotel), (Stage.)	4.00 P. M.
" Niagara Falls, (N. Y. C. & H. R. R. R.)	8.21 P. M.	" Saranac Inn (Station), (A. & St. L. R'y.)	4.20 "
" Buffalo, " "	9.15 "	" Lake Placid, (Stage.)	2.00 "
" Rochester, " "	11.05 "	" Saranac Village, (A. & St. L. R'y.)	4.00 "
" Syracuse, (R., W. & O. R. R.)	1.15 A. M.	" Saranac Junction, " "	4.35 "
		" Paul Smith's (Hotel), (Stage.)	4.10 "
L've Norwood, (C. V. R. R.)	6.55 A. M.	" Paul Smith's (Station), (A. & St. L. R'y.)	4.51 "
" Malone, " "	8.05 "	" Loon Lake House, (Stage.)	4.60 "
" Malone (Union Stat'n, A. & St. L. R'y)	8.20 "	" Loon Lake (Station), (A. & St. L. R'y)	5.22 "
Arr. Mountain View, " "	9.03 "	" Mountain View, " "	5.55 "
" Loon Lake, " "	9.35 "	Arr. Malone, (Union Stat'n) " "	6.30 "
" Loon Lake House, (Stage.)	10.00 "	" Malone, (C. V. R. R.)	6.35 "
" Paul Smith's, (A. & St. L. R'y.)	10.02 "	" Norwood, " "	7.30 "
" Paul Smith's Hotel, (Stage.)	10.30 "		
" Saranac Junction, (A. & St. L. R'y.)	10.15 "	Arr. Syracuse, (R., W. & O. R. R.)	3.45 A. M.
" Saranac Village, " "	10.40 "	" Rochester, (N. Y. C. & H. R. R. R.)	5.55 "
" Lake Placid, (Stage.)	12.15 P. M.	" Buffalo, " "	7.45 "
" Saranac Inn (Station), (A. & St. L. R'y.)	10.25 A. M.	" Niagara Falls, " "	7.44 "
" Saranac Inn (Hotel), (Stage.)	10.40 "	" Detroit, (Mich. Cent.)	8.35 P. M.
" Hotel Wawbeek, (Steamer.)	2.45 P. M.	" Chicago, " "	7.55 A. M.
" Tupper Lake Junc. (A. & St. L. R'y.)	11.15 A. M.	Arr. Utica, (R., W. & O. R. R.)	12.30 A. M.
" Childwold, " "	11.30 "	" Albany, (N. Y. C. & H. R. R. R.)	3.05 "
" Childwold Park House, (Stage,)	12.30 P. M.	" New York, " "	7.30 "

⟶ SOUTHERN DIVISION. ⟶

TO THE SOUTHWESTERN ADIRONDACKS.			FROM THE SOUTHWESTERN ADIRONDACKS.		
	Daily, except Sunday.	Daily.		Daily, except Sunday.	
L've Buffalo, "	1.15 P. M.	9.15 P. M.	L've Head of 4th Lake, (Str)		5.45 P. M.
" Rochester, "	2.40 "	11.05 "	" Old Forge, (Stage,)	5.30 A. M.	7.15 "
" Syracuse, (N. Y. C.)	4.15 "	1.20 A. M.	" Fulton Chain, (A. & St. L.)	5.45 "	7.30 "
" Utica, (R., W. & O.)	5.50 "	3.50 "	" White Lake, "	7.14 "	8.18 "
L've New York, (N. Y. C.)	7.30 A. M.	8.00 P. M.	" Remsen, "	7.55 " / 8.25 "	9.15 "
" Albany, "	1.35 P. M.	11.55 P. M.	" Trenton Falls, "	8.38 "	9.25 "
L've Herkimer, (A. & St. L. R'y)	5.20 P. M.	5.30 A. M.	Arr. Herkimer, "	9.50 "	10.30 "
" Trenton Falls, "	6.28 "	6.30 "	Arr. Albany, (N. Y. C.)	12.55 P. M.	1.30 A. M
" Remsen, "	6.55 "	6.45 "	" New York, "	6.41 "	6.30 "
" White Lake, "	7.45 "	7.14 "	" Utica, (R., W. & O.)	8.50 A. M.	10.05 P. M.
Arr. Fulton Chain, "	8.45 "	8.00 "	" Syracuse, "	12.45 P. M.	11.32 "
" Old Forge, (Stage)	9.00 "	8.15 "	" Rochester, "	3.47 "	1.25 A. M
" Head of 4th Lake, (Str)		10.00 "	Arr. Buffalo, (N. Y. C.)	5.10 "	3.15 "

*Except Sunday.

EDWARD M. BURNS,
GENERAL MANAGER,
HERKIMER, N. Y.

W. SEWARD WEBB,
PRESIDENT.
NEW YORK

H. D. CARTER,
ASS'T GEN. FREIGHT & PASS. AG'T
HERKIMER, N. Y.

the Northern Division were routed via the Rome, Watertown and Ogdensburg to Norwood where they were transferred to the Ogdensburg & Lake Champlain for the run to Malone. At Malone, the New York trains were routed southward to Lake Placid and Childwold. (Adirondack Museum Library)

It must have been a matter of immense personal satisfaction to Dr. W. Seward Webb as the rails drew together. He had inspired his forces with a degree of loyalty that is rarely seen according to Charles Burnett, who continued his tribute:

> The Doctor made frequent trips over the work, travelling on foot, horseback, handcar or construction train as opportunity offered. He knew every engineer, every contractor and sub-contractor, every foreman and every engineman and conductor by name. He never failed to stop and shake hands with them. He asked intelligent questions and showed sympathetic understanding of their difficulties and problems. He was prompt to help them over the rough spots with every resource at his command. He had the qualities of magnetism and leadership in a remarkable degree. He was generous to a fault. It is surprising that a man of his distinguished lineage and with all his environment of wealth and social position, should have been so genuinely democratic. He was loved and respected by everyone on the job, from the highest to the lowest. They would go to any lengths to please him. As one of the engineeers expressed it, "There was not a man on the line but would stand on his head for the Doctor."

The date for the driving of the final spike on the Adirondack and St. Lawrence Railway was set for October 12, 1892. Burnett's report on this event has been repeated time and again but we cannot improve or embellish it:

> Finally on October 12th, about a half mile south of Twitchell Creek Bridge, the two ends met and the last spike was driven. There was no ceremony, but much jubilation. The honor of driving the last spike was awarded to a young assistant engineer. He was undoubtedly a better engineer than he was a tracklayer for he swung at the spike a dozen times before he hit it, much to the disgust of the Negroes and Indians.

It is too bad that there was no record made of any dignitaries being present, particularly Dr. Webb or Chief Engineer W. N. Roberts or his Assistant Chiefs. Apparently no photographs were taken of this event for none have ever come to light.

Regular scheduled trains were running on October 24, 1892. The NEW YORK TIMES reported the schedule called for leaving New York at 7:30 P. M., arriving in Montreal about 9:00 A. M. and the return trip leaving Montreal about 4:15 P. M. and arriving in New York at 7:45 A. M.

There was much work to be done, of course, to bring the railroad up to a first class condition. Reballasting track was necessary; temporary trestles had to be filled in within the near future; banks and cuts had to be widened and stabilized; temporary culverts had to be replaced with more permanent types. Burnett said that nine steam shovels and twenty-seven work trains of thirty cars each were kept busy for months making the improvements.

In 1894 the inspector for the Railroad Commissioners of the State of New York made a report of his findings and here are some of the interesting facts. The single track, standard gauge line was laid with seventy-five pound steel rails. All the switches were "split points" and excellently cared for. The targets and guides were well painted and the guards were well braced. There were thirty-three solid steel floor structures on masonry, fifty-one pile and pile bent trestles, some seven deck plate girder bridges, eleven through plate girders, two riveted trusses, twenty-four separate minor openings and two trussed stringer openings.

The Mohawk and Malone Railway was leased to the New York Central and Hudson River Railroad on May 1, 1893 after having been in operation for about seven months. Henceforth it became the Adirondack Division of the New York Central and one of the first things that happened was the change in operation with through trains starting from and terminating at the Union Station at Utica instead of Herkimer. Trains were operated over the Rome, Watertown and Ogdensburg tracks, formerly the Utica and Black River Railroad to Remsen where they were shifted over to the Mohawk and Malone tracks.

For the ten month period ending April 30, 1893 the Mohawk and Malone Railway company reported to the Railroad Commissioners of the State of New York the following data:

> Capital Stock authorized by law or charter and now outstanding — 45,000 shares with a total par value of $4,500,000.
> The number of stockholders was 21.
> Funded debt; First Mortgage, four percent gold bonds, dated July 1, 1892, 99 year term, $2,500,000.
>
> Total cost of road $6,817,313.39
> Locamotives $174,283.04
> Passenger cars $74,603,88
> Freight & other cars $23,344.57
> Gross earnings first ten months $188,600.15
> Operating deficit $79,349.88
> Number of Passengers carried 137,276
> Number of tons of freight carried 71,297
> Locomotives 14
> First class passenger cars 10
> Second class passenger cars 2

Baggage, mail & express cars	2
Box freight cars	20
Flat freight cars	50
Caboose, 8 wheel cars.....................	6

The reason for the ten month report was that it covered the period the Mohawk and Malone Railway operated as an independent company and the last two months starting May 1st, 1893 were under the control of the New York Central and Hudson River Railroad.

Some of the locomotives were turned over to the Central Vermont Railway under a mortgage agreement and it is understood that some of the rolling stock of the Herkimer, Newport and Poland Narrow Gauge Railway was converted to standard gauge rolling stock and this also became Central Vermont property.

It is not readily apparent when the stock of the Mohawk and Malone Railway Company was actually purchased from the twenty-one stockholders listed in 1893 by the New York Central and Hudson River Railroad but by 1901 the number of stockholders was reduced to thirteen. In 1913 the Public Service Commission, Second District, of the State of New York authorized the merger of the Mohawk and Malone Railway Company into the New York Central and Hudson River Railroad as the later road now owned 100% of the capital stock of the Mohawk & Malone.

Moody's reported in 1976 that $1,489,000 of the bonds were still outstanding with no interest having been paid since 1969.

In January 1979 the WALL STREET JOURNAL reported that the Penn Central Corporation was settling with the holders of the Mohawk and Malone Railway bonds by turning over to them $197,000 in cash and about $1.8 millions in a new Series A Penn Central bonds.

The New York Central operated the Mohawk and Malone Railway as the Adirondack Division most of the time since it came under its control. There were periods of reorganization when it operated differently such as in 1907 when it was part of the Middle Division and in 1908–1909 when it was part of the Mohawk Divison but it was universally considered as the Adirondack Divison and this included, as always, the section from Herkimer to Remsen and in later years, the section from Herkimer to Poland even though no longer connected with the main line to Malone.

MOHAWK & MALONE RAILWAY CO.

Adirondack & St. Lawrence Line

LOCAL TIME TABLE—NORTHBOUND.

TO THE ADIRONDACKS, MONTREAL, ETC.

Dist. f'm Herk'er	STATIONS. April 23d, 1893.	Adirondack and Montreal Express. *47	Day Express. †21	Mail. †1	Mail. †5	Freight. †61
	Lv. NEW YORK, (N. Y. C.)..	7 00 pm	11 59 pm	....	10 00 am	....
....	" Poughkeepsie, "	9 15 "	3 10 am	....	10.00 "	....
....	" Albany, "	11.15 "	8.25 "	....	1.35 pm	....
....	Ar. Herkimer, "	1.20 am	11.07 "	....	4.17 "	....
	Lv. BUFFALO, (N. Y. C.)..	3.50 am	4 40 am	....	8 50 am	....
....	" Rochester, "	6 15 "	6.50 "	....	10.30 "	....
....	" Syracuse, "	8.45 "	9.40 "	....	1 30 pm	....
....	" Utica, "	10.25 "	11.20 "	6 00 am	3.25 "	....
....	Ar. Herkimer, "	10.50 "	11.45 "	6 30 "	3.55 "	....
.0	Lv. HERKIMER,..	1.30 am	11.50 am	7.00 am	5.00 pm	2.35 pm
3 3	" Kast Bridge..	....	f 11.59 "	f 7 07	5.09 "	2.46 "
5 2	" Countryman's..	....	f 12.03 pm	f 7.11	5.14 "	2.54 "
7 0	" County House..	....	f 12.07 "	f 7.15	5.18 "	3.00 "
8 7	" Middleville..	d 1 47 am	12.11 "	7.19 "	5.22 "	3.16 "
11.2	" Fenner's Grove..	....	f 12 17 "	f 7.24 "	5 27 "	3 30 "
13 0	" Newport..	d 1.55 am	12 21 "	7.28 "	5.31 "	3.45 "
16 4	" Poland..	d 2 01 "	12.28 "	7 35 "	5.39 "	4 04 "
2 4	" Gravesville..	....	....	f 7 43	5.49 "	....
23.6	" TRENTON FALLS..	....	f 12 45 pm	f 7.50 "	5.56 "	4 50 "
25.5	Ar. PROSPECT..	....	12.49 "	7 54 "	6.00 "	5.15 "
....	Lv. (Junction Hinckley Br.)..	....	....	....	6.05 "	6.10 "
27 6	Ar. REMSEN..	2 22 am	12.55 pm	8 00 am	6 10 "	6.30 "
....	Lv. REMSEN..	....	....	....	....	6.45 "
31 6	" Honnedaga..	....	f 1 03 pm	....	....	7 08 "
35.5	" Forestport..	....	1.12 "	....	....	7.28 "
42.4	" White Lake..	....	1 28 "	....	....	8.02 "
47.5	" Otter Lake..	....	f 1.42 "	....	....	8.30 "
49 4	" McKeever..	....	f 1 45 "	....	....	8.40 "
58 0	" FULTON CHAIN..	3 20 am	2 06 "	....	....	9 30 "
69 0	" Big Moose..	....	2.30 "	....	....	10.25 "
77 6	" Beaver River..	....	2.49 "	....	....	11.15 "
80 2	" Little Rapids. (Private)..	....	....	....	....	....
87 1	" Ne-ha-sa-ne.. (Stations.)..	....	....	....	....	....
90.7	" Bog Lake..	....	f 3 17 pm	....	....	12.25 am
99 7	" Horseshoe Pond..	....	f 3 37 "	....	....	1.02 "
106.9	" Childwold..	....	f 3 53 "	....	....	1 32 "
113 4	Ar. TUPPER LAKE JUNC..	....	....	....	....	2.00 "
						No. 63.
	Lv. TUPPER LAKE JUNC..	5.10 am	4 10 pm	....	5.25 am	....
128 4	" Saranac Inn..	x 5.36 "	4 38 "	....	6 30 "	....
131 4	Ar. LAKE CLEAR..	5.43 "	4 47 "	....	7 00 "	....
	Lv. (Junction Saranac Br.)..	....	....	....	....	7 25 am
136 6	" Paul Smith's..	x 5.57 am	4 59 pm	....	....	7 31 "
138 9	" Rainbow Lake..	....	f 5 02 "	....	....	7 37 "
144.0	" Lake Kushaqua..	....	f 5.12 "	....	....	8.02 "
149 2	" Loon Lake..	x 6.14 am	5 20 "	....	....	8.35 "
160.2	" Mountain View..	....	f 5 42 "	....	....	9.20 "
162.5	" Owl's Head..	....	5 46 "	....	....	9.40 "
169 1	" Whippleville..	....	f 6.01 "	....	....	10.10 "
173.1	Ar. MALONE (Union Station)..	7.05 am	6.10 "	....	....	10.30 "
	Lv. Malone (St. L. & A.)..	7.10 am	6 15 pm	....	....	....
....	" Huntingdon, "	7.45 "	6 51 "	....	....	....
....	" Coteau Junc."	8 24 "	7 30 "	....	....	....
....	Ar. Montreal (G. T. Ry.)..	9.20 "	8 30 "	....	....	....
....	Ar. Ottawa (C. A. Ry.)..	11.20 am	....	....	....	....

HINCKLEY BRANCH.

From the Main Line.		Dist. bet. Sta.	STATIONS	To the Main Line.	
Way F'g't †78	Way F'g't †71			Way F'g't †72	Way F'g't †74
pm	pm			pm	pm
.... 5.25	2.30	.0 Ar. .....HINCKLEY.....Lv.		2.45	5 45
5.15	2 20	2.8 Lv......... Prospect ....Ar.		3 00	6.05

SARANAC BRANCH.

From the Main Line.				Dist. bet. Sta.	STATIONS.	To the Main Line.			
*57 Daily	†55	†58	*51 Daily			*50 Daily	†52	†54	*56 Daily
pm	pm	am	am			am	am	pm	pm
9.20	6.00	11.15	6.10	.0 Ar.....SARANAC LAKE.....Lv.		5.15	10.20	4 20	8.35
9.00	10 50	5.50		5.6 Lv......... Lake Clear.....Ar.		5.40	10.40	4.45	8.55

* Daily. † Daily except Sunday. ‡ Daily except Saturday.
f Train stops when signaled, for passengers.
d Train stops to leave passengers holding tickets from Utica or points beyond, and from Albany or points beyond. x Train stops to leave passengers from Herkimer or points beyond and on signal to take on passengers for Malone or points beyond.
Freight trains carry passengers in caboose cars.

MOHAWK & MALONE RAILWAY CO.

Adirondack & St. Lawrence Line

LOCAL TIME TABLE—SOUTHBOUND.

FROM THE ADIRONDACKS, MONTREAL, ETC.

Dist. f'm Malone.	STATIONS. April 23d, 1893.	Day Express. †86	N. Y. Express. *44	Mail. †2	Mail. †4	Freight. †64
....	Lv. OTTAWA (C. A. Ry.)..	....	3.25 pm	....	....	....
....	" MONTREAL (G. T. Ry)..	7.00 am	5.30 pm	....	....	....
....	" Coteau Junc. (St. L. & A.)..	8.00 "	6.35 "	....	....	....
....	" Huntingdon, "	8 40 "	7 13 "	....	....	....
....	" Malone, "	9.15 "	7.45 "	....	....	....
0	Lv. MALONE (Union Station)..	9.20 am	7 50 pm	....	....	2 05 pm
4.0	" Whippleville..	f9.27 "	....	....	....	2.20 "
10 6	" Owl's Head..	9.40 "	....	....	....	2.45 "
12.9	" Mountain View..	f9.45 "	....	....	....	2 55 "
24.9	" Loon Lake..	10 09 "	x8.32 pm	....	....	3.50 "
29.1	" Lake Kushaqua..	f10.16 "	....	....	....	4.10 "
34.2	" Rainbow Lake..	f10 26 "	....	....	....	4.35 "
36.6	" Paul Smith's..	f10 32 "	x8.50 pm	....	....	4 50 "
41.7	" LAKE CLEAR..	10.42 "	9.00 "	....	....	....
....	" (Junc. Saranac Branch)..	....	....	....	....	5 35 pm
44.7	" Saranac Inn..	f10.47 am	x9 05 pm	....	....	6.06 "
59.7	Ar. TUPPER LAKE JUNC..	....	....	....	....	7.20 "
						†62
	Lv. TUPPER LAKE JUNC..	11.20 am	9 30 pm	....	....	7 00 am
66.2	" Childwold..	f11 34 "	....	....	....	7 25 "
73.4	" Horseshoe Pond..	f11.49 "	....	....	....	7.57 "
82.4	" Hog Lake..	f12 08 pm	....	....	....	8.36 "
88.0	" Ne-ha-sa-ne.. (Private)..	....	....	....	....	....
92.9	" Little Rapids. (Stations)..	....	....	....	....	....
95.5	" Beaver River..	....	....	....	....	9.37 am
104 1	" Big Moose..	f12 36 pm	....	....	....	10.16 "
115 1	" FULTON CHAIN..	1.16 "	11.30 pm	....	....	11 05 "
123.7	" McKeever..	f1 37 "	....	....	....	11.46 "
126.6	" Otter Lake..	f1.42 "	....	....	....	11 58 "
130.7	" White Lake..	1.52 "	....	....	....	12.30 pm
137.6	" Forestport..	2.16 "	....	....	....	1.12 "
141.5	" Honnedaga..	f2.28 "	....	....	....	1 30 "
144.5	" REMSEN..	2.25 "	12 20 am	8 25 am	6.45 pm	2.05 "
147 6	Ar. PROSPECT..	2.31 "	....	8.30 "	6.49 "	2.20 "
....	Lv. (Junc. Hinckley Branch)..	....	....	8 35 "	....	3.05 "
149.5	" TRENTON FALLS..	f2.38 pm	....	f8 39	f6.52 "	3.15 "
152 7	" Gravesville..	....	....	f8.45	f6.57 "	....
156.7	" Poland..	2.55 pm	d12 42 am	8.54 "	7.06 "	4 04 pm
160.1	" Newport..	3.05 "	d12.48 "	9 02 "	7.12 "	4.20 "
161.9	" Fenner's Grove..	f3.09 "	....	f9.05 "	f7.16 "	4.29 "
164.4	" Middleville..	3 16 "	d12 56 am	9.10 "	7.21 "	4.42 "
166.1	" County House..	f3.20 "	....	f9.14 "	f7.24 "	4.50 "
167.9	" Countryman's..	f3.24 "	....	f9.18 "	f7.27 "	4.57 "
169.8	" Kast Bridge..	f3.28 "	....	f9.22 "	f7.31 "	5.09 "
173.1	Ar. HERKIMER..	3.35 "	1.15 am	9.30 "	7.38 "	5.25 "
....	Lv. Herkimer (N. Y. C.)..	3.55 pm	1 15 am	10.00 am	7 39 pm	....
....	Ar. Albany, "	6 50 "	3 20 "	12.55 pm	10.25 "	....
....	" Poughkeepsie, "	....	5 30 "	3 50 "	....	....
....	" NEW YORK, "	10.30 "	7.45 "	6 41 "	....	....
....	Lv. Herkimer, (N. Y. C.)..	4.17 pm	1.34 am	10 03 am	8 31 pm	....
....	Ar. Utica, "	6.45 "	2.55 "	10.35 "	9 05 "	....
....	" Syracuse, "	8.35 "	5.45 "	12 45 pm	11.10 "	....
....	" Rochester, "	11.10 "	5 45 "	3.47 "	1.25 am	....
....	" BUFFALO, "	11.40 "	7 30 "	5.10 "	3.15 "	....

HINCKLEY BRANCH.

From the Main Line.		Dist. bet. Sta.	STATIONS.	To the Main Line.	
Way F'g't †78	Way F'g't †71			Way F'g't †72	Way F'g't †74
pm	pm			pm	pm
5.25	2.30	.0 Ar.......HINCKLEY......Lv.		2.45	5 45
5 15	2.20	2.8 Lv......... Prospect.........Ar.		3 00	6.05

SARANAC BRANCH.

From the Main Line.				Dist. bet. Sta.	STATIONS.	To the Main Line.			
*57 D'y	†55	†58	*51 D'y			*50 D'y	†52	†54	*56 D'y
pm	pm	am	am			am	am	pm	pm
9.20	6.00	11.15	6 10	.0 Ar.....SARANAC LAKE.....Lv.		5.15	10.20	4.20	8.35
9.00	5.35	10.50		5.6 Lv......... Lake Clear.....Ar.		5.40	10.40	4.45	8.55

* Daily. † Daily except Sunday. ¶ Daily except Monday. f Train stops when signaled, for passengers.
d Train stops on signal to take on passengers for Utica or points beyond and for Albany or points beyond.
x Train stops on signal to take on passengers for Herkimer or points beyond and to leave passengers from Malone or points beyond.
Freight trains carry passengers in caboose cars.

This time table was issued the next spring after the Adirondack & St. Lawrence Railway was completed and turned over to the Mohawk & Malone Railway Company for operation.

CHAPTER XI
On to Montreal

We have observed that the railroad reached Valleyfield from Malone on January 11, 1892. The Malone and St. Lawrence Railway had been incorporated on September 11, 1891. It was to operate from Malone northerly and join the St. Lawrence and Adirondack in the Town of Burke, a distance of approximately twelve miles or less, in fact, to the international boundary line. Trains were thus able to leave Malone via the Malone and St. Lawrence to the international boundary; via St. Lawrence and Adirondack to Valleyfield; via the Canada Atlantic Railway to Coteau Junction; via Grand Trunk Railway, arriving in Montreal at the Central Station. This distance was 75 miles from Malone.

Dr. Webb took control of the Malone and St. Lawrence in June 1892 and leased it to the Central Vermont. Commencing October 24, 1892 when the line between Herkimer and Malone was placed in service, solid trains were run through to Montreal. The Central Vermont continued to operate the St. Lawrence and Adirondack Railway for a couple of years under a temporary agreement with Dr. Webb. On March 1, 1894 he cancelled the former arrangements and turned the operation over to the New York Central and Hudson River Railroad.

On November 18, 1895 the Malone and St. Lawrence Railway Company and the St. Lawrence and Adirondack Railway Company were consolidated. This consolidation became effective in 1896 according to the NEW YORK TIMES of June 26th. During the period for 1894 to June 1896 several changes in the route were being made.

The Southwestern Railway Company was organized by Dr. Webb and it built thirteen and one quarter miles of railroad from Beauharnois to Caughnawaga Junction (Adirondack Junction). The Southwestern leased the Beauharnois Junction Railway from the Grand Trunk Railway. This leased line was from Valleyfield to Beauharnois, a distance of nearly thirteen miles. The newly constructed line and the leased line all became part of the "new" St. Lawrence and

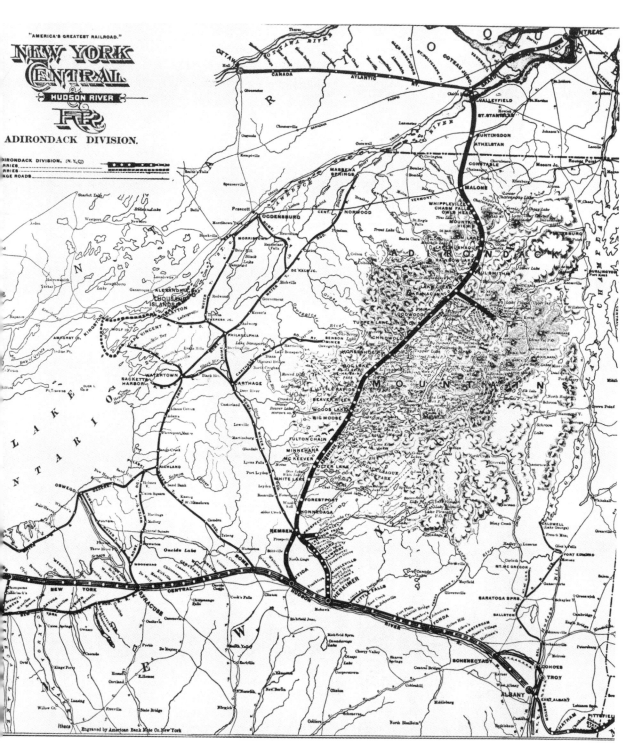

Dated about 1895 the map shows the Adirondack Division being routed through Cotteau Junction and the Grand Trunk to Montreal. (Edward Baumgardner collection)

ST. LAWRENCE AND ADIRONDACK RAILWAY COMPANY.

INCORPORATED UNDER THE LAWS OF THE STATE OF NEW YORK AND DOMINION OF CANADA.

SHARES $100 EACH.

CAPITAL STOCK $4,300,000.

NUMBER A234

COUNTERSIGNED, NEW YORK,

THE STANDARD TRUST COMPANY, of NEW YORK,

TRANSFER AGENTS.

BY

SECRETARY.

PRESIDENT.

TREASURER.

THIS CERTIFIES THAT

In Witness Whereof

COLONIAL TRUST COMPANY

REGISTRAR.

FIRST OFFICER.

COUNTERSIGNED & REGISTERED

CERTIFICATE FOR LESS THAN ONE HUNDRED SHARES

Adirondack Railway which obtained trackage rights over the Canadian Pacific from Adirondack Junction and ran through to Montreal arriving at Windsor Station. This distance from Malone was about 65 miles. It was ten miles shorter than the previous route from Malone to Montreal and much better adapted for increased speeds.

In the annual report to the Railroad Commissioners for 1896, the St. Lawrence and Adirondack reported leasing 12 locomotives, 8 passenger cars and 68 flat cars, cabooses and service cars. This number of leased rolling stock continued to decrease during the following years as it was replaced by New York Central equipment. The reports do not show that the St. Lawrence and Adirondack owned any locomotives or rolling stock. On June 26, 1896 the NEW YORK TIMES had reported:

> In the early part of this month, a corporation entitled the St. Lawrence and Adirondack Equipment Company was formed, with a capital of $225,000 to manufacture, sell, and lease locomotives, cars and other railroad equipment.

Undoubtedly this is where the ownership of all of the St. Lawrence and Adirondack Railway equipment lies.

Through service was established via the new route to Montreal on August 16, 1896. However, shortly after that Burnett reported:

> Commencing June 1, 1898, Dr. Webb entered into an agreement whereby the New York Central conducted the operations of this line without participating in the profits or sharing in the losses of such operations. This arrangement continued until July 1, 1905 when the New York Central purchased the entire outstanding stock of the St. Lawrence and Adirondack Railway and Dr. Webb retired from the last connection with an enterprise which he had so brilliantly and successfully consumated.

Apparently the locomotives and some of the other rolling stock that was owned by the St. Lawrence and Adirondack Equipment Company was transferred by that company to the New York Central or to the Rutland Railroad.

A little data contained in the 1897 REPORT OF THE RAILROAD COMMISSIONERS may be of interest:

10,960 shares of capital stock at $100 par value.
Number of stockholders was 18.
First Mortgage Bonds, dated July 1, 1896, one hundred year term, totalled $800,000.
Gross earnings — $135,189.
Profit for the year — $2,000.

Cost of the road — $1,896,363.21
Number of passengers carried — 102,069
Tons of freight carried — 147,938
Lumber; coal; agricultural products, other than flour and grain; and manufactured goods made up 86% of the freight moved.
Number of employees — 175.

The 1900 REPORT stated:

The maximum curve on the St. Lawrence and Adirondack is five degrees.
The grade on the St. Lawrence and Adirondack is almost continuous from the Canadian line to Malone, at the rate of 106 feet to the mile.

Published jointly by the Mohawk and Malone Railway and the St. Lawrence and Adirondack Railway (in 1896) was a booklet of over forty-five pages entitled RULES AND REGULATIONS — FREIGHT DEPARTMENT. It is a very interesting book and contains detailed rules for the employees. Its description of some of the articles carried as freight gives an insight on the type of merchandise transported in those years. For one interested in technical details there is a considerable amount of information contained in these rules and regulations. The joint publishing of a manual by both companies indicates how closely allied the companies were and by the same token it denotes that a definite separation of the two companies existed at that time.

A customhouse was established at Malone and all trains were subject to inspection by the custom agents. The years of the eighteenth or liquor prohibition amendment to the Constitution of the United States were especially busy years for the customs agents. Tales of the usual and bizarre attempts to bring intoxicants into the United States as well as to transport cigarettes into Canada have been heard for years. These tales are really deserving of an account of their own.

Suburban service was offered from Valleyfield to Montreal and in 1920, for instance, there were four trains each way between these two stations as well as the two regular express trains. The commuter service from Malone north was discontinued in 1957. The last Utica to Montreal through train had run on April 26, 1953.

According to the 1976 MOODY'S TRANSPORTATION MANUAL, the New York Central, who owned all of the outstanding stock, had last leased the St. Lawrence and Adirondack Railway for 99 years from January 1, 1937. There are two series of bonds, one maturing on July 1, 1996 with $590,000 outstanding in 1976 and the other maturing October 1, 1996 with $352,000 outstanding in 1976.

In 1958 passenger service on the Adirondack Division was discontinued between Lake Clear Junction and Malone and by 1960 the abandonment of all service north of Lake Clear Junction had occurred. A couple of years later the tracks were removed and the right-of-way turned over to the Niagara-Mohawk Power Company.

In 1961 the last train was run on the Rutland Railroad and this left Malone without direct freight service by a railroad.

At the present time, Montreal and Malone freight traffic is routed from Massena over Canadian National tracks to Huntingdon. At Huntingdon the Malone traffic is accumulated and sent south to that place on a weekly basis. There are about twenty regular patrons at Malone with three of them doing three quarters of the total business. The Montreal freight is sent north over the old St. Lawrence and Adirondack tracks to Adirondack Junction and then into Montreal. So the Old St. Lawrence and Adirondack Railway continues to be kept in operation by its Consolidated Rail Corporation (CON-RAIL) control and its subsidy by the State of New York.

In its August 1978 NEW YORK STATE RAIL PLAN ANNUAL UPDATE the New York State Department of Transportation reported:

> A negotiated solution on this line is currently in the discussion phase. The Department will continue to subsidize and study this line while negotiations continue.

There are those who advocate that with the rebuilding of the Remsen to Lake Placid line that the rails north from Lake Clear Junction to Malone should be relaid and the through route to Montreal be again put into operation. The idea of monorail construction and operation for the entire distance from Utica to Montreal has been advanced. In this modern age all things are possible and the future alone will bring the St. Lawrence and Adirondack Railway to its ultimate destiny.

CHAPTER XII
The Branch Lines

THE HINCKLEY BRANCH

When Dr. Webb purchased the Herkimer, Newport and Poland Narrow Gauge Railway he also acquired a charter for the Mohawk Valley and Northern Railway Company that was to operate a railroad between Poland and Nobleborough, a place several miles farther upstream on the West Canada Creek. On September 10, 1891 the Herkimer, Newport and Poland Extension Railway was incorporated to operate a railroad between Poland and Northwood, which was also upstream on the West Canada Creek from Poland and was located between Gang Mill (Hinckley) and Nobleborough.

Dr. Webb is reported to have promised the interim owners of the Herkimer, Newport and Poland Narrow Gauge that when he built north from Poland he would build a railroad to Gang Mill. The name Gang Mill came from the type of saws used to make multiple cuts at one time in the large saw mill and planing mill that Gardner Hinckley and Theodore P. Ballou had erected on the West Canada Creek. This mill was supposed to have the largest capacity of any water power mill in that part of the country so it can be seen that a railroad would be very advantageous.

The surveyors were at work on the line north of Poland early in the Spring of 1891. The BOONVILLE HERALD carried several items concerning this:

March 26, 1891 — Work actually begun on Mohawk Valley and Northern Railroad at a point near Hinckley. A. C. Hall of Trenton Falls Lumber Company had the honor of breaking ground and taking out the first shovelful of dirt. Mr. Hall was active in getting the line to Hinckley.

April 2, 1891 — Again the surveyors are with us. Engineer Ward told us that there was a possibility that the road might be extended beyond Hinckley.

April 23, 1891 — Herschel Roberts, engineer in charge of Mohawk and Northern Railroad will establish his permanent quarters here in Prospect. He has leased an office in the Walters Block.

60

The trestle leading into Hinckley. The station was on the south or east side of the West Canada Creek. It was washed away in the flood of 1901 but was rebuilt. The Hinckley Fibre Company mills are in the background on both sides of the creek. (Harter collection)

The depot at Hinckley. Circa 1910. (Helen Schermerhorn)

HERKIMER AND REMSEN BRANCH

Miles	STATIONS	71 Ex Sun	73 Sun only	75 Ex Sun	185 Mixed Sun only	77 Ex Sun	79 Ex Sun		
0	Lv. New York	‡ 9 PM 44	AM	12 AM 25	12 AM 25	12 AM 25	10 AM 30		
143	Lv. Albany	2 05	.....	7 25	8 00	9 15	1 50		
223	Ar. Herkimer	4 40	.....	10 01	10 20	12 10	4 10		
0	Lv. Utica	5 05	7 05	9 25	.....	.....	5 10		
15	Ar. Herkimer	5 32	7 36	9 43	.....	.....	5 37		
0	Lv. Herkimer	f6 55	7 45	10 25	11 10	12 20	6 50		
4	Lv. Kast Bridge	f7 02	f7 52	f10 32	11 23	f12 27	f6 57		
6	Lv. Countryman's	f7 07	f7 57	f10 38	f11 27	f12 31	f6 02		
7	Lv. County Home	f7 12	f8 02	f10 44	f11 31	f12 36	f6 07		
9	Lv. Middleville	7 17	8 07	10 50	11 40	12 41	6 13		
14	Lv. Newport	7 27	8 18	11 00	12 02	12 49	6 23		
17	Lv. Poland	7 34	8 26	11 10	12 13	12 57	6 31		
22	Lv. Gravesville	f7 43	f8 37	.....	.....	f1 06	f6 39		
24	Lv. Trenton Chasm	f7 50	8 43	.....	f12 47	f1 15	f6 48		
26	Ar. Prospect Jct	7 56	8 54	.....	12 55	1 17	6 55		
26	Lv. Prospect Jct	7 56	.....	.....	.....	1 17	7 00		
29	Ar. Hinckley	8 03	.....	.....	.....	1 24	7 12		
0	Lv. Hinckley	8 04	.....	.....	.....	1 26	.....		
3	Ar. Prospect Jct	8 16	.....	.....	.....	1 38	.....		
26	Lv. Prospect Jct	8 22	8 54	.....	12 55	1 38	7 00		
28	Ar. Remsen	8 AM 27	9 AM 00	AM	1 PM 05	1 PM 43	7 PM 05		

Miles	STATIONS	70 Ex Sun	72 Ex Sun	184 Mixed Sun only	74 Ex Sun	76 Ex Sun	78 Sun only		
0	Lv. Remsen	8 AM 07	AM	3 PM 10	3 PM 45	6 PM 50	7 PM 12		
3	Ar. Prospect Jct	8 12	.....	3 20	3 51	6 55	7 17		
0	Lv. Prospect Jct	.....	.....	.....	3 52	7 00	.....		
3	Ar. Hinckley	.....	.....	.....	4 05	7 12	.....		
0	Lv. Hinckley	8 04	.....	.....	4 06	7 13	.....		
3	Ar. Prospect Jct	8 16	.....	.....	4 14	7 20	.....		
3	Lv. Prospect Jct	8 22	.....	3 20	4 15	7 20	7 17		
4	Lv. Trenton Chasm	f8 27	.....	f3 25	f4 19	f7 25	7 21		
7	Lv. Gravesville	f8 34	.....	f3 38	f4 25	f7 31	f7 29		
12	Lv. Poland	8 43	11 20	3 50	4 32	7 40	7 39		
15	Lv. Newport	9 52	11 28	3 58	4 40	7 48	7 49		
19	Lv. Middleville	9 02	11 40	4 10	4 49	7 56	7 59		
21	Lv. County Home	f9 07	f11 43	f4 14	f4 52	f7 59	f8 03		
23	Lv. Countryman's	f9 11	f11 47	f4 19	f4 56	f8 02	f8 07		
25	Lv. Kast Bridge	f9 15	f11 52	f4 33	f5 00	f8 06	f8 12		
28	Ar. Herkimer	9 20	11 59	4 45	5 10	8 15	8 20		
0	Lv. Herkimer	10 01	12 10	.....	.....	9 24	8 22		
15	Ar. Utica	10 30	12 40	.....	.....	9 49	8 50		
0	Lv. Herkimer	9 48	12 44	5 57	5 37	9 46	9 46		
81	Ar. Albany	11 45	2 30	8 35	8 35	12 10	12 10		
223	Ar. New York	3 PM 45	5 PM 50	PM	PM	5 AM 05	5 AM 05		

FULTON CHAIN RAILWAY AND FULTON NAVIGATION CO.
For Old Forge and Points on Fulton Chain of Lakes

STATIONS		107 Daily	171 Ex Sun	173 Sun Only	111 Daily	101 Ex Sun	103 Ex Sun	179 Ex Sun
Lv. Fulton Chain	F.C.	6 20	9 45	10 25	11 15	3 12	3 48	8 16
Ar. Old Forge	Ry.	6 30	9 55	10 35	11 25	3 22	3 58	8 26
Lv. Old Forge		7 15	10 00	10 45	11 35	.....	4 00	8 30
Ar. Bald Mtn. House		8 00	10 35	11 15	f	.....	4 45	f
Ar. Eagle Bay		9 35	11 45	12 20	f	.....	6 18	f
Ar. Cedar Island Camp		9 45	11 50	12 27	f	.....	6 28	f
Ar. Rocky Point Inn		9 57	11 57	12 33	f	.....	6 35	f
Ar. Arrow Head		10 10	12 07	12 41	f	.....	6 41	f
Ar. The Wood		10 12	12 10	12 43	f	.....	6 42	f
Ar. Inlet Station		10 15	12 15	12 45	12 30	.....	6 43	10 00

STATIONS		170 Ex Sun	106 Daily	102 Ex Sun	114 Ex Sun	176 Ex Sun	178 Sun Only	112 Daily
Lv. Inlet Station		AM	7 30	11 00	PM	3 10	3 15	6 45
Lv. The Wood		.....	7 32	11 01	.....	3 12	3 17	6 46
Lv. Arrow Head		.....	7 34	11 02	.....	3 14	3 19	6 47
Lv. Rocky Point Inn		.....	7 40	11 06	.....	3 23	3 31	6 55
Lv. Cedar Island Camp		.....	7 46	11 12	.....	3 28	3 40	7 00
Lv. Eagle Bay		.....	7 50	11 15	.....	3 33	3 50	7 05
Lv. Bald Mtn. House		.....	9 05	12 30	.....	4 35	5 05	8 15
Ar. Old Forge		.....	9 50	1 15	.....	5 15	5 45	8 55
Lv. Old Forge	F.C.	6 50	10 05	1 40	3 25	5 30	5 55	9 15
Ar. Fulton Chain	Ry.	6 58	10 15	1 50	3 35	5 40	6 05	9 25

ADDITIONAL LOCAL SERVICE ON FOURTH LAKE

Read Down				STATIONS		Read Up		
	Ex Sun	Ex Sun	Daily			Ex Sun	Ex Sun	Daily
	PM	PM	AM			PM	PM	PM
.....	4 55	1 45	6 35	Lv. ...... Eagle Bay ...... Ar.		1 05	4 15	8 30
.....	5 00	1 50	6 45	Lv. ...... Cedar Island ...... Ar.		12 55	4 10	8 23
.....	5 10	2 00	6 55	Lv. ...... Rocky Point Inn ...... Ar.		12 45	4 00	8 13
.....	5 20	2 10	7 05	Lv. ...... Inlet Station ...... Ar.		12 40	3 50	8 03
.....	5 25	2 17	7 15	Lv. ...... Arrow Head ...... Ar.		12 33	3 43	7 58
.....	5 30	2 20	7 20	Lv. ...... Camp Neodak ...... Ar.		12 30	3 40	7 55
.....	5 35	2 25	7 30	Ar. ...... Grand View House ...... Lv.		12 20	3 35	7 45

For Explanation of Reference Marks and Notes, see page 13

These pages from a 1912 time table shows very handily all of the branches of the Adirondack Division including the

RAQUETTE LAKE RY. AND RAQUETTE LAKE TRANSPORTATION CO.
For Fourth Lake, Raquette Lake and Blue Mountain Lakes

207	253	STATIONS	262	212	214	
Daily	Ex Sun		Ex Sun	Ex Sun	Sun Only	
PM	AM		PM	AM	AM	
....	7 10	7 45	Lv..New York (G.C.Term.) Ar.	10 50	7 03	7 03	....
....	7 21	7 55	Lv...New York (125th St.) Ar.	10 39	6 50	6 50	....
11 05	11 10	Lv......Albany.......Ar.	7 15	2 55	2 55	....
3 00	1 40	Lv......Utica.......Ar.	4 25	12 45	12 45	....
5 05	.....	Ar.....Fulton Chain.....Lv.	2 42	11 00	11 00	....
....	4 07	Ar......Carter......Lv.	2 23	.....	.....	
5 35	.....	Lv.....Fulton Chain.....Ar.	.....	9 45	10 35	
5 52	4 10	Lv......Carter......Ar.	2 15	9 30	10 10	
f5 59	f4 17	Ar......Rondaxe......Lv.	2 08	f9 23	f10 04	
6 12	4 30	Ar...Minnow Brook...Lv.	1 54	9 09	9 50	
f6 19	f4 37	Ar.....Fairview.....Lv.	f1 43	f9 03	f9 44	
f6 24	f4 42	Ar...Skenowane...Lv.	f1 44	f8 59	f9 39	
6 30	4 48	Ar.....Eagle Bay.....Lv.	1 40	8 55	9 35	
f6 39	f4 57	Ar....Uncas Road....Lv.	f1 27	f8 42	f9 22	
7 00	5 15	Ar.....Raquette Lake.....Lv.	1 15	8 30	9 10	
7 30	5 20	Lv....Raquette Lake (St'r).Ar.	12 05	7 20	7 50	
7 40	5 25	Ar.......Antlers.......Lv.	11 50	7 10	7 40	
8 25	6 15	Ar..Marion River Carry..Lv.	11 00	6 15	6 45	
8 50	6 40	Ar..Dalys (Utowana Lake).Lv.	10 40	5 50	6 20	
9 20	7 10	Ar.....Eagle Nest.....Lv.	10 10	5 20	5 50	
9 40	7 30	Ar..Blue Mountain Lake..Lv.	9 50	5 00	5 30	
AM	PM		PM	PM	PM	

SARANAC BRANCH AND DELAWARE & HUDSON R. R.

STATIONS	41 Daily	43 Daily	9 Daily	45 Ex Sun	47 Daily	1 Ex Sun	49 Ex Sun	51 Daily	53 Daily
	AM	AM	AM	PM	PM	PM	PM	PM	PM
Lv. Lake Clear Jct...........	6 12	7 16	8 05	12 15	2 05	5 40	6 30	8 35	11 30
Ar. Saranac Lake...........	6 30	7 35	8 25	12 30	2 25	6 58	6 50	8 55	11 50
Lv. Saranac Lake (D. & H)	6 55	7 45	9 35	12 35	2 35	7 00	7 00	.....	.....
Ar. Raybrook (D. & H).....	zz	zz	f9 43	f12 42	2 44	f7 07	f7 07	.....	.....
Ar. Lake Placid (D. & H).....	7 15	8 05	9 55	12 55	3 00	7 20	7 20	.....	.....
	AM	AM	AM	PM	PM	PM	PM		

STATIONS	42 Daily	44 Daily	46 Daily	8 Ex Sun	48 Ex Sun	50 Daily	52 Ex Sun	54 Ex Sat	56 Daily	10 Daily
	AM	AM	AM	AM	AM	PM	PM	PM	PM	PM
Lv. Lake Placid (D. & H.)....	.....	6 20	.....	9 15	10 50	1 10	5 30	.....	7 50	.....
Lv. Raybrook (D. & H).....	.....	f6 27	.....	f9 22	f10 56	f1 18	5 38	.....	zz	.....
Ar. Saranac Lake (D. & H)....	.....	6 35	.....	9 35	11 10	1 30	5 50	.....	8 05	.....
Lv. Saranac Lake...........	5 35	6 40	7 00	10 30	11 30	1 35	5 58	7 50	8 15	10 50
Ar. Lake Clear Jct...........	5 55	6 58	7 16	10 50	11 50	1 50	6 15	8 10	8 35	11 10
	AM	AM	AM	AM	AM	PM	PM	PM	PM	PM

ST. LAWRENCE AND ADIRONDACK BRANCH

STATIONS	21 Ex Sun	23 Ex Sun	25 Ex Sun	5 Daily	27 Ex Sun	29 Ex Sun	11 Daily	31 Sun only	33 Sat only	3 Ex Sun
	AM	AM	AM	AM	PM	PM	PM	PM	PM	PM
Lv. Malone.............	.....	.....	6 10	7 38	.....	.....	3 30	.....	.....	8 00
Lv. Constable...........	.....	.....	6 19	z	.....	.....	3 40	.....	.....	8 09
Lv. Athelstan...........	.....	.....	6 41	8 07	.....	.....	3 57	.....	.....	8 24
Lv. Huntingdon........	.....	.....	6 51	8 16	.....	.....	4 03	.....	.....	8 33
Lv. New Erin..........	.....	.....	f7 00	n	.....	.....	f4 10	.....	.....	.....
Lv. St. Stanislas.......	.....	.....	7 08	z	.....	.....	4 16	.....	.....	8 46
Lv. Valleyfield.........	5 20	6 40	7 25	8 48	12 25	3 15	4 28	7 30	k3 20	8 57
Lv. Cecile Jc...........	f5 24	6 44	7 29	n	12 f29	3 19	.....	f7 35	k8 25	f9 01
Lv. St. Timothee.......	5 31	6 51	7 36	9 00	12 36	3 26	4 36	7 41	k8 31	9 08
Lv. Melocheville.......	5 40	7 00	7 45	n	12 f45	f3 35	.....	7 49	k8 f40	.....
Lv. Beauharnois.......	5 47	7 07	7 52	9 14	12 52	3 42	4 50	8 05	k8 47	9 22
Lv. Maple Grove.......	5 51	7 11	f7 56	n	12 f56	f3 46	.....	8 09	k8 f51	.....
Lv. Bellevue...........	5 55	7 15	8 00	n	1 00	3 50	.....	8 15	k8 f55	f9 28
Lv. Woodlands.........	5 59	7 19	8 04	f9 23	1 04	3 54	.....	8 21	k8 59	f9 35
Lv. Chateauguay.......	6 05	7 25	8 10	9 28	1 10	4 00	5 05	8 33	k9 05	9 40
Lv. Primeau...........	f6 11	.....	f8 16	n	f1 16	f4 06	.....	f8 42	k9 f11	.....
Lv. Adirondack Jc.......	6 20	.....	8 25	n	.....	4 15	.....	8 50	.....	.....
Ar. Montreal (Windsor Sta.)	6 50	8 10	8 50	10 05	1 50	4 45	5 40	9 20	9 50	10 15
	AM	AM	AM	AM	PM	PM	PM	PM	PM	PM

STATIONS	20 Ex Sun	2 Ex Sun	22 Sun Only	24 Ex Sun	26 Sat only	28 Ex Sun	30 Ex Sun	32 Ex Sun	34 Daily	4 Sun only	36 Sat only	38
	AM	AM	AM	AM	AM	PM	PM	PM	PM	PM	PM	PM
Lv. Montreal (Windsor Sta.)	7 15	8 00	9 30	9 40	1k00	1 35	3 50	5 12	6 25	7 15	10 15	k11 30
Lv. Adirondack Jct.....	7 4	h8 25	10 05	.....	.....	2 05	.....	.....	6 55	h7 39	10 45	.....
Lv. Primeau...........	.....	.....	10 f11	10 f15	k1 f35	f2 10	.....	.....	f7 00	.....	f10 50	k12 f04
Lv. Chateauguay	7 57	.....	10 20	10 24	k1 44	2 18	4 28	5 56	7 09	7 48	10 59	k12 13
Lv. Woodlands	f8 04	.....	10 26	10 29	k1 49	2 23	4 33	6 01	7 14	f7 52	11 04	k12 18
Lv. Bellevue	f8 09	.....	10 31	10 f34	k1 54	2 28	4 38	6 06	7 19	.....	11 09	k12 f24
Lv. Maple Grove	f8 14	.....	10 36	10 f38	k1 f58	f2 32	f4 43	6 10	7 23	.....	11 13	k12 f28
Lv. Beauharnois	8 20	8 47	10 41	10 43	k2 03	2 37	4 50	6 15	7 28	8 05	11 18	k12 34
Lv. Melocheville	f8 25	.....	10 49	10 f50	k2 f10	f2 44	f4 57	6 22	7 35	.....	f11 25	k12 f41
Lv. St. Timothee	8 35	9 00	10 53	10 54	k2 18	2 53	5 06	6 30	7 43	f8 18	11 33	k12 45
Lv. Cecile Jct.	f8 42	.....	11 f07	11 f05	k2 f25	f3 00	5 13	f6 37	f7 50	f8 25	f11 40	k12 f54
Lv. Valleyfield	8 49	9 13	11 25	11 10	k2 30	3 05	5 21	6 42	7 55	8 33	11 45	k 1 00
Lv. St. Stanislas	9 02	.....	11 35	.....	.....	.....	5 31	.....	8 46	.....	.....	.....
Lv. New Erin	f9 07	.....	11 f41	.....	.....	.....	f5 36	.....	.....	.....	.....	.....
Lv. Huntingdon	9 16	9 36	11 50	.....	.....	.....	5 46	.....	.....	9 00	.....	.....
Lv. Athelstan	9 23	9 43	11 57	.....	.....	.....	5 53	.....	.....	9 09	.....	.....
Lv. Constable	9 38	.....	12 12	.....	.....	.....	6 08	.....	.....	s9 24	.....	.....
Ar. Malone	9 55	10 15	12 30	.....	.....	.....	6 25	.....	.....	9 44	.....	.....
	AM	AM	PM	AM	PM	PM	PM	PM	PM	PM	PM	AM

For Explanation of Reference Marks and Notes, see page 13

Fulton Navigation Company and Raquette Lake Transportation Company.

July 16, 1891 — Captain Sullivan finding it very difficult. The soil on the Gang Mill branch (Hinckley) branch is hard and stony. The work here is not so far advanced as that between Poland and Trenton Falls.

June 16, 1892 — Trains are running on the new railroad all the way through to Hinckley.

The route laid out to reach Hinckley was a branch line off the main line at Prospect Junction, and the distance was 2.65 miles. The surveyors laid out a route as far as Northwood but rails were never laid north of Hinckley. There was quite a lot of track laid on the north side of the West Canada so that the Hinckley Fibre Company on that side could be served as well as the Trenton Lumber Company. On the south side of the creek near where Hinckley Fibre Company had a plant there was a pulp mill also. The station was on the south side of the West Canada.

Although the earliest timetables do not indicate it, a station stop was instituted at Summit Street in the Village of Prospect. This was a little over a mile from Prospect Junction. The normal operation of passenger trains that made the stop at Hinckley station was to back in on the branch line over the wye at Prospect Junction and then head out after the station stop was made. No mention has been found of any trains operating between Prospect Junction and Hinckley as branch line trains. The maximum grade on the branch line was 64 feet per mile.

There was a pile trestle built of hemlock and spruce at Hinckley where the station spur crossed the West Canada Creek. This trestle was the subject of some discussion by the State Railroad Inspector. In his 1900 report he recommended that it be rebuilt promptly. His suggestion had to be carried out because on December 15, 1901 the lumber company dam gave way and the logs hurtling down the creek carried the trestle along with them. The trestle was rebuilt in 1902, the inspector reported and said, "Although it was in good condition, it is not a proper structure to use at the crossing of a stream of the character of the West Canada Creek and should be replaced with a span bridge on masonry." As far as is known, the bridge was never built.

The name Gang Mill was discontinued and Hinckley was used henceforth. The lumber company was known as the Trenton Lumber Company. The Hinckley Fibre Company had establishments on both sides of the Creek. The Fibre Company used pulpwood, iron pyrites and limestone to make sulphite fibre. This resulted in considerable business for the railroad as some of the raw materials were brought in by rail as well as the finished product being shipped out by rail. The importation of sulphite fibre from Scandinavia at a lower cost than it could be manufactured in Hinckley caused the eventual shut down of the company's operations at Hinckley.

At Northwood there was a factory that produced eight carloads of charcoal, one and half cars of wood alcohol and two cars of acetate monthly. This firm was destroyed when the great dam at Hinckley was built and flooded out the area where the firm was located.

In its prime days the Hinckley Branch was reported to be the best paying stretch of track on the whole railroad. As high as five hundred men were at work in the fibre mill and saw mill and there were seven hotels in the village.

In 1927 the Public Service Commission allowed the New York Central to close the Hinckley passenger station because of low revenues and in 1931 the branch line was abandoned altogether and the tracks were torn up in due time. Today New York State Highway Route 365 has been built, in part, over the old Hinckley Branch right-of-way.

THE SARANAC BRANCH

Construction on the Saranac Branch preceded nearly all other construction on the Adirondack and St. Lawrence. John Hurd's Northern Adirondack Railroad had reached Tupper Lake in 1889. The terminal of this road was in the Village of Tupper Lake and was 1.74 miles from where Dr. Webb's road proposed to cross the Northern Adirondack at Tupper Lake Junction. Despite any animosity that existed between John Hurd and Dr. Webb, the fact remained that the Northern Adirondack was a common carrier and was utilized to transport the necessary equipment, materials and manpower needed to build the new railroad.

As soon as possible after his April 2, 1891 visit to Malone, Dr. Webb set his surveyors to work seeking out a line to the Saranacs. Encountering the difficulty of getting through the State lands promptly, it was determined to effect a trackage arrangement with Hurd's Northern Adironack Railroad from Moira to Tupper Lake and build a spur from there to Saranac Lake with the hope of reaching there by July first. The spur would pass near Saranac Inn and part of it would be later used as the main line from Tupper Lake Junction to what was later named Lake Clear Junction but at first designated as Saranac Junction. Trains would then be routed north from the Mohawk Valley via the Rome, Watertown and Ogdensburg, then east to Tupper Lake over the Northern Adirondack and then to Saranac Lake over the newly constructed Adirondack and St. Lawrence.

Thomas G. Alvord in his report published in the New York Herald on June 1, 1891 said:

> The scenery about the Saranac Inn, or a little further along is beautiful and bursts upon one suddenly. This comfortable old house with President Cleveland's cottage by its side, stands at the head of a superb lake, with great mountains rising in the distance beyond it. I found that there had been opposition on the part of Dr. Ward, Mr. Riddle and others in the association to the railroad scheme, until Dr. Webb considerately moved the road two miles away from the house, when Dr. Ward concluded that Dr. Webb was one of the finest gentlemen that ever lived, and the association immediately gave him the right of way over its many thousand acres. Everyone now about the place is listening for the locomotive, but don't want it to sound too loud.

The trouble in getting the right of way laid out north of Tupper Lake has been outlined earlier and this problem delayed the new railroad reaching to Saranac Lake at its intended time but with the land question solved the road was in operation from Malone south to Saranac Lake by July 16, 1892.

In 1878 the State of New York authorized the construction of a railroad, owned by the State, from Plattsburgh to Dannemora to transport men, supplies, fuel and any other necessary materials needed at Clinton Prison in Dannemora. This road never was incorporated but was known as the Plattsburgh and Dannemora.

In 1879 the Plattsburgh and Dannemora was leased to the Chateaugay Railway Company, a company organized to extend the three foot, narrow gauge line to the iron deposits at Lyon Mountain about 18 miles west of Dannemora. In 1886 the road was extended to Loon Lake and on December 5, 1887 it was open for traffic from Plattsburgh to Saranac Lake, a distance of 73 miles. There were changes in the corporate name during the next few years but the Delaware and Hudson Company had a substantial interest in the road from its early days.

The Saranac and Lake Placid Railroad was organized in 1890 and was a standard gauge railroad running between Saranac Lake and Lake Placid. Although built as a standard gauge road, a third rail was laid so that the Chateaugay trains could run over the ten mile new road all the way to Lake Placid.

In 1903 the Chateaugay Railway Company, the Chateaugay Railroad Company and the Saranac and Lake Placid Railroad Company were formally consolidated and the Delaware and Hudson was in control of the new company known as the Chateaugay and Lake Placid Railway Company. In 1902 the rebuilding of the railroad to standard

Station at Saranac Lake, N.Y. Both the Delaware and Hudson and the Saranac Branch of the New York Central came in to this station. (Harter collection)

Saranac Lake station in June 1974. (Harter collection)

Track side of Saranac Lake station in June 1974. (Harter collection)

Considerable research went into the establishment of the date of this wreck. The best estimate that could be made was September 1915. Apparently a New York Central passenger train ran into the rear of a Delaware & Hudson freight train in the general vicinity of Raybrook. (McKnight collection)

Taken about 1929 by an unknown photographer showing southbound train approaching Raybrook station. (Michael Kudish collection)

Mrs. MacKenzie stated: "Unfortunately this photo is a bit fuzzy, it had to be enlarged from a tiny snapshot, almost useless in its original state. I place this scene circa 1900. I believe the station is in the center at left (this was a converted house). Note the third rail which was laid to accommodate both the narrow gauge Chateaugay Railroad and the standard gauge cars of the New York Central." (Mary MacKenzie collection)

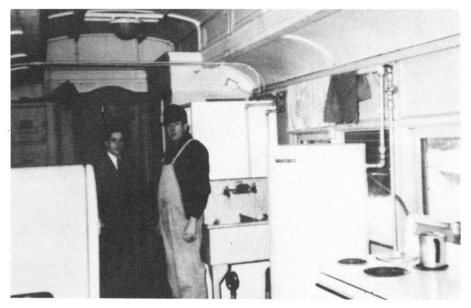

For the last years that passenger service ran into Lake Placid the New York Central fixed up two coaches, one for the train crew and one for the engine crew to use during their layovers. Dormitory, kitchen, dining and lounge facilities were provided. (Albert A. Hess collection)

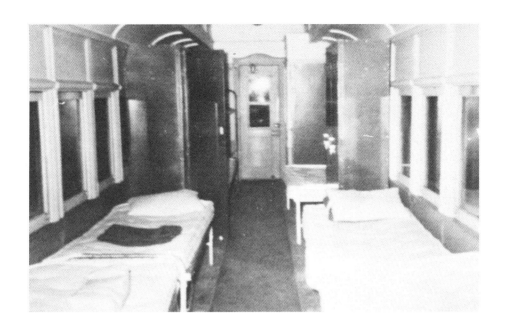

The turntable at Lake Placid. (Michael Kudish collection)

gauge was undertaken and this project was completed in 1903 and the line was leased to the Delaware and Hudson for a period of 500 years.

When the Adirondack and St. Lawrence reached Saranac Lake in 1892 over its six and one-half mile Saranac Branch, the July 16th timetable showed an arrival at Saranac Junction (Lake Clear Junction) at 10:15 A. M., Saranac Village at 10:40 A. M. and Lake Placid, by stage, at 12:15 P. M. At the time the Adironadack and St. Lawrence had its own station near or in what was later known as the Saranac yards.

Apparently a change in trains was necessary in the first year or years so that Adirondack and St. Lawrence passengers could reach Lake Placid by rail but at an undetermined later date it appears that the New York Central trains were run all the way into Lake Placid Station which, incidentally, was located in Newman, down the hill from the Village of Lake Placid.

The report of the State Railroad Inspector following an 1899 inspection of the Chateaugay Railroad said:

> The (Chateaugay) road is single track and three foot gauge, excepting that portion from Saranac Lake to Lake Placid, where a third rail standard gauge is laid to accommodate the cars of the Mohawk and Malone Railway, which are run upon the tracks of the Chateaugay Railroad between those points. (Apparently the inspector was including the Saranac and Lake Placid Railroad as part of the Chateaugay system.)

F. Ray McKnight studied the handling of the New York Central trains between Saranac Lake and Lake Placid but was not able to verify definite dates in the change pattern. Apparently the cars were run over the line to Lake Placid as the inspector reported in 1899 but it is not certain whether they were hauled by Saranac and Lake Placid engines or by New York Central engines or exactly who the engine crews worked for. It seems that they ran under Delaware and Hudson rules for sure.

Eventually the New York Central did run all the way into Lake Placid with their own locomotives and crews but the date that started remains unsettled.

In 1940 the Delaware and Hudson was allowed to abandon the twenty-seven mile stretch of trackage between Plumadore and Saranac Lake. This paralleled the New York Central and trackage rights were secured by the Delaware and Hudson over the New York Central tracks between these points.

On November 1, 1946 the Interstate Commerce Commission allowed the Delaware and Hudson to abandon all of the line beyond

Lyon Mountain and to sell the ten miles of track between Saranac Lake and Lake Placid (the Saranac and Lake Placid Railroad) to the New York Central. The Central was at last in complete control of the railroad into Lake Placid. In 1957 when passenger service north of Lake Clear Junction was discontinued the trains ran to Lake Placid as a terminal. The New York Central set up two crew cars at Lake Placid. One was for the train crews and one for the engine crews. The cars had bunks and cooking facilities and the men utilized them while there on their lay-overs before starting back to Utica.

The Saranac–Lake Placid area has traditionally been a popular recreational area all year around. As early as February 3, 1900 the Utica SATURDAY GLOBE carried the following:

> Winter Carnival at Saranac Lake — There will be three days of enjoyable sport at Saranac Lake during the winter carnival, Tuesday, Wednesday and Thursday of next week. Among the attractions will be hockey matches, skating races, fancy skating, coasting, tobogganing, snowshoeing, masquerade skating, grand parade of sleighs and floats, storming the ice palace, etc., John Nillson, champion speedy and acrobatic skater, and Miss Minnie Cummings, a noted fancy and figure skater, will give exhibitions. Excursion rates via New York Central from Utica, also from Herkimer and stations on the Adirondack Division to Saranac Lake and return. Tickets good going January 29, 30 and 31 or February 1, returning on or before February 5.

The New York Central Lines continued to advertise special fares to the Winter Carnival at Saranac Lake through the years. Some interesting items concerning the recreational traffic are gleaned from the NEW YORK CENTRAL LINES MAGAZINE:

> October 1928 — Boston-Lake Placid Sleeping Car Service — Begining Sunday, September 30, Boston-Lake Placid sleeping car service was operated as follows:
>
> Westbound, Boston to Lake Placid, Fridays only, twelve section drawing room car in New York second No. 21 and Adirondack Division No. 5, October 5, to October 26 inclusive and December 14 to March 22 inclusive.
>
> Eastbound, the service moves in Adirondack No. 4 — Main Line No. 8 B. & A. 12, same type of car, September 30 to October 28, inclusive, and December 16 to March 24, inclusive.
>
> December 1928 — An extra train, without dining car, will be operated on days of heavy overnight winter travel from New York to the Adirondack Mountains. The train which will handle all of the sleeping car business on the dates specified in this paragraph will leave New York at 7:30 P.M., arrinving at Utica at 1:10 A.M., and follow the regular schedule of Adirondack Division No. 5 beyond. The extra train will

move December 21, 22, 23, 24, 25, 26, 27, 28 and February 8 and 21. On these dates regular New York-Lake Placid and New York-Montreal cars ordinarily moving in second No. 21 will move in the extra train. A Boston-Lake Placid sleeper leaving Boston December 21, December 28 and Febraury 8 only will be handled in the extra train from Albany.

Other pertinent items from the LAKE PLACID NEWS are:

September 7, 1935 — The Delaware and Hudson Railway station was a busy place Monday evening with the annual Labor Day exodus from this resort. 41 pullmans and coaches left the station in four sections carrying vacationists back to their homes in New York, Boston, Buffalo and points en route. The crowd included 190 persons here on a New York Central holiday excursion. Many reservations for Monday night were reported cancelled, due to the sudden change to warm weather conditions.

The makeup of the trains which filled all available space on the local tracks included four club cars, 30 sleepers to New York, one to Boston, two to Buffalo, two baggage cars and seven engines. The crowd leaving Monday was estimated to be under that of Labor Day last year.

January 1, 1936 — The first snow train to be sent here from Buffalo will arrive Saturday morning, February 8. According to C. A. Rebling, district passenger agent of the New York Central lines, who has been in charge of arrangements, the department stores of Buffalo have been conducting an intensive promotion campaign for the snow train in featuring winter sports equipment for Lake Placid during the past week.

Arrivals on the snow train, in addition to the amusement they will find for themselves on nearby ski trails, will be here for the National A.A.U. senior bobsled Championships on Saturday and Sunday mornings. A special program of ski events is being planned by James Littlejohn, ski instructor at the arena. The train arrives Saturday morning and leaves Sunday night.

November 20, 1936 — Railroads Plan to Enlarge Snow Train Service — Will Have Special Cars for Rental of Ski Equipment — With the rapid approach of the winter sports season, railroads are making elaborate plans to take the urban population to the snow fields in upstate New York.

More than 5,000 New Yorkers becam addicted to winter sports last year and weekend and Sunday snow trains were jammed with skiing, snowshoeing and bobsledding enthusiasts.

The New York Central announced that the success of snow trains last year was so great that an enlarged program is being planned this year for the Adirondacks, Catskill Mountains, with special cars for the rental and sale of skis, ski clothes and other equipment.

The company this year will arrange hotel accommodations for

The depot at Lake Placid is now occupied by the Lake Placid-North Elba Historical Society. It is used for meetings and as a museum.

The track side was pretty well grown over in 1976 when these photos were taken but some of the tracks still remained. (Harter collection)

weekend passengers for Old Forge, North Creek, Fort Ticonderoga and the Catskills.

Beginning January 8, if snow conditions are favorable, the New York Central will run two trips every weekend, one to either Old Forge, North Creek, Fort Ticonderoga and the other to the Catskills. Excursions will also be run to Lake Placid, Montreal and the Laurentians.

F. Ray McKnight has preserved copies of some of the block sheets (Station Record of Train Movements) from the Saranac Inn station. On September 6, 1937, train No. 10 southbound is shown as running in three extra sections. Ray's comments on the train movements through Saranac Inn station on January 2, 1939 are highly interesting:

> The sheet for January 2, 1939 gives a good idea of the business generated by the "ski trains." This shows five specials out of Lake Placid for New York taking in approximately 45 sleepers! Note too the use of the main line high wheeled K-3 engines — 4703, 4693, 4673 and 10-wheelers 844, 845, 876. An engine shortage due to the K-11 class oil burners which were not in service made it necessary to bring in off line engines. I recall that the 4693 had a difficult time getting her train started out of Saranac Lake. Our engineers were not used to those high drivers and eight cars was a heavy train. Never heard how they made out getting over Big Moose, they may have got a second engine at Tupper Lake.

World War II intervened and following that the better plowed highways, better equipped automobiles and installation of more and nearer ski slopes forced the cancellations of the snow specials but it must be doubted though, if the comradeship of these memorable trains was ever exceeded by any other method of transportation.

There were only a few recorded mishaps of any magnitude on the Saranac Branch. One occurred in September 1915 when a New York Central train, southbound from Lake Placid, struck the rear of a Delaware and Hudson freight train headed for Plattsburgh. The accident occurred in the vicinity of Raybrook and resulted in the destruction of the caboose and four or five freight cars.

A serious derailment took place in October 1916 and the LAKE PLACID NEWS reported:

> Thrown by a defective rail on Tuesday near the Ray Brook crossing, the noon Central train out of Lake Placid containing two Pullmans, two day coaches, and two baggage cars, broke over a 15-foot enbankment injuring nine persons.
>
> The train left Ray Brook at 11:43 and was just getting under way when, taking the loop at about 30 miles an hour the outside rail gave

way, plunging one of the cars over the embankment, taking the whole string except the engine with it.

There were about 30 people on the train at the time of the accident. Twelve were in the forward day coach, with the rest distributed throughout the train.

The wrecking crew and train from Tupper Lake arrived at about 3 o'clock and working all night had the wreckage cleared and the track relaid for the morning trains.

New York Central engine No. 3092 exploded in the Saranac yards in September 1929 with the usual serious outcome of such accidents.

The depot at Saranac Lake is still standing but in need of considerable rehabilitation in 1976. The same could be said for the depot at Raybrook. However, the Lake Placid-North Elba Historical Society has the Lake Placid depot and uses it for a combined museum and meeting place. It is in fine repair and well maintained. Adjacent to the Lake Placid depot is an old dining car that was a gift to the Historical Society. It has been refurbished to quite an extent but was not restored to its original appearance.

CHAPTER XIII
The Connecting Roads

THE FULTON CHAIN RAILWAY

No sooner had the first regularly scheduled train discharged passengers at the Fulton Chain Station, two miles from the head of navigation of the Fulton Chain of Lakes at Old Forge, than it was realized that transportation to and from Old Forge was going to be a problem. A company was organized and Victor Adams of Little Falls, N.Y. was one of the chief promoters. The officers and directors were all residents of either Little Falls or Lowville and it appears that none of them were allied with William Seward Webb's interests. On February 15, 1896 the Fulton Chain Railroad Company applied for a certificate under section 59 of the Railroad Law.

Filed with the application were several interesting and intriguing affidavits. Thomas E. Ehrehart, a civil engineer from Newburgh, N.Y. made the survey and his affidavit read in part:

> That the length of said railroad is two miles; that the maximum grade is one percent; that it connects with the Adirondack and St. Lawrence at Fulton Chain and runs to the docks at Old Forge where it connects with steam boat navigation; that the probable cost of said railroad will be as follows —
>
> | | |
> |---|---:|
> | Earth works, 19,700 yards at 15m | $2955.00 |
> | Tracks, ties, rails, etc. | 7725.00 |
> | Engineering | 400.00 |
> | Right of Way | 1500.00 |
> | Legal expenses | 750.00 |
>
> Together with the cost of building depots, freight houses, docks, bridges and trestles and purchasing rolling stock.

To the best of my knowledge and belief, the scheme is feasible, that freight cars may be run at Old Forge on to barges or scows and towed to the head of Fourth Lake without rehandling, twelve miles farther up.

C. M. Barrett, the proprietor of the Bald Mountain House at Third Lake of the Fulton Chain went into much more detail. There is a tremendous amount of local background in his 750 word statement. He said he had been proprietor of the Forge House for nine years and the proprietor of the Moose River House "at the beginning of the wooden railroad of Mrs. DeCamp" for about six years. He went on to say:

> The Fulton Chain was formerly reached from Boonville "by 25 miles partly very bad road." About eight years ago Mrs. DeCamp and associates built a wooden track from Moose River to Minnehaha and then carried people by steamer Fawn to within a mile of Old Forge. Since Dr. Webb's road has been constructed the travel to the Fulton Chain has grown very large and is steadily increasing.

Mr. Barrett then listed about fifty hotels, boarding houses and cottages as well as the business establishments then on the Fulton Chain of lakes. His statement continues:

> I am reliably informed that a number of hotels will build large additions and that a great number of new cottages will be erected. The steamers on these four lakes can carry about 300 people. Excursions to the lakes have not been run, at least no large ones, on account of the lack of carrying facilities from the Adirondack and St. Lawrence Railway to Old Forge over two miles of usually bad road. The number of vehicles for carrying passengers from the railroad to steamboat navigation has been entirely inadequate and has been a serious hindrance to the public and has prevented invalids from coming in as they cannot endure the trip over such bad roads and the dilapidated conveyances and the public has been to my knowledge been complaining bitterly about the miserable condition of that part of the general route. The access to the Adirondacks via Fulton Chain is the easiest of all and all the prominent parts of them can be reached by steamer, boat and easy carriage barring the aforesaid highway to Old Forge. As the through travel via Racquette Lake has increased considerably with the last few years this road subjects these tourists to the same discomforts as the visitors of the Fulton Chain. I believe that the construction and operation of a railroad from Fulton Chain Station to Old Forge is needed for the further development of this region, for the comfort and health of the general public and for the further prosperity of the settler now living here all or part of the time. If the access to this main gateway of the Adirondacks is not made more approachable and easier to all I have no doubt that in course of time travel will reach the great level plateau of the lake region by some other way. As there is in the whole region no other chain of lakes which offers the same advantages to tourists, sportsmen and invalids. I believe that such a railroad is demanded by public necessity.

Robert Dalton stated that he was a guide and was thoroughly familiar with the area. His comments about the situation although lengthy gave a significant insight on just how good the "Good Old Days" were when it came to travelling:

The connecting road from Fulton Chain Station to Old Forge, a little over two miles long, is of light sand mixed with vegetable muck. After rains the road becomes impassable and repairs have been made to no avail. During several months of the year, in the spring and fall, the road is in very bad and dangerous condition. During the dry season the road is very dusty. The vehicles used for the transporting of passengers are old fashioned second hand omnibusses and farm wagons with crude tops fastened on and some wagons without springs whatever.

The horses used for drawing the vehicles are the same used by their owners in the lumber woods and on the farm and the time used in average to make the trips of two miles is three quarters of an hour or more. The drivers of the conveyances are extremely awkward and, when large crowds arrive, perfectly helpless. There is no organized stage company and anybody with a horse and wagon becomes a common carrier. The mail is carried on a one horse rig and not on the stages, but during the height of the season the mail is carried on the baggage wagons as the mail is too heavy.

All of the wagons existing at Old Forge and Fulton Chain, including lumber wagons, stages, busses, carryalls, carriages and buggies have a capacity of carrying passengers not exceeding one hundred and twenty-five people. As trains have landed often three hundred and more people it would take three trips to take this number over to the steamboard landing and certainly would require one more trip for the baggage so that in such a case the people either had to walk or stay on the sands of the desert around Fulton Chain. It would be impossible to get all of these wagons to draw passengers at any one time. Tourists and sportsmen have often expressed their indignation and disgust at this condition of things and many people have told me that they would never return to here unless the conditions and facilities to reach navigation were greatly improved.

Mr. Dalton listed the steamers then operating on the Fulton Chain of Lakes. He mentioned the *S. S. Stowell, S. S. Zyp, S. S. Fulton,* one large and one small freight steamer. He also listed the following "houses of public entertainment" from the Forge pond to the head of Fourth Lake and the numbers represent the capacity which in nearly every case was being expanded: The Forge House (200), Barrett House (100), Powers House (70), Miner House (15), Don Wood's (20), Cedar Island House (75), Rocky Point Inn (100) and Fred Hess' (40). Besides these he mentioned the boarders taken at the many cottages.

Ex-President Benjamin Harrison even sent a letter expressing his thoughts that the proposed railroad would be a great public convenience. Edwin N. Arnold and Frederick Hess of the Hess House on Fourth Lake were others that filed affidavits. Mr. Hess also listed the steamers on the lake and added the *Minnie H.*

Theodore Seeber who identified himself as a boat builder. He also reviewed the very difficult land travel situation about Old Forge but being true to his trade he added considerable information about the lake steamers and boats. In capsule form, here is what he described:

In 1885 I brought to the Fulton Chain a small steamer, the *Hunter,* capacity 40 persons, cost $900. The *Hunter* was run for six seasons and then sunk, being not worth repairing.

In 1887 the *Eddie S.,* capacity 15 persons, cost about $600, which was built by me at Boonville, was brought in. It was run for two years, then I sold her to outside parties.

About 1888 I built the *Fulton,* 80 persons capacity, a cabin boat, cost $2100, for the well known Jack Shephard, which boat has been run ever since.

About 1890 two small steamers were added, the *Buella,* capacity 20 persons, cost about $700, and the *Old Forge,* capacity 40 persons, cost about $900, both were second handed and now out of commission and useless.

About two years ago (1894) the steamer *ZYP,* capacity about 50 persons, cost $1000, was built in Rome and brought here.

In 1894 the *Stowell* was built by Captain Sweet with my assistance. It is a fine substantial boat of 150 persons capacity and cost about $7000.

On Seventh Lake there is the steamer *Gazelle,* capacity 30 persons and cost $600.

On Eighth Lake a small steamer of 20 persons capacity operates. This steamer cost about $500.

With the completion of the Adirondack and St. Lawrence Railway the travel over and to the Fulton Chain has increased many times. I estimate that in the days of the buckboard travel from Boonville the total number of tourists going past Old Forge did not exceed 1200 per year which did include all of the visitors for the Upper Chain of Lakes and part of the Moose River tract who now reach those regions from stations below and above Fulton Chain Station by correct routes. I estimate that the number of people travelling either way past Old Forge to points of destination amounts now to 25,000 per year. (Mr Seeber concludes his statement with a review of the now familiar complaints about the travel difficulties between Fulton Chain Station and Old Forge and concludes with) . . . I believe that the construction of a railroad is demanded by public necessity and will result in the greatest development of this section of the Adirondacks and the Valleys of the Middle Branch of the Moose River and Fulton Chain of Lakes and the headwaters of the Racquette River from Blue Mountain down.

Reputed to be the first excursion train to Old Forge. Shed at left is on the site of the later station. The steam boat in the background is the C. L. STOWELL. 1896. (Harter collection)

The Forge House apparently taken from a steamboat. Small building in foreground is the first railroad station at Old Forge. Circa 1896. (Harter collection)

Another view of the first excursion train into Old Forge. 1896. (Harter collection)

Railroad bridge between Fulton Chain and Old Forge about 1908. (Denio collection)

Fulton Chain Railway,
·1901· No. 15
Pass C. E. Snyder & family
Director: F. C. Ry
W Webb
President.

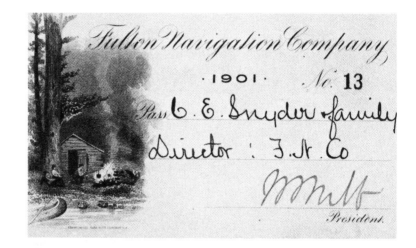

Fulton Navigation Company,
·1901· No. 13
Pass C. E. Snyder & family
Director: F. N. Co
W Webb
President.

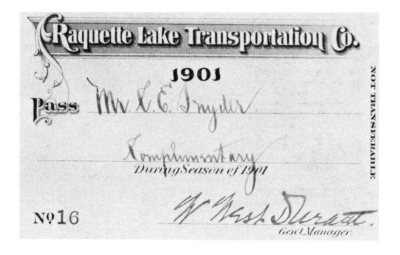

Raquette Lake Transportation Co.
1901
Pass Mr. C. E. Snyder
Complimentary
During Season of 1901
W. West Durant
Gen'l Manager.
No 16

NOT TRANSFERABLE

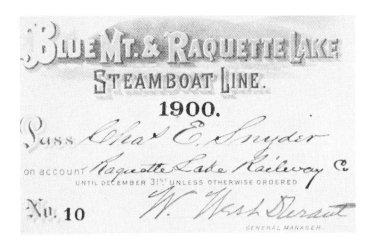

BLUE MT. & RAQUETTE LAKE
STEAMBOAT LINE.
1900.
Pass *Chas E. Snyder*
on account *Raquette Lake Railway Co.*
UNTIL DECEMBER 31ST UNLESS OTHERWISE ORDERED
No. 10
W. West Durant
GENERAL MANAGER

New York Central No. 929 leaving Old Forge depot for Fulton Chain Station. Circa 1910. (Fred C. Miller collection)

With such an array of statements testifying to the necessity of this two mile railroad as a public convenience it is not surprising that the Board of Railroad Commissioners granted the application for the construction of the railroad from Fulton Chain Station on the Adirondack and St. Lawrence Railway to the head of navigation on the Fulton Chain of Lakes at Old Forge.

The new company soon ran into difficulty as this statement from the 1897 REPORT OF THE RAILROAD COMMISSIONERS indicates:

> After the organization of the Fulton Chain Railroad Company, and in May 1896, a contract was entered into with James Campbell of Lowville, N.Y., for the construction of the road including ties, rails, bridges, etc., the contractor to furnish all materials and labor for the contract. The contractor has failed to complete the work according to his contract, and no settlement has been made with him. Pending a settlement with the contractor, and with the consent of the trustees for the bond-holders, the road has been operated, but no financial statement can now be made.
>
> Two cars and a locomotive have been purchased by notes indorsed by the directors, acting individually, and the same have been used, but no financial statement can be rendered until the road is formally accepted.

By 1901 Dr. Webb had apparently taken over the Fulton Chain Railroad as evidenced by the Railroad Commissioners saying:

> The reorganization of this property under foreclosure proceedings has not yet been completed. Owing to the fact that no books, papers or records of any kind came into the possession of the present owners of the property it is impossible to give any information prior to May 1901. This property is being operated at present by the New York Central and Hudson River Railroad Company under a tentative agreement with the owners, represented by William Seward Webb, and the company. And this report covers the period of such operation, viz.: May and June 1901.

In 1902 the Fulton Chain Railroad Company was sold and reorganized as the Fulton Chain Railway Company. The track repairs were being made by the section men of the Mohawk and Hudson and the motive power and passenger cars of the New York Central and Hudson River Railroad were used.

After the death of Mr. Huntington in 1900, Dr. Webb was elected president of the Raquette Lake Railway and also of several transportation companies which he and his associates acquired at about that time. They included the Fulton Chain Railroad, The Fulton Navigation Company, operating the steamers on the Fulton

Chain of Lakes and the Raquette Lake Transportation Company, operating steamers on Raquette and Blue Mountain Lakes and a tiny railroad in between. Under his direction many improvements were made in the equipment and service of these companies, greatly to the advantage to this entire region.

The OFFICIAL GUIDE OF THE RAILWAYS in 1905 shows the Fulton Navigation Company maintaining a regular schedule of boats departing from the Old Forge station of the Fulton Chain Railway. Boats made regular connections with four trains a day each way. The boats also made connections with the Raquette Lake Railway at Eagle Bay.

In 1906, the railway reported it carried nearly 20,000 passengers and over 2,700 tons of freight, with a slight profit resulting. It certainly is worthwhile to list the 1906 directors of this two mile long railroad:

J. Pierpont Morgan	Robert Bacon
Charles H. Tweed	H. E. Huntington
W. Seward Webb	Arabella D. Huntington
Isaac E. Gates	Harry Payne Whitney
Chauncey M. Depew	Edward M. Burns
Frank A. Harrington	W. Pierson Hamilton
Alfred G. Vanderbilt	

Charles E. Snyder, Secretary and General Counsel
Clarence Morgan, Treasurer

Beginning about 1906 and continuing every winter until 1922 one of the great freight producing items was ice. It is understood that the most or all of this ice was stored by the New York Central in its own icehouses and was used to refrigerate milk cars and other such units requiring cooling. The Fulton Chain Railway was authorized by the Public Service Commission in 1908 to establish a special rate of fifteen cents per net ton on ice in carloads between Old Forge and Fulton Chain Station.

In 1908 the company reported originating only 89 tons of freight outside of the ice business but handled 1418 tons of incoming freight. Certainly not enough revenue could be derived from that source to keep the road running.

In 1914 the passenger revenue was threatened by the Public Service Commission certifying that public convenience and necessity required the operation by Samuel A. Smith of a stage route (or auto bus line) between Fulton Chain Station and Old Forge. Evidently Smith didn't avail himself of the certification because in 1915 the

From the Forge House showing Railroad Depot and Steamboat Landing. Circa 1909. (Harter collection)

Steamer UNCAS on the Fulton Chain of Lakes. Circa 1913. (Harter collection)

Steamer NEHASANE at Bald Mountain Landing. Circa 1914. (Harter collection)

Steamer CLEARWATER on the Fulton Chain of Lakes. Circa 1924. (Harter collection)

Commission granted the certificate of convenience and necessity to Maurice Callahan who had been or still was the superintendent of the Fulton Chain Navigation Company. Callahan was authorized to carry passengers, baggage and freight by automobile between Fulton Chain Station and Old Forge.

On March 2, 1917 the Public Service Commission of the Second District granted permission to the New York Central Railroad Company to purchase the Fulton Chain Railway by assuming the indebtedness of the subsidiary line. Most of the indebtedness was to the New York Central. The same order applied to the Raquette Lake Railway Company.

In an order permitting the Fulton Chain Railway to suspend operations except during June, July, August and September of 1918, the commission made note that the railroad had been in existence for 20 years and had always suspended operations from October to May.

The Utica-Old Forge Transportation Company, a bus line, had been established and in 1929 it reported that it had received $9,671 in operating revenues and the cost of operation was $9,214.

What business the little railroad had continued to decrease and the Interstate Commerce Commission authorized the abandonment on July 11, 1932. The two mile shortline had been smothered by the increased use of private automobiles on better highways which permitted greater and wider access to the Adirondacks than the Mohawk and Malone and Fulton Chain Railways could provide.

One of the most unusual services ever offered in the name of railroads was the mail route around the Fulton Chain of Lakes from Old Forge to Fourth Lake and return. A steamer or in later years a motor launch was designated as a mail boat and made deliveries and pickups from camp to camp all around the lakes. Most of the mail was passed hand to hand from the camp docks without the mail boat coming to a full halt. Mail picked up was postmarked "INLET AND OLD FORGE R.P.O." signifying Railway Post Office and most of the postmarks besides the date included the designation "TR" and a number signifying Train No. 1 or Train No. 4 or whatever the proper number was. All of this gave birth to the phrase "The only service like it in the world. A railway post office run on a boat like a Rural Free Delivery route."

Although we have dwelt in quite some detail with the Fulton Chain Railway it was done to emphasize the conditions prevailing before the Adirondack and St. Lawrence Railway was built and the profound influence the opening of the railroad had on the entire Adirondack area. The primitive means of communication and travel were limited to the most hardy or venturesome individuals. With the opening of the last link to the Fulton Chain of Lakes the days of expanded use of the North Woods were at hand. At no other point on the entire railroad were the conditions so conducive to the utilization of recreational opportunities as those offered in the Fulton Chain area. The great American public is still enjoying itself there, winter and summer, spring and fall.

THE RAQUETTE LAKE RAILWAY

The building of the Raquette Lake Railway was due to one or more very good reasons. It probably was a combination of all the reasons advanced that eventually led to an application for permission to conduct and operate an eighteen mile railroad from Clearwater on the Adirondack and St. Lawrence Railway to Raquette Lake.

One reason given was the need for former governor John A. Dix to reach the market with millions of board feet of lumber which he had cut in the Rondaxe Lake area. John Dix had laid a couple of miles of lumbering railroad from Clearwater to haul his timber. W. W. Durant is usually credited with the idea to hitch on to this lumber railroad and extend it to the foot of Raquette Lake where there was a little settlement sometimes listed as Durant, later Raquette Lake Village. Such a railroad would give considerably better access to properties that Durant owned on Raquette Lake and the vicinity thereof.

Two reasons have been attributed to the Collis P. Huntington family who had purchased Camp Pine Knot on Raquette Lake from W. W. Durant. It has been reported that Mrs. Huntington was so dissatisfied with the rigors of travel up the Fulton Chain of Lakes by steamer and then by various transfers using boats and buckboards on so called roads that she served notice that she would not visit their camp again until she came by rail. To put it bluntly, Mrs. Huntington is supposed to have said, that if her husband could build a transcontinental railroad there was no reason that he could not build one to reach their camp on Raquette Lake.

Charles H. Burnett attributes the building of the road to Mr. Huntington himself:

> Mr. Huntington spent his summers at Pine Knot Camp, coming by train to Old Forge, where he left his two private cars and traversed the Fulton Chain of Lakes and Brown Track Inlet by a series of small steamers and a number of carries — a very tedious trip. One day Mr. Huntington had to content himself with a seat on a keg of nails all the way from Old Forge to the head of Fourth Lake. He was thoroughly disgusted and decided that the time had come to build a railroad.

Raquette Lake Railway No. 1. This is the third engine that the Raquette Lake numbered as # 1. (H. K. Vollrath collection)

Raquette Lake Railway No. 2. This is Raquette Lakes first engine # 2. (Railway Hist. Soc. of Northern New York)

Raquette Lake Railway south of Eagle Bay. Circa 1920. (Harter collection)

This apparently is the morning train coming in from New York to Raquette Lake directly with the Raquette Lake engine needing the help of a New York Central with this 7 or 8 car train. (Edward Baumgardner collection)

THE GENERAL STORE   CARTER N.Y.   N.H.

South end of the station and the general store at Carter. Circa 1914. (Gerald Smith collection)

The Eagle Bay depot, now a tavern. 1974. (Harter collection)

Steamer ADIRONDACK on Raquette Lake. In background is the terminal area of the railroad and the ramp for loading freight cars on scows for towing across Raquette Lake. The shed on the rise was a shelter for private cars while their owners were at their camps in the neighborhood. (Harter collection)

This picture from a postcard on the back of which the correspondent wrote "Raquette Lake, April 11, 1917. The picture is the scow coming in with a box car, this car has been up through Raquette Lake on the scow and across the little railraod to Blue Mountain Lake, then across Blue Mountain Lake on a scow to Blue Mountain Lake Village. Now it is back to go out on our line." (Edward Baumgardner)

J. Pierpont Morgan was the owner of a beautiful camp called "Uncas" on Lake Mohegan. Mr. Durant was the owner of a camp on Shedd Lake called "Sagamore Lodge" which he afterward sold to Alfred G. Vanderbilt. William C. Whitney and Harry Payne Whitney were owners of extensive lands near Raquette Lake and Dr. Webb still possessed a large share of his holdings in the John Brown Tract. Mr. Huntington had no difficulty in persuading these friends and neighbors to join him in the building of the Raquette Lake Railway. Chauncey Depew also became a member of the board of directors.

In 1892 Dr. Webb had had George C. Ward make a survey for a railroad to the Raquette Lake shore but the line was not built at that time.

On March 23, 1899 the NEW YORK TIMES printed the following:

THE RAQUETTE LAKE RAILWAY — Believed to be for the Benefit of a Few Rich Men — Albany, March 22 — The application of the Raquette Lake Railway Company, recently incorporated, for permission to construct a nineteen-mile railroad in the Adirondacks will be heard by the State Railroad Commission on Wednesday next. The company must convince the Railroad Commissioners that public necessity and convenience requires the construction of the road. The company prefers to operate the road by air power, but if this is not feasible electricity will be utilized. The reason for this preference is to lessen the liability of fire in the woods. There is always liable to be a leakage from feed wires, which it is hoped to obviate by air power.

The charter was approved on April 11, 1899. There was a discrepancy between the charter and the actual method of operation of this road. The Raquette Lake Railway had applied for permission to operate as a street railway by air power or electricity along a highway leading from Clearwater to Raquette Lake. The air power and electricity were advanced as the proposed power sources because of the forest fire threat then being experienced in the Adirondacks. The highway was more or less nonexistent except in a couple of places. Maps were prepared showing sections of the DURANT ROAD (part of former projected highway from Clearwater to Raquette Lake) in the town of Long Lake West and in the Town of Inlet. Red lines were used to indicate where the Raquette Lake Railway would run in these sections of highway. However, no one seemed to challenge the projected railway and permission was given on June 20, 1900 for the railway to use oil-burning steam locomotives. Motive power was secured from the New York Central and that company's rolling stock was utilized for both passengers and freight. Trackage rights from Clearwater to Fulton Chain, a distance of 6.14 miles were secured.

Construction was started in April 1899 and was completed in about five months. The MORNING HERALD reported on September 12, 1899:

> CLEARWATER-RAQUET LAKE — The New Railroad Between These Two Points Practically Open — Raquet Lake, Sept. 11 — (Special) — C. P. Huntington left New York City in his private car Saturday morning (September 9) for Raquet Lake, arriving here that evening over the new railroad from Clearwater. This is the first time any one has ever made this through trip by rail from New York.
>
> The Clearwater and Raquet Lake Railroad is now practically open, and it is expected that it will soon be ready for business.

The officials decided not to throw the road open to the public so late in the year. According to the railroad inspector, he examined the railroad on January 30 and 31, 1900 and said the track was all laid but no stations had been built. He did report:

> The railroad passes through an almost unbroken forest of principally spruce and hardwood timber, the entire distance. A narrow strip, about 50 feet in width, has been cleared to provide for it. The construction company is using one small, soft coal-burning locomotive for transporting its laborers and materials, and at the same time, is carrying any freight offered for transportation, also passengers desiring to ride, and charges are made for so doing. No regular trains are run, but it is understood that connection will be made with the afternoon passenger trains on the Mohawk and Malone Railway. A caboose is attached to the train, in which passengers and employes ride. The New York Central and Hudson River Railroad Company run a log train over that portion of the road from Clearwater Junction to near Eagle Bay, a distance of about six miles. Mr. G. C. Ward, engineer for the Railway Construction Company, with office at Eagle Bay station, is in charge of the property.
>
> The maximum grade is 132 feet per mile; the maximum curve, 11 degrees. The rail used is 67 pound, second hand steel, connected by 36 inch angle plates, with 4 bolts, and is in good condition.

Charles H. Burnett said that Mr. Huntington made a hobby of the project and that they used to tell him (Burnett) that Southern Pacific affairs had little chance for consideration when Raquette Lake matters were to the fore. The little road had the most distinguished Board of Directors of any road its size in the world. It included Mr. Huntington, Mr. Morgan, Dr. Webb, the two Whitneys, Mr. Durant and Senator Depew.

Collis P. Huntington is regarded as the prime mover of the Raquette Lake Railway and as Burnett said, it was his hobby, but unfortunately he was not able to enjoy it for very long as he died in

August 1900. Dr. W. Seward Webb was elected president and made improvements in equipment and service on the railroad and on the subsidiary companies allied with it.

The Raquette Lake Railway was officially opened to the public on July 1, 1900. Summer service consisted of two trains daily in each direction, one was a day train and the other carried sleeper cars. Obviously the balance of the year could not support such service and it varied from one train a day to a three days a week schedule in later years.

Examination of the earlier employee time tables indicate that the night train from Raquette Lake ran into Fulton Chain Station over the six mile trackage rights and in the morning picked up the sleeping cars at Fulton Chain Station for the trip to the Raquette Lake terminal. Albert Hess, who was an Adirondack Division conductor, said that sometimes there would be an extra train for Raquette Lake and the crew would make the entire run from Utica but normally the Raquette Lake-Clearwater trains were all handled by the same crew and their run was restricted to that road.

On December 5, 1900, President Webb issued a general order:

> Commencing January first, 1900, the operating department of the Raquette Lake Railway Company will be conducted by the New York Central and Hudson River Railroad Company.
>
> All agents and other employes will from that date make their reports accordingly.

In the 1901 railroad inspector's report it says:

> At Clearwater there is a combination passenger and freight station of good design, new and properly equipped. At Eagle Bay, which is near the head of Fourth Lake on the Fulton Chain, there is also a new and convenient freight and passenger station. At Raquette Lake a commodious freight and passenger station with restaurant included, all new and of modern design, neatly and properly finished. The other stations are small, about 12 × 12, with covered shed about the same dimensions and at these no agents are employed.

In the 1901 financial report the railway reported that the cost of construction had been $467,768.77. It also reported that $33,168.83 had been spent for 3 locomotives; passenger car; mail, baggage and express car; freight and other cars; bridges, floats and tugs. The last items were for use in connection with the Raquette Lake Transportation Company.

In 1906 the company reported that total operating income was over $28,000 but it left a deficit of nearly $4,000 and a total deficit had accumulated as of June 30, 1906 of over $42,000. This operating ratio was never to improve.

The first two decades of the twentieth century were the best years of the Raquette Lake Railway. The well-to-do arrived at Raquette Lake in their private railroad cars which were left on a siding or under a shed which covered a spur track just beyond the station. Pullman service was available from New York City.

One of the most unusual incidents in railroading occurred in August 1908. Heavy traffic had developed from a large excursion and the little 4-6-0 bringing the train into Raquette Lake ran short of water and had to leave the train near Uncas and try to make the water tank at Raquette Lake. Apparently the engineer realized that he was taking too great a chance and so had to draw the fire. He secured a horse to pull the dead engine into the water tank at the terminal. But it all turned out well, the engine was fired up and went back towards Uncas for the train. Some enterprising photographer took a picture of the engine being towed and the mischance was recorded for posterity.

World War I had a great effect on the opulent society. The cost of maintaining and using such luxury items as private railroad cars and the cost of staffing large estates became overbearing. Highways were being built that were bringing the great out-of-doors to where many people could enjoy it.

The railroads were beginning to see a difference in their short line operational expense ratios and this was to become an increasing bugaboo to them in the years to come especially during the depression years of the 1930's.

Harold K. Hochshild in his LIFE AND LEISURE IN THE ADIRONDACKS says that ice was cut the first part of the winter at Old Forge. When the ice within one half mile of the railroad had been cut, the equipment was moved to Raquette Lake. This ice was also used by the New York Central Railroad. In 1908 the Public Service Commission authorized the Raquette Lake Railway to establish a special rate of twenty cents per ton on carloads of ice, minimum weight twenty-five tons, from Rondaxe, N. Y. and Raquette Lake, N. Y. to Clearwater, N. Y.

In 1911 the company reported 13,692 tons of outgoing freight, 92% of which was forest products of some type. 2,776 tons of incoming freight was handled. Ice was not listed as a commodity. Probably this was due to its being transported for the New York Central icehouses at Utica, Syracuse and Weehawken. The ice contract which the Callahan interests had with the New York Central started in 1906 with 20,000 tons and rose to as high as 50,000 tons. This was harvested partly at Old Forge and partly at Raquette Lake.

In 1912 the name of the junction point of the Mohawk and Malone Railway and the Raquette Lake Railway at Clearwater was changed to Carter.

On November 9, 1913 a serious wreck occurred on the line. The BOONVILLE HERALD of November 13 describes the sad event:

> Storm Blows Tree Across Raquette Track and Engine Plunges Down Embankment — Raquette Lake, Nov. 10 — Three men were killed in a wreck on the Raquette Lake Railroad yesterday afternoon. They are Benjamin Hall, engineer; John Case, fireman and A. G. Lashaway, brakeman, all of this village.
>
> The train was running from Carter to this place when 'it struck a large tree which had been blown across the track during a storm earlier in the day. The locomotive tumbled down a steep embankment. The cars remained on the Roadbed. There was a long delay in getting assistance. Conductor John Rank was obliged to walk six and one half miles to reach the nearest telegraph and because of wire trouble the operator was unable to get word to any outside point for a long time. Engineer Hall was 58 years old and for years was an engineer on the main line of the Central. He formerly lived in Oneida.

F. Ray McKnight said that there was a serious mishap in the early part of 1915:

> . . . during the winter of 1914–15 Father (Orville McKnight) was working second trick at Carter and has told me that one night an "ice extra" (back then train loads of ice were shipped out) came out of the Raquette Lake and ran into some cars standing on the south leg of the wye. The coal boards broke in the tender and the fireman was buried under about two tons of coal.

On March 14, 1917 the Public Service Commission of the Second District granted permission to the New York Central Railroad Company to acquire and hold the entire capital stock of the Raquette Lake Railway Company by assuming the indebtedness of the company. By 1921 POOR'S MANUAL OF RAILROADS was reporting that in 1920 the Raquette Lake Railway operated at a deficit of over $40,000.

In 1925 a new highway was projected between Seventh Lake of the Fulton Chain of Lakes and Raquette Lake with an eventual extension to Blue Mountain Lake and north from there. This boded no good for the well being of the Raquette Lake Railway.

On May 14, 1932 the Raquette Lake Railway Company and the New York Central Railroad Company filed a joint application with the Interstate Commerce Commission for permission for the

Raquette Lake to abandon its entire line of railroad and for the New York Central to abandon operations of said line. About the same time the Raquette Lake had sought permission from the New York State Public Service Commission to abandon all stations on the line. Protests were filed and the State Commission held a hearing on June 15, 1932 and on the following August 9th denied the petition and required the Raquette Lake to maintain serviceable facilities for the convenience of the public during the summer season of each year, from June 15th to September 30th, inclusive.

We have noted that in 1916 the New York Central took over the Raquette Lake capital stock and cancelled the debts thereof and later cancelled the mortgage bonds. By 1928 the debt for deficit operations had accumulated to over $326,000 and the New York Central cancelled this indebtedness and among other things, obligated itself to assume all deficits from operation of the line in the future.

In January 1934 the matter was again submitted to the Interstate Commerce Commission. At that time service consisted of one mixed train making three round trips weekly during the fall, spring, and winter months. During the summer months the New York Central rendered through passenger train service, including Pullman service, between New York City and places on the Raquette Lake line. The schedule of these trains were not stated to the Commission. However, the record shows that during the summer season of 1931, about 200 Pullman cars were operated over the line. The locomotives used were about the smallest type in service on the Central as restrictions prevented the use of larger locomotives.

Here is a quotation from the Interstate Commerce Commission Docket No. 9403:

> The New York Central contends that as a result of the construction of improved highways, most of the traffic to and from the summer resorts is now handled by automobiles; that an improved highway, constructed in 1930, between Thendara and Raquette Lake, roughly parallels the line its entire length; that passenger traffic can be handled by busses from trains on its Adirondack division serving Thendara; that a considerable amount of pulpwood and natural ice have been shipped over the line in the past, but the pulpwood production has ceased and there is no longer any demand for natural ice; that the only freight now handled over the line consists of small quantities of inbound coal, gasoline, oil, and occasional shipments of material used in the construction of highways; and that operation of the line has resulted in heavy deficits during past years.

The Interstate Commerce Commission report also said that in 1933 the line operated from June 15 to September 15. Outbound

RAQUETTE LAKE RAILWAY LOCOMOTIVES

Eng. No.	Type	Class	Dimensions	Previous Numbers	Prev. Classes	Bldr.	Date	C/N	Rebuilt	Date Acquired	Dispos.
1st/1	4-6-0	F*	18 × 24-57	105,100	NYC&HR 495-658-2003-2163	C	Rome	12/87	314		5/1902	Ser. WA 2/4/1914
2nd/1	4-8-0	X-3	20 × 26-57	143,000	BC 69-NYC&HR 2629-3629-629-81	H-50b,H-3	Schen.	2/98	4700		3/21/14	Scr. 2/15/16
3rd/1	2-6-0	E-1g	20 × 28-63	160,000	NYC&HR 1764	V-2,E-10,E-3a	Schen.	8/00	5506	W. Alby 10/1905	1916	Reno. NYC 1928 and Scr. 12/12/47
1st/2	4-6-0	F	18 × 24-57	105,100	NYC&HR 535-678-2023-2183	C	Schen.	11/87	2442		5/1902	Scr. WA 4/25/12
2nd/2	4-8-0	H-3*	20× 26-57	143,000	BC 64-NYC&HR 2624-3624	H-50b	Schen.	2/97	4532		4/8/12	Scr. WA 1/4/15
3rd/2	2-6-0	E-1f	20 × 28-63	159,200	NYC&HR 1767	V-1,E-9,E-3	Bald.	4/00	17638	W. Alby 4/1904	12/28/14	Reno. NYC 1927 and Scr. 11/5/41

*Engine 1st 1 reclassed Fa
*Engine 2nd 2 reclassed X-3

F. Ray McKnight Collection   Compiled by Edward L. May

freight consisted of 1 carload of cordwood and 1 carload of miscellaneous commodities. Inbound freight consisted of a total of 1208 tons mostly coal and petroleum products. The total number of passengers handled was 4779. Total revenues were $5,600 and expenses which included nothing for maintenance of way and structures was over $13,600 showing an operating deficit of $8,000.

Those protesting the abandonment advanced many arguments but none sufficiently impressed the Commission enough to stop it from issuing a certificate permitting the Raquette Lake Railway Company to abandon its entire line of railroad and the New York Central Railroad Company to abandon the operation of the line effective a month after the decision was made on February 27, 1934. But this in effect permitted the discontinuance as of the end of the 1933 season and the Public Service Commission gives the date as September 30, 1933.

THE MARION RIVER CARRY RAILWAY

In 1871 the Adirondack Railroad had reached North Creek and despite sporadic efforts that was to remain as its passenger terminal. The Blue Mountain Lake Stage and Transportation Company was organized for the purpose of transporting passengers from North Creek to Blue Mountain Lake and points on Raquette Lake served by the Raquette Lake Steamboats and Blue Mountain Lake Steamboats. It was about a thirty mile trip via buckboard from the railhead to Blue Mountain Lake and the ride left much to be desired and travel over the route was one of discomfort especially to the ladies.

William West Durant had built and developed steamboat lines on Raquette Lake and Blue Mountain Lake and inaugurated through service between the two. However, it was necessary for his patrons to walk the distance across Bassett's Carry later called the Marion River Carry. In 1878 Durant built a dam at the upper end of the carry to raise the water level and in 1890 he rebuilt a dam at the outlet of Raquette Lake to facilitate the steamboats reaching selected docking sites.

With the coming of the Raquette Lake Railway in 1900, Durant saw the solution of his troubles and he is supposed to have been one of those who first advanced the building of this line. In 1899 Durant started construction of a railroad across the Marion River Carry to effect an adequate through route. This route was from Raquette Lake Station, at one time named Durant, to the Marion River Carry by steamboat, cross the three-quarter mile carry by railroad and reboard

Steamer ADIRONDACK at Marion River Carry. (Harter collection)

Loading the Marion River Carry Railroad train. (Harter collection)

Marion River Carry Railroad train enroute across the Carry. (Harter collection)

RAQUETTE LAKE STEAMBOATS.	BLUE MTN. LAKE STEAMBOATS.
MARION RIVER	**BLUE MOUNTAIN LAKE**
TO	TO
KENWILLS.	**MARION RIVER CARRY.**
R13	R13
940	940

Two-part ticket for Raquette Lake and Blue Mountain Lake steamboats.

Blue Mountain Lake Stage and Transportation Company.

No. 7   Blue Mt. Lake, July 12 1886

To Agents.   Special Ticket.

The bearer, Mr. Whittmore has engaged seats in Patent Covered Buckboard Carriages, Through No. Creek to Blue Mountain Lake. Party of 4

Price $ 11 00 Paid.

Buckboard No.   J. F. Mitchell Supt

Before the route through the Fulton Chain and Raquette Lake was opened, Blue Mountain Lake was reached by stage from the Adirondack Railway Company at North Creek. The ticket was stamped on the back as sold on Sept. 17, 1886.

Issued by Blue Mountain Lake Stage & Transportation Co.

ONE PASSAGE.

BLUE MOUNTAIN LAKE

— TO —

NORTH CREEK.

George Leavitt, Supt.

344

a steamer for the balance of the trip through the Eckford Chain of Lakes (Utowana, Eagle and Blue Mountain).

In 1900 the rails were laid and Durant had purchased a small locomotive to draw the three ex-street railway horsecars he had purchased in Brooklyn. This locomotive proved to be underpowered so he rented a switch engine from the New York Central. This engine proved to be too heavy and too expensive to operate. He thereupon ordered an 0-4-0 saddle tank engine from the H. K. Porter Locomotive Works at Pittsburgh and when it was received it proved to be just what was needed. It did not have a tender, it was coaled at each end of its run with a small reserve pile of coal carried in the corner of the cab.

Drawing the three cars, the capacity was about 125 per trip which took only a matter of five minutes or so. Durant is said to have had the idea that through sleeping car service could be established from New York City to Blue Mountain Lake. This would involve the sleeping car being transferred to a car float at Raquette Lake Station, towed across Raquette Lake and up the Marion River to the dock at the Carry. It would then be hauled across the Carry and reloaded on another car float for its final journey through Utowana, Eagle and Blue Mountain Lakes to the terminal. The Pullman Company did not take to the idea of risking these valuable cars on such a hazardous journey and the sleeping cars were unloaded at Raquette Lake Station and the passengers transported by steamer, the Carry Railroad and again by steamer to their destination. Another reason for the abandonment of the idea of transporting the passenger cars via car float was the long time it would take to tow a car float across Raquette Lake.

The transportation of freight cars by car float was a more practical idea and they were ferried over the lakes and used the Carry railroad. The car floats had been built in 1900 and proved inadequate in later years when the empty cars weighed as much as loaded cars had in 1900. Between 1920 and 1925 three of the larger cars foundered in Raquette and Blue Mountain Lakes. Starting in 1926 the standard cars were unloaded at Raquette Lake and the freight reloaded on a boxcar small enough for the aging car floats.

In 1901 the steamboat lines and the railroad were reorganized as the Raquette Lake Transportation Company and Dr. W. Seward Webb became president. In 1909, A. Buchanan, Jr., Supervisor of Equipment, was instructed by the Public Service Commission, Second District to make an inspection of the Marion River Carry Railway. This inspection was made in accordance with a request made by the

Forest, Fish, and Game Commission. His report, although a little lengthy, gives a full description of this unique railroad when it was operating during its good years:

The gauge is 4 feet 8½ inches and the road is seven-eighths mile long. Connection is made between two points on the Marion River through which navigation is impossible. By this method transportation is possible between Raquette Lake and Blue Mountain Lake. A private right of way 200 feet in width is used, and is laid with steel rails weighing 60 pounds per yard. Ties are spaced about 24 inches and roadbed is well ballasted with gravel. The Blue Mountain terminal is 25 feet higher than the Raquette Lake terminal. The railroad is nearly a continuous curve, with three or four short tangents. The condition is good for the light equipment and speed of trains, 5 minutes being used in running the seven-eighths mile.

The equipment consists of one Porter tank locomotive and three light open street cars for passenger traffic. The locomotive is of the tank type, and anthracite coal is used; was built in 1901 by H. K. Porter & Co.; weighs 15 tons, all on drivers, no trucks or tender; boiler steam pressure 140 lbs. per sq. in.; cylinders 11-in. diameter by 16-in. stroke, air and steam brakes on all wheels; link and pin coupler is used; the condition is good throughout except spark-arrester, which is in exceptionally bad condition.

Light open cars, formerly used as street horse cars, are used for passenger traffic, and are number 1, 2, and 3; Nos 1 and 2 have 10 horizontal reversible seats with a seating capacity of about 40 persons; No. 3 is equipped with camp stools, a number of which are in poor condition and generally unsafe. Cars are equipped with hand brakes. Link and pin couplers are used; bell signals on each car; cars are protected with side rails which are placed in position by train crew before train is in motion; all trips are made in daylight and no lighting equipment is furnished. Cars are freshly painted and clean.

The season usually opens May 5th and is closed November 10th. Passenger traffic consists largely of excursionists from Raquette Lake to Blue Mountain Lake. Freight traffic consists largely of parcel freight. A freight float is in operation on Raquette Lake and Blue Mountain Lake, and by this method loaded cars are received from the Raquette Lake Railroad and transported by means of freight floats and the Marion River Carry Railway to all lake points; lumber, coal and other bulk freight is handled in this manner. Each year between 50 and 60 cars of freight are handled.

Link and pin couplers are used throughout. On the passenger cars there does not seem to be any particular danger to employees as cars remain coupled and cars are so light they can be pushed against locomotive by one man to make coupling. On the locomotive the condition is different; locomotive being backed on to lake floats to handle heavily loaded freight cars the liability of injury to employees is considerable, and I believe the locomotive should be equipped with automatic couplers.

RECOMMENDATIONS: That camp stools in passenger car No. 3 be removed and replaced with stationary seats; that the locomotive be equipped with automatic couplers; that the spark-arresters in locomotve be put in good condition at once and so maintained.

In 1923 the heirs of the orginal organizers of the Raquette Lake Transportation Company sold the company to Maurice Callahan who had managed it for twenty years. During the 1920's Callahan had built some smaller car floats for the purpose of transporting automobiles.

In 1940 Douglas S. Dales writing for the RAILROAD MAGAZINE gave the figures of from 8,000 to 10,000 passengers a year. He did not state his source for these figures. The Marion River Carry Railway was not listed as such with the Board of Railroad Commissioners or the Public Service Commission. Although the railroad had been known by various unofficial names, such as the Marion River Railroad, the Carry Railroad and the Marion River Railway, it was actually an integral part of Durant's unincorporated Blue Mountain and Raquette Lake Steamship Line and apparently carried the same status when the reorganization to Raquette Lake Transportation Company took place.

With the opening of a new highway from Raquette Lake to Blue Mountain Lake, the need for the roundabout means of travel was no longer needed. The little train made its last regular run on September 15, 1929 and on October 2nd the locomotive and surviving passenger car was moved into the train shed near the lower terminal.

The Raquette Lake Transportation Company operated its steamboats as public carriers until 1930 on Raquette Lake and the Eckford lakes.

The Marion River Carry locomotive and cars remained at the old train shed at the Carry for over twenty-five years. In time the title of the rolling stock and right-of-way was transferred to the Raquette Lake Supply Company. The rails were reportedly torn up for scrap in 1939. Richard Sanders Allen stated in his article on the Carry Railroad in the YORK STATE TRADITION, Spring 1965, that the railroad property was eventually acquired by Herbert A. Birrell of Raquette Lake. He donated what was left of the unique and famous train for a permanent exhibit at the Adirondack Museum.

In 1955 the locomotive and the remains of the cars were hauled to the Museum at Blue Mountain Lake where one car was rebuilt from the parts of the three. The builder's plate had disappeared from the front of the engine and for the last quarter century it has been the fond hope that it show up again from somewheres so it could be reinstalled in its proper place at the Adirondack Museum.

Douglas Dales gave the Raquette Lake Railway an exceptional classification when he stated that on occasion the railroad made special trips for persons traveling through the lake region by canoe. The minimum tariff of one dollar for such trips probably stands as an all time record low for the cost of chartering a special train.

THE GRASSE RIVER RAILROAD

Childwold, 106.7 miles from Herkimer, 100.5 miles from Utica, became the junction point of the Grasse River Railroad and the Mohawk and Malone Railway.

William L. Sykes had organized the Emporium Lumber Company in Pennsylvania in the 1880's. By the first decade of the 20th Century it became evident that the lumber company would have to have a new base of operations if it was to continue in the business. The first purchase of land in New York State was 18,000 acres in the township of Clare, St. Lawrence County in 1905. Originally planning to operate a sawmill at or near Canton, the plan was revised and a new location was sought.

A point on a tributary of the Raquette River about ten miles west of Tupper Lake was selected and a small community named Conifer was built there, about one and one half miles from Childwold. This was in 1910, five years after the first land purchases. The new sawmill was in operation in the summer of 1911. The TUPPER LAKE HERALD reported on July 7, 1911:

> Childwold — One would imagine a 4th of July celebration was taking place from the booming of dynamite blasting rocks and other obstructions on the new right-of-way of the Emporium Lumber Company.

In 1912 a new company was formed, The Emporium Forestry Company. There was no real change except that the three sons of William L. Sykes assumed executive positions in the new company.

The railroad from Childwold Junction was extended to Cranberry Lake by 1913 along with miles of logging branches or trams as they called them, being put down through the forest. The line to Cranberry Lake was more carefully and substantially built and became popular enough that the Grasse River sought a certificate to operate as a common carrier for the approximately sixteen miles from Childwold to Cranberry Lake Village. The operations of the

Grasse River Railroad No. 68. At Cranberry Lake on June 226, 1936. (R. W. Biermann)

| 7 | 8 | 9 | 10 | 11 | 12 | 13 | 14 | 15 | 16 | 17 | 18 | 19 | 20 | 21 | 22 | 23 | 24 | 25 | 26 | 27 | 28 | 29 | 30 | 31 |
| JAN | FEB | MAR | APR | MAY | JUN | JUL | AUG | SEP | OCT | NOV | DEC | DAY | 1 | 2 | 3 | 4 | 5 | 6 |

GRASSE RIVER RAILROAD

7440

TRAIN TICKET

Good for One Continuous Passage between Stations notched for this day and train only.

(Patented, The Macdonald Mfg. Co., Cleveland, Ohio.)

Columns (top reading): FULL FARE | HALF FARE | 5 cts. paid | 10 | 15 | 20 | 25 | 30 | 35 | 40 | 45 | 50 | 55 | 60 | 65 | 70 | 75 | 80 | CHILDWOLD–N. Y. C. | CONIFER | GRASSE RIVER CLUB | SHURTLEFF | CLARKS | CRANBERRY LAKE

Columns (bottom reading): FULL FARE | HALF FARE | 5 | 10 | 15 | 20 | 25 | 30 | 35 | 40 | 45 | 50 | 55 | 60 | 65 | 70 | 75 | 80 | N. Y. C.–CHILDWOLD | CONIFER | GRASSE RIVER CLUB | SHURTLEFF | CLARKS | CRANBERRY LAKE

Ticket, Grasse River Railroad.

LUMBER YARD AND MILL CONIFER N.Y.   Photo. by H.M.Beach.   No 27.

Grasse River Railroad in foreground and Emporium Forestry Company yards at Conifer. Circa 1915. (Harter collection)

Grasse River Railroad were kept separate from the Emporium logging branches. The Public Service Commission, in 1916, authorized the purchase from the Emporium company of 16.87 miles of railroad plus the land, buildings, 4 locomotives, 2 gasoline cars, 37 freight cars and 3 passnger cars besides all other stores belonging to the railroad operation. This method of operation became effective on May 15, 1916.

The forestry company extended the trams for several years and at the high point in 1937 it was estimated that there was nearly a hundred miles of logging branches in use. Ordinarily Shay engines were used on the logging roads. Rod engines were in use on the main line.

One remarkable fact according to William Gove was that neither the Grasse River Railroad nor its logging railroad ever had a known major accident.

Various home-built motor cars were used through the years on the main line.

The depression years had the same effect on the Emporium Forestry Company and the Grasse River Railroad Corporation. In 1930 Emporium begain to sell off some of its cut over timberland holdings and by 1941 some of the logging rails were being lifted. In 1948 the rails on the Grasse River line were taken up from Cranberry Lake Village to near Conifer, leaving only about two miles of railroad from Conifer to Childwold Station.

In 1949 the Heywood-Wakefield Company bought most of Sykes remaining properties including the railroad. However, a serious fire in November 1957 was the death blow to the industry and the little railroad.

Throughout the years of its operation this railroad had fed many cars of lumber to the Mohawk and Malone and in turn generated considerable incoming shipments by rail. Its demise was only one more of the serious losses of traffic for the Adirondack Division.

William Gove has written a very interesting and detailed history of the Grasse River Railroad and the Emporium Lumber Company. This is part of RAILS IN THE NORTH WOODS published by North Country Books and it is recommended for those seeking more information on the Sykes' enterprise.

PAUL SMITH'S ELECTRIC LIGHT AND POWER AND RAILROAD COMPANY

Apollos Smith was born in Milton, Vermont in 1825. In early life he shortened his name to Paul by which name he was thenceforth known. He first settled near Loon Lake in Franklin County and quickly established a reputation as a hunter and a popular guide. In 1852 he opened a hunter's home to accommodate visitors from New York City who came to the North Woods to hunt. His early business endeavor proving successful, he built a seventeen room hotel on Lower St. Regis Lake about 1859.

The nearest railroad was thirty-seven miles away at "Point of Rocks," the southern terminus of the Plattsburgh Railroad near Au Sable Forks. This left a forty-two mile journey over rough mountain roads and it took all day. In spite of the remote location and the very poor means of transportation, Paul Smith's as it was known now, continued to thrive and expand. By 1875 the establishment had grown to a three story structure with a hundred guest capacity. There was a separate house for the guides who at that time numbered nearly sixty. In the 1870's Paul Smith bought 13,000 acres of St. Regis land. Eventually his holdings grew to as much as 40,000 acres. He sold many campsites to his wealthy clientele. He became the prime supplier for all food, fuel, lumber, building supplies and sporting equipment and this buiness grew to a considerable extent.

The transportation problem began to improve when the narrow gauge Chateaugay Ore and Iron Company railroad reached Loon Lake in 1886 and was extended the next year to Saranac Lake. The station at Bloomingdale became known as Paul Smith's Station and was approximately seven miles from the Lower St. Regis Lake hotel. This was a great improvement as it took about one and one half hours to travel the distance by tally-ho.

John Hurd was busy extending his Northern Adirondack railroad towards Tupper Lake and when it reached Brandon in 1886 it provided another station near Paul Smith's and naturally Brandon was listed as Paul Smith's Station on the Northern Adirondack Railway. This railroad being a standard guage road provided a means of routing sleeping and drawing room cars from New York City to close proximity to Paul Smith's hotel. The Northern Adirondack Railway stressed this in their time tables using the slogan "Direct Route to Paul Smith's Station."

When the Adirondack and St. Lawrence Railway was opened in 1892, Paul Smith's Station was established at approximately milepost 137. This station in later years was known as Gabriels. This, of course, was the nearest of all to Lower St. Regis Lake and naturally became the favorite station. Nevertheless Paul Smith was faced with making connections with three railroads with as many as fourteen trains daily.

Paul Smith had become interested in electric power as far back as 1890 when he generated electricity for his hotel at his Keese Mills plant. After the turn of the century he developed hydro-electric plants at Union Falls and Franklin Falls and he purchased the Saranac Lake Electric Company. These interests were incorporated on July 10, 1905 as the Paul Smith's Electric Light and Power Company.

After a dozen years elapsed, with his stages and tally-ho making connections with the various railroads, Paul Smith conceived the idea of building a railroad from his hostelry direct to the Mohawk and Malone Railway. It was quickly evident that electricity was the most feasible power for it was readily available. The distance was the shortest to the station presently being used on the M. & M. but the contours of the land prohibited the construction of a right-of-way to this point. In 1904 Smith had M. J. Corbett make a survey and a line was located through to Lake Clear Junction, seven miles to the south. The highest point on the line was approximately 70 feet higher than the junction and the hotel.

In his monograph PAUL SMITH'S ELECTRIC RAILWAY, Michael Kudish writes:

> It was relatively easy to electrify the railroad so Paul Smith ordered an electric interurban combine car. J. C. Brill of Philadelphia built the body while General Electric of Schenectady provided the motors and electrical equipment; according to Mr. James Brown of Bloomingdale, the car cost $25,000 and supposedly the whole railroad cost $75,000.

Construction of the line took place during 1905 and 1906. The Public Service Commission reports indicate that the Paul Smith's Electric Light and Power Company incorporated in 1905, and was permitted to amend its certificate under Section 21 of the Railroad Law on May 2, 1906. The new title was the Paul Smith's Electric Light and Power and Railroad Company. On August 1, 1906 the Railroad Commissioners of the State of New York agreed that public convenience and necessity required the construction of the railroad.

At least one 4-4-0 locomotive was purchased from the New York Central and possibly another one was used during the construction period with the steam engine being used up to the time that the electric car was received. Undoubtedly steam was called upon during some periods but there does not seem to be much information on this subject nor is there any mention made about fighting snow.

The electric operation of the railroad was virtually unique. It was the only road in New York State to use a trolley line at the side of the right-of-way. Alternating current of 5,200 volts was carried in the trolley wire and was converted to 600 volt direct current in the car.

This was first done with a rectifier but later a motor generator set was used. The 600 volt direct current was used in motors mounted on the trucks adjacent to the axles.

The earliest time table is one of August 20, 1906 and this is generally accepted as the date on which the railroad was placed in service.

All trains on the New York Central were met at Lake Clear Junction and this resulted in five trains each day, except Sunday, with 30 minutes allowed for the seven mile distance. At the time that the new rail service became available, the station on the Adirondack Division known as Paul Smith's was renamed Gabriels and the stage service was discontinued. Likewise the stage service to Bloomingdale on the Delaware and Hudson and to Brandon on the New York and Ottawa, being no longer needed, were discontinued.

There was no turntable or wye to use to reverse the direction of the electric car after it was received in the fall of 1906 so it was always headed the same way, the mail baggage end towards Lake Clear Junction. Freight and passenger cars were pushed to the hotel terminal and were pulled to the Lake Clear Junction terminal. Pullman sleeping cars and private cars were switched by New York Central locomotives onto the electrified Paul Smith's track at Lake Clear Junction and then they were pushed to the hotel.

Once again we turn to the annual report of the Public Service Commission for a description of the locomotives and passenger car equipment and repair facilities of the Paul Smith's Elctric Light and Power and Railroad Company. A report made in 1909 makes interesting reading:

> The locomotive equipment consists of one American type locomotive, No. 1, in good general condition; locomotive was purchased second-hand from the N. Y. C. & H. R. R. R. Co.; built in 1888 at West Albany; boiler steam pressure 145 lbs.; size of cylinder 18-in. diameter by 24-in. stroke; weight on drivers 65,500 lbs.; total weight of locomotive 98,500 lbs.; total weight of locomotive and tender 169,200 lbs.; railroad is electrically operated and steam locomotive is used only when electric locomotive is out of service.

> The steam railroad passenger car equipment consists of one passenger car, No. 1636, in good condition; car is heated with steam and equipped with Pintsch gas, oil lamps, low back plush covered reversible seats, and parcel racks; seating capacity 62 passengers; car is not equipped with lavatory or drinking water, and none are required on a railroad 7 miles in length; emergency tools are in good condition and properly located; car is equipped with Westinghouse air brake and signal apparatus, cast iron truck wheels, metal brake beams, and automatic couplers.

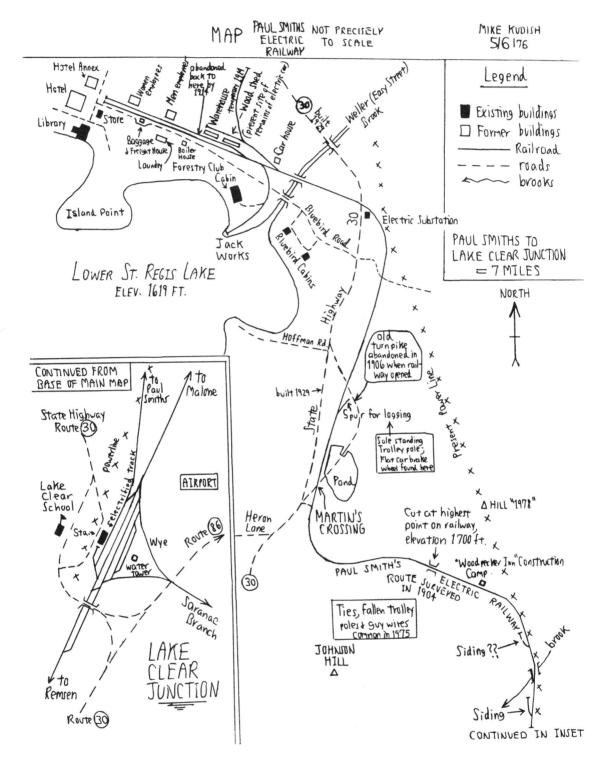

MAP PAUL SMITHS NOT PRECISELY ELECTRIC TO SCALE RAILWAY

MIKE KUDISH
5/6/76

Legend

- ■ Existing buildings
- □ Former buildings
- —— Railroad
- – – – roads
- ↜ brooks

PAUL SMITHS TO
LAKE CLEAR JUNCTION
= 7 MILES

NORTH

Hotel Annex

Hotel

Library

Store

Women Employees

Men employees

abandoned back to here by 1914

Warehouse

trolleyman 1941

Wood shed (present site of remains of electric car)

Car house

built 1918

Weller (Easy Street) Brook

Baggage & Freight House

Boiler House

Laundry

Forestry Club Cabin

Island Point

Jack Works

Bluebird Cabins

Bluebird Road

30

Electric Substation

LOWER ST. REGIS LAKE
ELEV. 1619 FT.

Highway

Hoffman Rd.

Old turnpike abandoned in 1906 when railway opened

built 1929 →

Spur for logging

Sole standing Trolley pole; Flat car brake wheel found here

Present Power Line

CONTINUED FROM BASE OF MAIN MAP

to Paul Smiths

to Malone

State Highway Route 30

Powerline

Electrified track

Lake Clear School

Store

Water Tower

Wye

Route 86

Heron Lane

30

Pond

MARTIN'S CROSSING

△ HILL "1978"

Cut at highest point on railway, elevation 1700 ft.

"Woodpecker Inn" Construction Camp

AIRPORT

Saranac Branch

LAKE CLEAR JUNCTION

PAUL SMITH'S ELECTRIC RAILWAY ROUTE SURVEYED IN 1904

Ties, fallen trolley poles & guy wires common in 1975

JOHNSON HILL △

Siding ??

brook

to Remsen

Route 30

Siding →

CONTINUED IN INSET

(Michael Kudish and Franklin County Historical and Museum Society)

Paul Smith with guests. Car 99 was an official business car or private car of the New York Central and Hudson River Railroad and apparently when the photo was taken some official of the railroad company was a guest of Paul Smith. Note the steam engine on the far end of this train. Circa 1906 to 1912. (Cubley Library, Paul Smith's College)

Stage coach used between Paul Smith's Hotel and the railroad stations, prior to the opening of Paul Smith's electric railroad. (Cubley Library, Paul Smith's College)

The electric motor car equipment consists of one combination electric motor, baggage, and passenger compartment car named *ST. REGIS CHAIN OF LAKES,* which is in good general condition; car is heated with electric heaters and lighted with electric lights; car is equipped with high back, leather covered reversible seats, and parcel racks; seating capacity 24 passengers; car is not equipped with lavatory or drinking water, and none are required on a railroad 7 miles in length; car is equipped with Westinghouse air brake and signal apparatus, metal truck frames, steel-tired wheels, metal brake beams, and automatic couplers.

This company, on account of its varied manufacturing interests, has a machine, blacksmith, and wood-working shop which is well equipped, and is in position to promptly make all necessary repairs.

Referring to reports to the Public Service Commission, we find that in 1908 the gross operating revenue was $12,279 with an operating expense of $5,600 leaving a net operating revenue of $6,679. In 1920 the gross revenues were $7,286 but the gross expenses were calculated at $13,394 with a resulting loss of $6,108. The railroad operating deficit was apparently covered by the profit made on the electric power sold but it is evident that the need for the railroad was dropping steadily.

Michael Kudish says that he found that the date of the closing of the Paul Smith's Railway was rather indefinite. A small gasoline powered jitney was in use the last three or four years of operation and it is generally accepted that it was closed down in 1932 but the rails remained for the next six or eight years.

The railroad being operated as it was for the benefit of the Paul Smith's organization and not running between communities, it is more than likely that it was run as a matter of convenience in its last years and no protests were made when it was finally discontinued.

The electric car, *ST. REGIS CHAIN OF LAKES,* was stripped of all electrical units and trucks and was well cleaned out inside but the shell continues to stand out in the open on the Paul Smith's College campus. Dr. Kudish has been trying for a number of years to find a place where this interesting relic might be placed under cover and perhaps restored somewhat, but so far he has been entirely unsuccessful in his efforts. The steam locomotive and other rolling stock seems to have disappeared, possibly scrapped at the time that the rails were taken up.

Probably the most complete history of the Paul Smith's Electric Railway was published as Volume 13 of the Franklin County Historical Reviews in 1976. Authored by Dr. Michael Kudish, Ph.D., of the Paul Smith's College of Arts and Sciences Faculty, it was published by the Franklin County Historical and Museum Society at Malone, N. Y.

Photo taken about 1928 shortly before the electric railroad as discontinued. The main hotel building in background burned in 1930. (Cubley Library, Paul Smith's College)

Picture taken on a rainy, overcast day, November 21, 1975. The electric car of Paul Smith's railroad has continued to deteriorate on this location. It must be moved in the coming spring and unless someone takes on the task of preserving the car it will probably be destroyed at that time. (Harter collection)

THE PARTLOW LAKE RAILWAY

One other short railroad, the Partlow Lake Railway was organized and a time table was published in the July 1905 OFFICIAL GUIDE. W. Seward Webb was the president and C. H. Burnett was the superintendent. This was listed as running from the Partlow station, just north of milepost 84 on the Adirondack and St. Lawrence to Sylvan Lake, a distance of five miles. It has been reported that the road operated with locomotives rented from the New York Central but little seems to be known about the operation of this railway. It probably was used for logging purposes on the Webb estate.

In 1905 New York Central Mohawk Division Employee's time table shows two passenger and two regular freight trains each way, made stops at Partlow. Shortly thereafter the station stop was removed from the time tables and nothing further seems to have been heard of the Partlow Lake Railway.

OTHER CONNECTING RAILROADS

It is not within the scope of this book to cover the larger railroads connecting with the Adirondack Division of the New York Central. These railroads would include: The Rutland Railroad at Malone; The Northern Adirondack, later the New York and Ottawa at Tupper Lake; The Utica and Black River, part of the Rome Watertown and Ogdensburg at Remsen; The Chateaugay branch of the Delaware and Hudson at Saranac Lake; and the Canadian railway connections north of the border.

Logging railroads along the Mohawk and Malone Railway provide a subject large enough to justify separate treatment. There were several of these logging roads feeding the Adirondack Division at one time or another and at one place or another. Some of them handled logs only, and others lumber, and some contributed the raw materials to factories existing near the railroad. However, none of these were common carriers like the Grasse River Railroad.

CHAPTER XIV
Forest Fires

The threat of forest fires was projected into the controversy of Dr. Webb's proposed railroad through the Adirondacks from the very first. It was a problem that stayed with the Mohawk and Malone all of the time that it operated but in a much lesser degree after its second decade. Much of the earlier fear of the danger of fire was derived from the destruction that occurred along the Northern Adirondack and the Chateaugay road. On August 31, 1890 the Chateaugay road had come under criticism in the NEW YORK TIMES:

> The havoc wrought by the railroads is apparent to visitors because nearly every one of them comes by rail. The first impressions of the Adirondacks are inevitably disappointing for every one expects to pass through forests. Yet in the seventy miles from Plattsburgh to Saranac Lake which one passes over on the Chateaugay Road, he does not go through forest at all. It is a rough, mountainous, rocky and sterile country with few live trees in sight. Much of the land is still blackened from the fires that have passed over it.

John Hurd's Northern Adirondack Railroad received the attention of the NEW YORK TIMES on May 15, 1891:

> The success of the scheme to pierce the heart of the Adirondacks with a railroad will mean the building of a road by the Delaware and Hudson (from North Creek) and the extension of the Chateaugay Road from Saranac Lake south. The woods would be gridironed. The finest forest preserve in the world would be ruined. Along Hurd's Railroad in the Adirondacks today there are burned spaces miles wide on each side of the tracks. Picture the situation with the New York Central running fast trains daily through the forests.

On May 21, 1891 the TIMES quoted Dr. Webb as saying that he was a large property holder and had no intentions of seeing the area devastated. Dr. Webb also said at that time that his railroad would not carry any timber that had been cut from logs less than twelve inches in diameter and furthermore it would not carry lumber or charcoal made from green timber.

A great deal of the foregoing was engendered by the opposition to Dr. W. Seward Webb's construction of the railroad from Herkimer to Malone. Many other articles appeared in newspapers protesting the building of the railroad and the forest fire danger was only one of the reasons advanced for the argument that the railroad should not be built.

Despite all good intentions, forest fires did occur on the Adirondack and St. Lawrence and were in many cases justifiably blamed on the railroad. It was, apparently, the rule that New York Central Form 1434, Report of Damages, was to be completed and sent to the Division Superintendent when damages of any type occurred and this was used to report on forest fires that section gangs discovered and/or extinguished. One such fire happened on May 17, 1894. The report read in part:

> Mr. W. S. Webb, Town of Wilmurt, County of Herkimer sustained damages by the burning of 3 or 4 acres of timberland set on fire by engine 730 attached to Train No. 50 going south. The fire was one half mile from Beaver River Station. This fire started from sparks thrown by Engine 730. The forest being very dry and a stiff breeze blowing, section men were unable to check the fire until it had burned over 3 or 4 acres of timber.

This was not an isolated incident. The author read a few such reports that have been preserved and in one case on May 12, 1894 a fire started by the same engine 730 was set down as the cause of a fire that burned about 125 acres of land near Forestport.

It might be noted that 1894 was a particularly dry year and the great fire at Hinckley, Minnesota in September of that year killed over 400 people and caused wide devastation.

Less than five years later the Village of Tupper Lake was almost totally destroyed on July 29 and 30, 1899. The summer of 1899 was marked as another very bad year. William F. Fox, Superintendent of Forests, State of New York said in his annual report that the season of 1899 was marked by the largest number of fires that had occurred at any one time during a long term of years. The summer was a season of unprecedented drought. He stated that of the 322 fires reported 24 were known to have been caused by locomotives. Of course, not all of these fires were caused by the Adirondack Division engines but the indication is given of the great danger that the railroad posed.

One of the interesting parts of Mr. Fox's report is the way he relied on the railroad for transportation. Starting on August 7th when the first fires broke out near Indian Lake, Mr. Fox was constantly on the move throughout the Adirondack area. He speaks of going from Loon Lake to Old Forge, and back and forth, and at one time he took the train south and then through Albany and north by the Adirondack Railroad of the Delaware and Hudson to North Creek, thence by horse to the Indian Lake area. On August 21st a rain rendered everything comparatively safe.

In an accompanying financial report Dr. Fox showed that the sum of $12,841.97 was expended in paying men to fight this series of fires. An explanatory note is attached which said that $146.46 was paid to the N. Y. C. & H. R. R. R. for a locomotive and special train which was used in moving parties of men to fires at distant points where there was no resident population, and where men could not otherwise be obtained. This train was in use for four days, part of the time both night and day. Many of the men were hired at Saranac Lake and the train operated between there and Loon Lake and Tupper Lake.

The year of 1903 was the next bad year. Between April 20 and June 8 of that year over 600,000 acres of timberland in northern New York were burned over. Gifford Pinchot, Forester, submitted a very detailed report of the FOREST FIRES IN THE ADIRONDACKS IN 1903 to James Wilson, Secretary of the United States Department of Agriculture. The report was prepared by H. M. Suter, Agent in the Bureau of Forestry. The report stated the cause of the fires was due to a protracted drought. In reviewing some of the worst fires Agent Suter said:

> Twelve thousand acres of the Nehasane Preserve were burned, with much damage to the beauty of the preserve and interference with the results of a working plan of the Bureau of Forestry under which lumbering was being done. The handsome and expensive camp buildings were saved by city fire engines hurried in on the railroad from Herkimer and Ilion. Powerful steam pumps mounted in a freight car protected a narrow belt of trees along the track.

Agent Suter discussed the organization and methods used in fighting these fires and then discussed the causes of them. He was very forthright as to what he believed were the greatest causes and these included besides the railroads, unauthorized burning of lumbering debris, carelessness of campers and the deliberate incendiarism for private gain or revenge. As for the railroad, Agent Suter stated:

> Inexcusable negligence and disregard of legal requirements and the rights of adjoining property has been charged against the railroads. Fully one-half of the fires due to carelessness caught from locomotives of the New York Central and the New York and Ottawa, and the

NYC & HR No. 1099 at Fulton Chain early 1900's. Note auxiliary engine back of smokestack driving a pump which was used for fire-fighting purposes. (H. K. Vollrath collection)

Fire train circa 1908. Water was carried on tank on flat car. (Harter collection)

Fire train stationed at NE-HA-SA-NE PARK Circa 1908. The fire pump was driven by the boiler in the ex-box car, and was supplied by the 6187 gallon tank on the flat car. (Photograph courtesy of The Adirondack Museum, Blue Mountain Lake, N.Y.)

NYC 2243 with a fire train. Pump is mounted on top of boiler. Circa 1910. (Photograph courtesy of The Adirondack Museum, Blue Mountain Lake, N.Y.)

Chateaugay, which upon June 1 became a part of the Delaware and Hudson system. A good many fires were also set by logging railroads. A map has been prepared that shows how the burned areas follow the path of certain railroads. The laws of the State require the equipment of locomotives with spark arresters and the observance of other precautions against fire. Had the railroad been compelled to adopt these safeguards at the beginning of the dangerous season, much loss would have been averted. The railroads themselves will be heavy sufferers in the long run from the devastation for which they are so largely responsible. There was a lack of proper patrol of tracks and indifference on the part of section men. Locomotives were not infrequently sent over the road hauling freight trains which taxed their capacity to the utmost. As a result sparks from the heavy exhaust were a constant cause of fire. For example, on May 5 a heavy excursion train, hauled by two locomotives, set almost continous fires for ten miles in the town of Fine.

Later in the season, and after the harm was done, locomotives were equipped with spark arresters. Ash pans and dampers were inspected thoroughly, freight trains were reduced to one-half their former tonnage, the apathy of the section men disappeared, and a track patrol was established.

The report concluded with the observation that should another long drought occur the State would be powerless under the system by which they then operated to prevent another dire calamity from forest fires. The prophecy was carried out in 1908. The UTICA SATURDAY GLOBE on October 3, 1908 carried a report "The Forest Fires In The Adirondacks." Excerpts from this article follow:

Never was rain more gratefully received than that of Monday, September 28, 1908, which temporarily at least, put an end to the destructive fires which were devastating a large section of the Adirondacks. Many black scars were left in the forest, which many years will be required to remove, and, at least one prosperous village — that of Long Lake West — was wiped out. Over 44,000 acres of forest land were burned over and 94 buildings in all were destroyed.

The fires in the Adirondacks were spread over a wide area and perhaps were at their worst in the vicinity of Nehasane Park, Bear Pond, Cranberry Lake, Long Lake West, Tupper Lake, Lake Clear Junction and in the district between Lake Placid and Saranac Lake. In the Saranac Lake region Col. William F. Fox, State Superintendent of Forests, had charge of the men fighting the fires.

Until Saturday evening it was believed that the fires had been brought under control, but with the rising of a stiff south wind the situation materially changed. One of the places immediately threatened was the valuable preserve of Dr. W. Seward Webb at Nehasane and in response to an urgent appeal for aid a squad of Utica firemen, with an engine and other apparatus, left for Nehasane, which is on the line of the M. & M. Railroad, Saturday night. Chief Sullivan, Commissioner Church and President of the Common Council Baker accompanied the firemen, who returned home Tuesday after the rains. The Uticans were not required to face the actual fires in the forest, but they performed valuable services on the preserve, drenching the buildings and immediate surroundings, thereby minimizing the danger of fire from stray sparks. The heat was oppressive and the smoke which rolled through the woods was very trying on the eyes and lungs.

The most spectacular features of the forest fires were the destruction of the little village of Long Lake West and the explosion there of 1,500 pounds of dynamite. The village contained a dozen dwellings, railroad station, a large hotel, a store and storehouse belonging to lumber dealers, a new electric light plant, a livery with accommodations for 200 horses, a schoolhouse and a large lumber yard. Every structure was consumed. The horses in the livery had been turned loose before the flames reached the village and found safety in flight and the residents fled by train to Tupper Lake. Soon after the flight of the villagers the 1,500 pounds of dynamite used in blasting out tree stumps exploded with a deafening roar which was distinctly heard at Nehasane, eight miles to the south.

Sunday afternoon the fires along the Mohawk & Malone Railroad seemed to reach the height of their intensity. Sweeping across the railroad they destroyed telegraph wires, interrupting communications between this city and Nehasane. Between Nehasane and Horseshoe, 12 miles to the north, the heat twisted the rails of the M.&M. road out of shape so that trains could not be sent over that section. The firefighters employed by the State and the various towns worked a total of over 16,000 days, and in addition the railroads furnished hundreds of men and large quantities of supplies.

One fortunate thing about the fire was that no human lives were lost, so far as is known. This providential outcome came very near being negated. One authority wrote that the population of Long Lake West was saved from death by the arrival of a New York Central Railroad train, just before the flames swept over the hamlet leaving nothing except bare rocks, the parched bones of the soil.

Immediately after the fire catastrophe of 1908 it was apparent to everyone, lumbermen, camp owners, private clubs and the general public that better protective measures must be placed in effect.

By October 12, 1908 the Public Service Commission was holding a hearing on the setting of fires by sparks from "locomotive engines." This hearing was held following the request of the State Forest, Fish and Game Commission. The Commission stated that in the forty days previous to September 29th that a survey showed that, on all railroads running through the Forest Preserve, over four hundred fires had been started on or adjacent to the right-of-way of these railroads. The Commission outlined the efforts made to control fires along the railroad but these were not enough and it was felt that using coal for fuel must be eliminated during the seasons of the year when there was danger of fire.

In FIFTY YEARS OF CONSERVATION IN NEW YORK STATE, Gurth Whipple wrote:

> On December 29, 1908 the Forest Commission called a meeting to determine what must be done to save the Forest Preserve. The problem was thoroughly discussed and after summing up the situation, the Commissioner appointed a committee which later submitted a report containing the best of the recommendations advanced at the meeting. Part of the plan including the burning of oil for fuel in railroad locomotives and a paid patrol of railroad properties under State supervision. The Forest, Fish and Game Commission petitioned the Public Service Commission to compel the railroads in the Forest Preserve to burn oil as fuel. The petition was bitterly fought by the railroads but the petition was granted and the railroads operating in the Forest Preserve were ordered to burn oil from 8 A. M. to 8 P. M. from April 15 to October 31 inclusive. The regulation had a tremendously beneficial effect in reducing the number of fires in the Adirondacks.
>
> It was noted that the oil burning question had arisen before and one railroad company, the Raquette Lake Railway, an oil-burning road, running from Clearwater to Durante (sic), nineteen miles, had no fires along its right-of-way. Timorously commenting on this fact the Commission report of 1902 said "but petroleum is much more expensive than coal" and the subject was dropped.

The Public Service Commission said in the report for 1909 that the railroad companies failed to prove to the saisfaction of the Commission that their locomotives, as they proposed to equip and maintain them, would be sufficiently free from the danger of throwing sparks and dropping fires from ash-pans to warrant the continuance of coal burning during the dry months. The evidence did show that coal burning locomotives, properly equipped, could be safely used at night, and the order provided accordingly.

The complete installation of oil burning equipment was to be effected by April 15, 1910 but at least two locomotives of the Mohawk and Malone were to be fitted with oil burning apparatus and placed in service by July 15, 1909. The Utica SATURDAY GLOBE reported that the oil-burners were used for the first time on Wednesday, July 14, 1909 and that they worked very satisfactorily. There were two engines converted to burn oil and number 2125 was the first to be placed in service. It was a ten-wheeler and had been rebuilt at the West Albany shops. Each engine has a storage capacity of 3,200 gallons of fuel oil, the tanks being placed in the space used on ordinary engines for coal. It was expected that storage tanks would be built in various locations along the railroad so that the fuel could be replenished as necessary but it was expected that the engine tank would contain more than enough fuel for the trip from Utica to Malone.

For the last year of fire season operation of the coal burners, careful inspection of the spark arresters and ash-pans were made by the Public Service Commission expert. At the first inspection, 26 of the 56 Adirondack Division engines were found to be defective and had to be immediately corrected. Even at that, the 54% passing mark achieved by the Division far exceeded the 22% mark received by all of the other railroads operating in the Forest Preserve.

The Public Service Commission Supervisor of Equipment in his 1909 report said that the two engines that the New York Central converted to oil burners were 2115 and 2131 which he later corrected to numbers 2125 and 2131, both of the ten-wheel type. Oil storage tanks were installed at Utica, Tupper Lake Junction and Malone Junction. The inspector made a trip in the cab on one of the first runs. He found fault in the way that the engine was "fired" and expected that considerable improvement would be made. He remarked that the engine was noiseless, as far as the oil burning was concerned. This last observation is quite at odds with the report given in the Herkimer newspaper of March 18, 1910 when it said:

> "The oil burning engines," said one familiar with them to a TELEGRAM reporter, makes a noise sufficient to almost awaken a whole town, this is the manner in which the oil is burned it causing a continuous series of explosions which would place a gasoline driven engine way in the shade. The report that oil burners will run through Herkimer instead of only to Forestport as heretofore, comes through unofficial railroad channels. If this is so the question is raised whether the trains at night time cannot be dispatched from the M. & M. yards instead of from the Central station in the central portion of the village or a shifting engine take the trains in and out of the village.

We are sure that everyone was pleased to learn that the amount of noise generated by an oil burner was nothing like it was described. It might noted though, that at that time there were two northbound trains, No. 15 and No. 19 and two southbound trains No. 16 and No. 18 that ran between Herkimer and Fulton Chain Station. This accounts for the reference to the possibility of changing engines at Forestport.

The New York Central maintained fire trains at strategic points in the early 1900's. There was one train made up of a tank mounted on a flat car and what appeared to be a former locomotive boiler was mounted in a freight car, with steam pumps probably mounted inside. This two unit train was drawn by whatever locomotive was available and was lettered "NE-HA-SA-NE PARK FIRE SERVICE." Work train locomotives were equipped with a steam fire pump mounted on top of the boiler in front of or in back of the steam dome as space permitted. The fire hoses were attached directly to the pumps on these engines and hose lines ran down the side of the engine. A tank car coupled behind the tender provided the water for fire fighting. Tank cars were stationed at Remsen, Thendara, Tupper Lake and Malone.

Later on modifications were made in the restrictions against the operation of coal burning locomotives. These had to do with the time of day when regularly scheduled trains were running late and with the operation of special inspection engines. Other modifications were made in the years to come as the weather conditions varied and permitted safe operation of coal burning locomotives within the period prescribed by the original Public Service Commission order.

In the 1915 annual report the Public Service Commission stated that no fires of any consequence had resulted in the Adirondack Preserve which were caused by a locomotive since the entering of its order in 1909. In 1915 also the commission reported that 97% of the New York Central engines were passing inspection on ash-pans and spark arresters.

The Central continued to request that the restriction order on coal burners be removed. It applied in 1919 and in 1921 but never succeeded in having the restrictions removed.

The New York State Conservation Department continued to improve the methods of fighting forest fires and adopted new devices such as portable pumps. The years of 1921, 1930 and 1934 were unusually dangerous years during the fire season but the fire loss was kept at an acceptably low figure. The railroads were contributing less and less to the forest fire statistics.

Throughout the years Employee's Time Tables carried special instructions on the Operation of Coal Burning Locomotives in the Forest Preserve. These instructions referred in part to ash pan slides and the dumping of ashes as well as watching for defects which might develop enroute. There were several other rules such as reporting of fires, available men to assist in extinguishing any fires, etc. When the steam locomotives were eventually replaced by diesel engines, the instructions were modified to eliminate the direct references to coal burning locomotive operation and the title was changed to Forest Preserve Territory Instructions but never-the-less the special instructions remained as an important part of the New York Central's operation in the Adirondack area.

CHAPTER XV
Memorabilia of a Railroad

By choice the author would have liked to title this the MEMOIRS OF A RAILROAD. A purist would say that memoirs are the memorial of an individual, or a history or narrative composed from personal experience, especially written by oneself. It is admitted that a railroad cannot write but what could be more personal than the multitude of happenings, recalled from numberless sources, but never-the-less a biography of an enormous, vibrant creation of man endowed with the breath and fire of a living creature? So we will settle for the more prosaic MEMORABILIA. However, we can remember that what follows in most cases, was born from the "Fairy Tale Railroad" that went from the Mohawk to the St. Lawrence through the Great Woods of the Adirondacks.

As we start out, what better way can we realize what the Adirondacks meant than by reading what Ernest W. Blue wrote following a lifetime career of close association with the North Woods as a District Forest Ranger:

> When I went to work for the State of New York in 1912 we were just beginning to erect fire observation towers on some of the higher mountains. There were no maps in those days to show the elevations so we just had to climb some peaks to see if they were suitable. Thus it was that I climbed a lot of mountains and now, as I look back over my life, I like to compare it with the ascent of a high mountain. You start out early in the morning; the air is fresh and cool and you make good progress. Then the trail gets rougher and steeper; the sun beats down and the flies torture you but you stumble on until you break through the last scrubby Balsams at timberline and fall exhausted at the summit. But you do not lie here for long. You are soon revived by the cool bracing air; you regain your feet and look back over the way you have come. You do not see the rough trails; you forget the struggle and the heat and the flies for you see only purple mountains, blue lakes and green timber and deep down in your heart you thank your God for the privilege of being an American and to have even a tiny part in the development of our land.

So we can say for the Mohawk and Malone Railway and the St. Lawrence and Adirondack Railway, together the Adirondack Division of the New York Central, they came, they struggled and they stayed to help develop, for all people, the use of the great Forest Preserve. When the time came, they receded into the wilderness to be born again if and when needed.

HERKIMER AS A TERMINAL

The principal office of the Herkimer, Newport and Poland Narrow Gauge Railway Company was always listed as being at Newport, N. Y. There is considerable doubt if any office building existed outside of perhaps the railroad station. Mr. George H. Thomas was the first secretary and treasurer and was at that time the president of the National Bank at Newport so undoubtedly that was where the railroad business was transacted. However, the railroad did use the facilities of the New York Central and Hudson River Railroad at Herkimer. The narrow gauge joined the Central right-of-way on Albany Street near King Street and became the fifth track along side of the main line. Passenger trains proceeded westerly until they stopped between Washington and Main Streets where passenger, baggage and express was unloaded. This brought the train directly opposite the Herkimer depot of the NYC&HRRR. At some time later an iron fence was erected between the main line and the fifth track but just when this fence was erected is very uncertain. Its purpose was to prevent the passengers from crossing the tracks except at the Main Street crossing.

The narrow gauge track continued westerly to a point west of Prospect Street where the freight facilities of the NYC&HRRR could be used.

In 1882 the HN&PNG was authorized to lay a third rail along Albany Street so that standard gauge cars could be shifted directly into the narrow gauge yards which were north of Albany Street, just east of King Street. In 1888 a Ramsey Hoist, for transferring trucks under freight cars was located at Herkimer and standard gauge cars of large capacity were then transported over the narrow gauge road. On February 14, 1888 the changing of car trucks led to a serious accident. David Snyder, foreman of the transfer works, was killed. Trucks were being changed underneath a car when the jack with which the car was being raised, slipped and let the car down. Mr. Snyder was caught and he was fatally injured.

Available records do not indicate whether this accident occurred before or after the Ramsey Hoist was installed. It is possible that a

NEW YORK CENTRAL LINES

UTICA TO MALONE
ADIRONDACK DIVISION

North-Bound In Effect June 25, 1916

STATIONS	5 Daily	7 Daily	9 Daily	71 Ex. Sun.	73 Sun. Only	11 Daily	1 Ex. Sun.	3 Ex. Sun.	15 Friday Only	79 Ex. Sun.
	PM	PM	PM	PM	PM	AM	AM	AM	PM	AM
Lv New York	7 10	7 10	7 10	11 30	11 30	2 49		7 45	12 30	10 30
" Albany	11 00	11 00	11 00	2 56	2 56	6 25	9 15	11 10	3 45	1 48
Lv Buffalo	8 00	9 00		1 15	1 15	4 10	7 30	7 40	1 00	1 00
Lv Utica	1 20	2 15	3 00	6 25	7 50	9 30	12 45	1 40	5 45	5 10
" Remsen	2 20	3 15	4 00	8 30	9 08	10 30	1 40	2 40	6 30	7 05
Ar Forestport	a	3f30	4f15	8 45	9 25	10 46	1 56	d	6i44	7 20
" White Lake	a	3f45	4f30	9 00	9 40	11 04	2 10	d		7 34
" Otter	a	3f56	4f42	9 10	9 52	11 16	2 22	d		7 44
" McKeever	a	4f01	4f46	9 13	9 57	11 22	2 27	d	7i05	7 48
" Fulton Chain	3 28	4 18	5 08	9 35	10 20	11 39	2 46	d	7 25	8 05
" Carter	a	4 40	5 33		LAST TRIP SEPT. 10	11 57	3 08	4 10	7i40	
" Big Moose	a	4 55	5 47			12 11	3 23	d	7i49	
" Beaver River	a	5 11	6 04			12 25	3 39	d	8i05	
" Brandreth	a	c	6f11			12 31	3 46	d		
" Nehasane	a	c	6f23			12f44	3f58	d		
" Long Lake West	a	5 45	6 33			12 57	4 11	d	8i34	
" Horse Shoe	a	5f54	6 48			1 07	4f21	d		
" Pleasant Lake	a	c	6f56			1f14	4f29	d		
" Childwold	a	6f08	7f02			1 20	4 35	d	8i55	
" Piercefield	a	6f13	7f08			1 29	4 42	d		
" Tupper Lake Jct.	5 28	6 22	7 20			1 40	4 52	5 33	9 10	
" Saranac Inn	a	6 56				2 15	5 25	6 10	9i44	
" Lake Clear Jct.	6 08	7 03	FIRST TRIP JULY 29 LAST TRIP SEPT. 9			2 23	5 30	6 16	9 50	
Ar Saranac Lake	6 40	7 35				2 55	5 58	6 50	10 18	
Ar Lake Placid	7 05	8 00				3 30		7 20	10 35	
Lv Lake Placid		6 20				1 25		5 30	LAST TRIP SEPT. 1	
Lv Saranac Lake	5 45	6 40				2 00		5 58		
Ar Gabriels	a b	7 30				2 43		6 24		
" Rainbow	a b	7 35				2 48		6f40		
" Onchiota	a b	7f40				2f53		6f45		
" Lake Kushaqua	a b	7 44				2 58		6f48		
" Loon Lake	6 48	7 54				3 07		6 58		
" Mountain View	a b m	8 15				3 26		7 22		
" Owls Head	a b	8 20				3 35		7 27		
Ar Malone	7 37	8 40				3 55		7 52		
Ar Montreal	10 10					6 35		10 15		
	AM	AM	AM	AM	AM	PM	PM	PM	PM	PM

a Stops on signal to receive passengers for North of Malone.
b Stops only to discharge sleeping car passengers from West of Utica.
c Stops on signal to receive or discharge passengers to and including July 28, and after September 9.
d Stops on signal to discharge passengers from Schenectady and East, and Syracuse and West.
f Stops on signal to receive or discharge passengers.
i Stops only to discharge passengers.
m Stops Monday only.

Form 149 R. McN. & Co.—5M 7-1-1916

NEW YORK CENTRAL LINES

MALONE TO UTICA
ADIRONDACK DIVISION

South-Bound In Effect June 25, 1916

STATIONS	70 Ex. Sun.	6 Daily	8 Ex. Sun.	2 Ex. Sun.	76 Ex. Sun.	78 Sun. Only	12 Daily	10 Daily	4 Daily
	AM	AM	PM	AM	PM	PM	PM	PM	PM
Lv Montreal				8 00			3†30		7 05
Lv Malone		6 00		10 47			*6 15		9 25
" Owls Head		6 33		11 22			6 52		
" Mountain View		6 39		11 29			6 59		z
" Loon Lake		7 07		11 51			7 21		10 26
" Lake Kushaqua		7 16		12f01			7 30		
" Onchiota		7f19	FIRST TRIP JULY 29 LAST TRIP SEPT. 9	12f05			7f35		
" Rainbow		7 24		12f13			7f41		
" Gabriels		7 30		12 19			7 47		
Ar Saranac Lake		8 12		1 00		LAST TRIP SEPT. 10	8 55		11 18
Ar Lake Placid		9 55		1 25					
Lv Lake Placid		6 20		11 30				7 50	
Lv Saranac Lake		7 00		12 05			7 35	8 16	10 25
Lv Lake Clear Jct.		7 50		12 39			8 10	8 45	10 57
" Saranac Inn		7 57		12 46			8 17	8 52	
" Tupper Lake Jct.		8 28	12 15	1 17			8 50	9 28	11 33
" Piercefield		8 38	12 25	a			9f00	b	
" Childwold		8 44	12 32	1f35			9f06	9f45	
" Pleasant Lake		8f50	12f38	a			9f12	b	
" Horse Shoe		8 57	12 45	a			9f18	b	
" Long Lake West		9 07	12 57	1f56			9 29	b	
" Nehasane		9f20	1f10	a			9f41	b	
" Brandreth		9 33	1 24	a			9 53	b	
" Beaver River		9 42	1 34	a			10f01	b	
" Big Moose		10 03	1 54	2 46			10 25	b	
" Carter		10 13	2 06	3 03			10 35	b	
" Fulton Chain	6 55	10 30	2 46	3 20	5 30	6 10	11 00	11 19	1 12
" McKeever	7 14	10 49	3 05	a	5 48	6 27	11f17	b	
" Otter	7 18	10f54	3 17	a	5 52	6 32	11f21	b	
" White Lake	7 29	11 04	3 26	a	6 02	6 43	11f31	b	
" Forestport	7 42	11 20	3 38	4f07	6 15	6 55	11f43	s b	
Ar Remsen	8 00	11 38	3 52	4 25	6 30	7 10	11 58	12 19	2 03
" Utica	9 15	12 15	4 35	5 10	9 10	d8 50	12 40	12 58	2 50
Ar Buffalo	5 10	5†30	10 55	10 55			7 15	7 15	8 20
Ar Albany	11 45	2 30	7 25	7 25	12 10	12 10	3 00	3 00	5 15
Ar New York	3 45	6 15	10 50	10 50	5 05	5 05	7 03	7 03	9 00
	PM	PM	PM	PM	AM	AM	AM	AM	AM

* Daily † Daily except Sunday.
a Stops on signal to receive or discharge passengers until July 28 inclusive, and after September 10; July 29 to September 9 inclusive stops only to discharge passengers from North of Malone.
b Stops only to receive sleeping car passengers for B. & A. R.R. and West of Utica.
d Via Herkimer.
f Stops on signal to receive or discharge passengers.
s Stops Sunday only. z Stops Saturday only

Trains No. 71, 73 & 79 ran from Herkimer to Fulton Chain via Remsen. Trains No. 70, 76 & 78 ran from Fulton Chain to Herkimer via Remsen. (Leon Johnson collection)

makeshift method of changing car trucks had been used up to the time of the accident and this led to the purchase and installation of a piece of equipment designed for the work to be done.

David Snyder was the father of Charles E. Snyder, the attorney who did much of the legal work involved in securing the right-of-way for the Adirondack and St. Lawrence Railway. He also represented that railroad and the New York Central and Hudson River Railroad in many legal actions in the years to come.

After the Herkimer, Newport and Poland was sold and widened to standard gauge, Herkimer's dream of being the main terminal for the Adirondack and St. Lawrence did not last long. In less than a year Tupper Lake, Malone and Montreal passenger trains were being routed out of the Utica terminal over the former Utica and Black River section of the Rome, Watertown and Ogdensburg Railroad to Remsen. There they were switched to the Adirondack and St. Lawrence Line. It is safe to assume that freight operations were changed about the same time and trains were made up in the Utica yards and routed north the same way.

Local passenger service was maintained between Herkimer and Fulton Chain Station. A combination milk and passenger train also ran daily to Prospect Junction where it turned on the "Y" there and returned to Herkimer.

TRESTLE FAILURE

January 6, 1899 was the date that the trestle at Herkimer failed under NYC&HRRR Engine 472. It was situated on the north side of East Albany Street, south east of the M&M yards. It supported a track which formed part of a "Y" between the M&M yards and the tracks of the NYC&HRRR. The land in the vicinity was very low and was often flooded by the waters of the West Canada Creek which was situated east about 600 feet from the "Y" track. Near the trestle was an opening under the New York Central tracks which was for the purpose of allowing the water of floods to pass underneath the tracks to the flat lands on the opposite side of the tracks and from there to the Mohawk River.

Engine 473 was proceeding over the trestle at 6:30 A. M. when the stringers failed on each simultaneously and not very rapidly, so that the engine was deposited in ice and water in an upright position. Two of the men in the cab escaped but Andrew Moore was drowned.

The flooding of the area was eliminated in later years by the construction of the dike along the west side of the West Canada Creek following the great flood of 1910. In general the trestle was located

Main Street crossing, Herkimer. Engine is on Mohawk & Malone track on north side of main line of N.Y.C. & H.R.R.R. Circa 1895. Banner on Manion & Fick building advertises O.U.A.M. & Horrocks Desk Company employee's outing at Sacandaga Park. (Sumner Wickwire collection)

"Sunday's wreck at Herkimer." This collision was between standard and narrow gauge engines. Definite information was never located. (Harter collection)

A general view of the results of the explosion of the roundhouse at Herkimer, August 19, 1901. (Herkimer County Historical Society)

Awaiting northbound train to come up from yards. M. & M. track in foreground north of protecting fence. N.Y.C. mainline in background. Herkimer depot at left. Circa 1910. (Herkimer County Historical Society.)

near where the M&M track crossed East Albany Street in later years to connect with the New York Central lines which were moved to the southern edge of the Village of Herkimer.

THE ROUNDHOUSE EXPLOSION

For an account of the terrible catastrophe which occurred on August 20, 1901 the UTICA SATURDAY GLOBE and one of the other newspapers supplied the following information.

Six men were killed and a large number of others suffered more or less serious injuries as the result of a terrific explosion of dynamite and powder which shook the village and vicinity like an earthquake. Thousands of dollars worth of property was destroyed in a twinkling of an eye and at least six men were dead or dying.

> The terrible disaster occurred in the old Mohawk & Malone round-house located in the railroad yards in the eastern part of the village. Since the Central-Hudson absorbed the Mohawk & Malone the building had been practically abandoned as a round-house and had been used as a storehouse. Jacob P. Rice of this village held the position of storekeeper for the company. The cause of the disaster is not known and probably never will be fully explained, as those who were in a position to tell were dead. In some way a fire started in the round-house about ten o'clock. Attention was first attracted to it by blowing of a whistle, which was at first thought to come from one of the manufacturing plants, but later it was learned that it was the whistle of one of the Central locomotives which was standing on a side-track near the round-house. It was at once assumed that it was an alarm of fire, but the members of the fire department who did not live somewhere near the yards were at first uncertain as to the location.

> That did not last long for suddenly the heavens were lighted up by a blinding flash, which was followed by a report the like of which was never heard in this section before. That was followed by a rain of bricks, stones, pieces of iron, etc., which extended over half the village. So loud was the report that it was heard for miles around. When the explosion came it shook the very earth. It scattered around a blaze of death; it sent missiles of destruction throughout the neighborhood; it smashed windows in scores of houses and bombarded their inmates with flying glass and nails; it exerted such a terrific energy that people in Little Falls and Frankfort, in Middleville and Fort Plain were affected by it, but worst of all, it sent six human souls into eternity. Suddenly, with a roar like an angry Niagara, the fire leaped into one mighty volume of destructive energy, hurling death and destruction in a wide radius and vomiting into the air a flame-permeated mass of ruin. Houses rocked on their foundations; timbers creaked and groaned and were sprung as the air rushed toward the created vacuum; blinds were

smashed, sashes were torn out and hurled through the air; doors were forced from their hinges; bricks tumbled from chimneys and a rain of glass fell on the streets where the power of the explosion reached. And in the darkness and confusion and shock of the moment scores of persons, injured by the flying missiles and glass and dazed by the suddenness of the catastrophe, fled in panic from their homes, over which it seemed the crack of doom had sounded. A strange and tragic surprise this from a building believed to be almost as non-combustible as a rock.

The explosion seemed to almost shake the people out of their houses, so quickly did the crowd turn out. There was a mad rush for the scene but many were deterred from going nearer than several hundred feet, owing to the fear of another explosion, the report having spread that a large quantity of dynamite was stored in a car near the burning ruins. That did not deter the members of the fire department from doing their duty, and never did a paid fire department work more nobly to save life or property than the members of the Fort Dayton Steamer Company and the Excelsior Hook and Ladder Company. In an incredibly short time they had lines of hose strung from hydrants in Folts, Green and Deimel streets, and soon several streams were pouring on the fiercely blazing heap of ruins. They soon had it under control, so that there was no danger of it spreading.

John Dak, the night-watchman, was one of those who briefly survived the holocaust. He was conscious when pulled from the flames and was questioned as to how and what happened. He was quoted as saying, "If I get well I'll tell all about it, but if I die no one will ever know anything about it." He could not be induced to explain and shortly thereafter dropped into a coma which continued up to the time of his death.

That part of the Village of Herkimer was known as "Brooklyn" and there was hardly a whole pane of glass to be found in the whole area. For an example, there was the residence of Mrs. Philip Burnop which was on Folts Street and located northeast of the round-house. Nearly every window was broken, and the doors were torn from their hinges. The clock which was on the mantle in the sitting room was hurled half way across the floor and broken in a hundred pieces. The window shades and lace curtains were torn away from nearly every window. Dishes were broken and strewn about the floor. The rear end of the house was forced away from the main building. The author's mother-in-law, Mrs. Florence Wells, was the daughter of the Mrs. Burnop referred to above. Mrs. Wells told me many times that the reports of that terrible event were not exaggerated. She said that the Burnop homestead showed visible evidence of the explosion for many, many years afterward.

There were many other tales of harrowing experiences which occurred that evening of August 20, 1901. Severe damage was incurred by the lumber yards and the knitting mills as well as places of business located several blocks from the explosion scene.

Incoming train on Mohawk and Malone track. Main line of N.Y.C. in foreground. Circa 1910. The large building in background was destroyed by fire in 1915. (Harter collection)

Locomotive working its way through ice. Snow plow # 232 being used on adjacent track. Herkimer flood, 1910. (Harter collection)

The West Canada Creek was blocked by ice and overflowed on February 28, 1910. The M. & M. yards are in upper right corner. The open, water covered area curving in front of locomotive is the M. & M. tracks to the north. (Harter collection)

East Albany Street, Herkimer. M. & M. track at right crosses street and heads north leaving the main line right of way. (Harter collection)

N.Y.C. 1901 in M. & M. yards at Herkimer, 1938. This may have been engine used on Little Falls & Dolgeville as that was stored in Herkimer overnight. (Harter collection)

At an inquest held by Coroner S. S. Richards, the railroad storekeeper, Jacob P. Rice, testified that there were on hand at the time of the fire and explosion, five boxes of dynamite, 250 pounds, and from 15 to 20 kegs of giant powder, 25 pounds to the keg. There were also quantities of gasoline and kerosene.

Naturally there were many questions raised as to the responsibility of the New York Central Railroad and to what extent reparations should be made. Some of these cases reached the courts as might be expected. The scars and memories of the village residents remained for many years thereafter.

ALBANY STREET

On October 6, 1908 the Herkimer Village Board of Trustees and the New York Central representatives were in conference over the questions as to whether the north track of the New York Central Railroad, known as the Mohawk and Malone track, should be moved towards the south so that a greater width would be given to Albany Street, east of Main Street. This subject was the matter of discussion for the next thirty-five years but nothing was ever changed while the New York Central tracks ran through the village over the land now known as State Street.

It appears that in 1905 the Board of Trustees of the village wanted to extend Albany Street west of Prospect Street. The railroad agreed to donate a strip of land for the Albany Street extension. In turn, among other concessions, the Village of Herkimer agreed that the railroad company could maintain, keep, use and repair the then present stub tracks and switches on Albany Street as they were at that time located, constructed and used.

The bridge over the Hydraulic Canal was the scene of many highway accidents, some very serious, as the south girder of the bridge projected out into the street. It was never changed as long as the M&M track ran through and along Albany Street.

ELECTRIFICATION

The Herkimer newspaper on July 23, 1909 printed a story on the electrification of the Herkimer-Remsen Division of the New York Central and Hudson River Railroad. It sounded perfectly wonderful. Extensions would be built to Piseco Lake, Morehouseville and Wilmurt and hourly service would be offered on the Herkimer-Remsen line.

That the newspaper article said it was bound to come may be true, but we are still waiting.

THE FLOOD AT HERKIMER

The Mohawk and Malone yards were located on the eastern side of the Village of Herkimer about 1000 to 1500 feet west of the normal channel of the West Canada Creek, sometimes referred to as the Kuyahoora River. Wide flats adjoined the creek channel and it was not remarkable for these flats to be inundated when the spring thaws came and broken ice began to pile up.

Preceding February 28, 1910 there had been cold weather which put a heavy coating of ice on the creek and its tributaries and then covered the land with masses of snow. Suddenly the weather turned from the cold of winter to mildness, accompanied by spring showers. Every brook and stream began to contribute a tremendous amount of water to the West Canada. A severe ice jam developed on the southern edge of the village and in the afternoon of the 28th the great flow of water broke the bounds of the creek channel and began to flood and push huge masses of ice over the area. The ice developed to a depth of several feet.

The Mohawk and Malone yards and the adjacent lumber yards of the West Canada Lumber Company and Snell Lumber Company were covered with ice and water. Eventually with the use of dynamite the ice jam was broken and the flood receded on Wednesday. The railroad used snow plows to push the blocks of ice, mixed with earth and other materials, off the tracks.

The flood damage in the village as a whole was tremendous. There was considerable damage around the M&M yards but all was quickly repaired and trains again used the track to the north.

A few years later a long dike was built to confine the West Canada to a more defined area and despite threatening conditions developing periodically through the years, the village was spared the ravages of another flood such as the one of 1910.

THE MONTREAL EXPRESS RUNS AGAIN

On June 11, 1917 one of the worst rain storms in immediate history hit the Central New York area.

The New York, Ontario and Western Railway was severely damaged in the vicinity of Oriskany Falls. The Delaware and Lackawanna suffered in the Sauquoit Valley. North of Utica the Montreal Express of the New York Central System was marooned near Holland Patent when a culvert was washed out just after the train had crossed over it and another culvert was swept away just before the train reached it. Nearly 100 passengers had to spend the day in Holland Patent while some went back to Utica by automobile.

The Adirondack train leaving Utica that day had to be rerouted by way of Herkimer and reached Lake Placid and other mountain resorts many hours behind schedule.

THE LOG TRAINS

The most poignant memory that the author has of the Mohawk and Malone was the arrival in Herkimer in the late afternoon of the log train from the North Woods. As we lived in the northeastern section of the village, the whistle of the locomotive as it approached the East German Street or Creek Road Crossing was very audible at our home. However, it seems as though the engineer never really believed that anyone would contest his train crossing the village street so he would not let the whistle reach top volume. It sounded more like a king-sized moan. My mother used to tell me that that was because the engine was tired after a long day's trip up into the mountains to get a train load of logs. The funny part of it all was, that I believed it and you know, I still like to think it was true!

The train had only a short distance to go after crossing German Street before it went into the siding at the Standard Desk Company sawmill which was located between the M&M tracks and Harter Street, north of Folts Street in Herkimer.

FAMILY RECOLLECTIONS

The author's father, aunt and uncle were born on the Hilts-Harter farm located between mileposts one and two on the HN&PNG. I asked my aunt, who was the eldest of the children, if she remembered the narrow gauge and she replied that she did indeed. Furthermore, she said that when the first formal train was run north, she placed herself too near the track and the engineer brought the train to a halt so that she could be induced to move back to a safe distance.

There is a culvert under the tracks at this location which lets the water of a small pond on the property drain towards the West Canada Creek. Most of the stone work in this culvert gives the appearance that it was part of the original culvert built in 1880.

A change in fortunes caused the family to move north to Kast Bridge. The two boys had reached the ages where going to town on the railroad was a weekly excusion. There was only one fly in the ointment and that was the fare. It was 7½¢. At first the boys thought that 15¢ should take care of the two of them but they were unable to convince the conductor of their viewpoint. So the next logical thing was to cut a penny in half on the farm anvil and the next week that is what they offered the conductor. He was to say the least, unhappy. Not only because two young smart alecks had outwitted him but he was left with only 14 cents and 2 unnegotiable half pennies instead of 16 cents. Needless to say the boys did not try to repeat the maneuver.

In later years my father was the foreman on the construction of the concrete retaining wall that was built along the so-called Dugway above Dempster's Bridge, near Countryman's Station. This wall was substantially built and is still there today. It was supposed to hold back the slip bank from coming down on the road. At that point the highway ran very close to the slipbank, separated from the railroad by a board fence and the West Canada Creek was just beyond the railroad. It was still the scene of numerous slides covering the highway and the railroad as well on occasion. This dangerous area was eliminated in the mid-sixties by the realignment of the West Canada Creek and moving the highway and railroad a considerable distance from the old "Dugway." Ironically, when in 1973, the Poland Branch stopped operations, the roadbed and its track between Kast Bridge and the one time Countryman's was undoubtedly the best piece of trackage on the whole Adirondack Division. In 1979 this was dismantled and if we can believe the newspaper reports, the tracks and ties were sent to Chicago to be used in subway construction there.

TRAGEDY AT NORTH HERKIMER

For a good many years, East German Street or the "Creek Road" was crossed twice by the M&M. The first time just at the edge of the residental section of Herkimer and the second time about a mile north, near the dam on the West Canada which diverted water for the Hydraulic Canal that ran through the village. This upper crossing was eliminated a number of years ago when a new highway was built entirely on the west side of the M&M track.

On December 6, 1920 tragedy struck the area when Mr. and Mrs. Joseph Wooster, Sr. of Middleville were killed when a train hit their automobile at the upper crossing. This great shock to the residents of the Valley had not worn off when on Friday, December 10th fate struck again. The UTICA SATURDAY GLOBE said:

> Within 600 feet of the spot where Mr. and Mrs. Joseph Wooster were killed on Monday, another tragedy of the rail, in which a Utican was killed, took place on Friday morning. The victim was Daniel J. Kelly, engineer of a train running between Remsen and Herkimer. The accident was due to the carlessness of a section gang which was working on

the roadbed. The men were engaged in repairing the roadbed and had removed a damaged rail, intending to replace it with a new one. They found, however, that the new rail was too long and some of the men were sent to saw off a part of it. No thought apparently was given to the train that was soon due in Herkimer and the damaged rail lay unfastened to the ties.

Suddenly the whistle of the train blew for the crossing and then frantic efforts were made but too late to secure the rail and make it safe for the passage of the train. The flagman was too far down the track, too distant to warn the approaching engineer in time. As the train bore down on the broken roadbed members of the crew waved thier arms. The brakes were applied but when the locomotive reached the displaced rail it lurched toward the Hydraulic Canal that parallels the railroad and with the tender pitched on its side into the water almost drawing after it the passenger coach, which was well filled with women on their way to Herkimer to do their Christmas shopping.

At the last moment Kelly on the right side of the cab leaped to the roadbed but fell and suffered a fractured skull which caused his death a short time later. Fireman Leon Smith on the left side leaped into the canal and swam to safety. On the passenger coach were 35 women, many of whom might have met with death or injury had the coach followed the engine and tender into the canal. Only the fact that Engineer Kelly stuck to his post until the brakes were applied prevented this added horror.

TROUBLES ON THE CENTRAL

There are days when it doesn't pay to own a railroad. March 27, 1913 was one of those days. The mainline of the New York Central was closed because of flooding near Little Falls, a bad washout at St. Johnsville and a section of the line completely washed out at Yosts.

The Central turned to its West Shore line to keep the trains running but unfortunately a landslide at the Mohawk grade south of Herkimer put one of the West Shore tracks out of business. Complications at Schuyler Junction caused further trouble.

The trolley line to Little Falls experienced trouble near the power house between Herkimer and Little Falls but kept the cars running pretty close to schedule.

Nothing came through all day on the Oneonta-Herkimer electric line owing to a big landslide south of Herkimer.

After reporting all of the preceding misfortunes, the Herkimer EVENING TELEGRAM reported:

Now this afternoon it is the M&M that gets held up by a slide at the "Dugway," an old trouble point owing to the steep earth bank bordering the road at this point and occasionally sending down water loosened

masses over the retaining wall. It was about two o'clock when this occurred today and the slide is described as an extensive one. It came
down as if by evil design just as the milk train due here at 2:15 reached
the point, and there was all the setting for a serious if not tragic wreck.
The watchful eye of Engineer Ezra French saw the first danger tokens,
however, and he put the emergency clutch on his train and shut off his
engine with a promptness that sent it into the mass at greatly reduced
speed, and only the forward trucks were carried out of place. Engineer
Harry Crandall has charge of the train. It, of course, remains crippled
at the place.

DEMPSTER'S BRIDGE

Accidents at grade crossings have always been the most sorrowful
part of railroading. No attempt has been made to do any research on
this type of catastrophe as far as this history is concerned but occasionally the subject makes its own appearance. One of these accidents
occurred on May 14, 1911 at Dempster's Bridge north of Kast
Bridge. At that point the highway crossed the West Canada Creek
through a covered bridge. Within a car length from the northern
portal of the bridge the Herkimer-Poland railroad crossed the highway.

On May 14, 1911 a car passed through the bridge and entered
the railroad crossing directly in front of a southbound, behind
schedule milk train. Four of the five passengers in the car were killed.

In an effort to eliminate the cause of such a tragedy, the side
boards were knocked off the bridge to improve visibility. It still remained a very hazardous site. In 1920–21 a new bridge was built at
this place. It was a poured concrete structure and designed whereby
the creek and the railroad were both crossed by the same bridge. This
bridge lasted until the late 1960's when the channel of the creek was
realigned and the need for a bridge no longer existed.

MIDDLEVILLE

The Herkimer, Newport and Poland Narrow Gauge Railway was
formally opened to Middleville on Tuesday, September 6, 1881. The
scheduled train was to consist of a combination baggage, mail and
smoker's car and one regular passenger coach.

It is sad to report that on November 23, 1881 the first fatality of
the new railroad occurred when Conductor Irving H. Griswold was
killed. The details of this melancholy event have been recorded earlier in the history of the railroad.

The automobile came out of the covered bridge, at right, in front of a southbound milk train on May 14, 1911 with the results shown. This sad accident at "Dempster's" caused four casualties. (Harter collection)

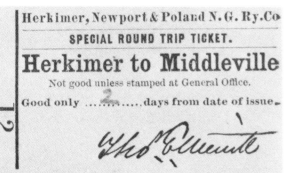

The original ticket was stamped on back showing the date of sale as August 23, 1883. (Herkimer County Historical Society)

The "Dugway" 4½ miles north of Herkimer. Picture was taken from M. & M. roadbed. Track curves around creek this side of highway. Mud & clay would slide off hillside and periodically slide off highway and block highway and railroad. After suffering with this danger point for 85 years it was corrected by changing the course of the creek 5 years before railroad closed operation. (Harter collection)

The depot at Middleville. Circa 1909. (Harter collection)

From Bridge Street south, Middleville. Station is at right. August, 1917. (Harter collection)

No. 9305 on the head end of a north bound train near Fishing Rocks Road north of Middleville. Circa March, 1968. (Richard Tucker)

Headed south, West Canada Creek bridge, north of Middleville. (Richard Tucker)

Crossing the West Canada Creek Ox-bow, south bridge, between Middleville and Newport, April 1978. (Harter collection)

The north bridge over the West Canada Creek Ox-bow, April 1978. Fenner's Grove was in between the two bridges. (Harter collection)

Historian G. A. Hardin stated that the railroad shops were located at Middleville and also that Frank M. Molineux did all of the painting for the railroad. Nothing further to substantiate these two items has been found.

Middleville was the place of business of Edward M. Burns who was such an important personage in both the Herkimer, Newport and Poland and the Adirondack and St. Lawrence Railways. He died in 1914 and is buried in the Middleville cemetery.

The freight and passenger station still stands in Middleville but in a very dilapidated condition. There is a postcard picture extant showing a neat, substantial building as the station at Middleville but just what happened to this building is uncertain. F. Ray McKnight worked there in 1940 and fortunately took a snapshot of the station at that time but the picture is of the building that is still standing.

FENNER'S GROVE

Between Newport and Middleville the southward flowing West Canada Creek creates an oxbow when it flows from the extreme eastern edge of the valley to the extreme western edge and then back towards the east. The construction of two bridges was necessary to carry the Herkimer, Newport and Poland over the creek. In between the bridges Fenner's Grove was located. This was described as a charming spot for Sunday School and society picnics.

The southern bridge was apparently designated as Jones' Crossing as this flag station appears on early timetables between Middleville and Fenner's Grove.

On March 5, 1891, the BOONVILLE HERALD reported:

> Newport — Ice carried away some of the supports under the bridge at Jones' Crossing last Wednesday (the day the New York Central men visited) weakening it to such an extent that the company has been afraid to run its engines or heavily loaded cars across it, but have shunted all passengers or freight across and an engine on the other side takes them on from that point. Temporary repairs were soon made.

In June of 1891 the narrow gauge railroad was changed to standard gauge on one Sunday. The two bridges demanded immediate attention. The BOONVILLE HERALD reported:

> Newport — Nov. 5, 1891 — Straightening of curves between Middleville and Newport is almost finished. Abutments of the first bridge are above water level and the second is nearly completed. No expense has been spared. Dr. Webb is evidently building a first class road.

This 4-6-0 was originally Adirondack & St. Lawrence No. 17. Renumbered to New York Central No. 2027, it arrives in Poland with a southbound passenger train. Circa 1900. (Gerald Coyne collection)

A NYC&HR 4-4-0 on the head-end just north of the depot in Poland. Circa 1900. (Helen Schermerhorn)

Train from the south arriving at Poland station. Circa 1910. (Harter collection)

Looking south on the Mohawk & Malone from north of the depot in Newport.
Note water tank. Circa 1911. (Richard Tucker)

Newport — January 21, 1892 — On Monday the trains ran over the new railroad between Middleville and Newport. The road is straightened but the passengers will miss the beautiful ride through Fenner's Grove.

The rubble of the earlier bridge is still visible just to the north of the southern bridge.

NEWPORT

Newport was always a staunch supporter of the railroad to Herkimer. Its philosophy may have been expressed in the Newport column of the Little Falls newspaper when it said, "Newport hath its charms and when we get the new railroad it is only hoped that the outer world may be brought to enjoy those charms with us."

Work at Newport on the narrow gauge road started on April 26, 1881 when H. W. Dexter commenced work with a "gang of hands" to build the roadbed on the west side of West Canada Creek. Henry W. Dexter was also a director of the railroad and when the HN&PNG secured a 2-4-4T type locomotive it was numbered as No. 2 and named *HENRY W. DEXTER*. This engine apparently was used mainly for construction and maintenance. There is some doubt that No. 2 was converted to standard gauge when the railroad was changed and the ultimate disposition of No. 2 is obscure.

When the possibility arose that the railroad from Herkimer might not be constructed because of financial troubles, Newport people redoubled their efforts and were able to see the plans carried out. On January 2, 1882 the railroad ran its first scheduled train from Herkimer. One hour and five minutes was the time allowed for the 13 mile trip but there was some work to be done along the way. Undoubtedly the trip even at this rate of speed seemed to be at express speeds after the days of the stage from Herkimer.

Newport at this time had a population of about 1,200 people. Considerable mercantile business was carried out there and cheese and other farm products were important items.

The principal office of the HN&PNG was listed at Newport. Mr. George H. Thomas, president of the National Bank at Newport was the treasurer and Thomas E. Merrit of Newport was the secretary. Edward M. Burns was, of course, the president.

A rather unusual type of derailment happened in January 1882 in Newport when a news item dated January 14 revealed:

Quite a severe accident occurred with the engine of the N. G. R. R. at this place last Saturday evening, at 6 P. M. The engine ran on the turntable, tipped up, letting the tender and engine run backward toward the West Canada Creek. The tender ran off the turntable, burying the trucks in the ground and striking an old log, just on the edge of the bank, about 15 feet above the creek. Had it run backward ten inches farther, it would certainly have gone over the embankment taking the engine with it into the creek. It took fifty or more men until about 4 o'clock Sunday morning to replace the engine and tender back on the turntable.

Another interesting item at Newport was the one on Friday, June 23, 1882 when it was reported that the Herkimer, Newport and Poland Narrow Gauge Railway Company had leased Mr. W. W. Swezcy's grove for the season and proposed to erect a platform, tables, etc., for the accommodation of picnic parties. The company invited inquiries by mail for further particulars. The HN&P certainly was early in recognizing the value of recreational areas as fare-getters.

In December 1882 a newspaper item stated that the baby train battled manfully with the snow and came through nearly on time being only 1½ hours late on Thursday.

One of the important sources of freight traffic was the cheese market. In a newspaper story on this subject, circa 1904, it was reported under Newport that:

> The Herkimer County Warehousing Company, of which W. D. Grant is president and principal owner, already have their large cold storage building and cheese warehouse in this village packed to the ceiling with this season's cheese. About 200,000 cheese have already been handled at the storage here this season, and as the building is filled to its utmost, much of the cheese purchased by Mr. Grant of late has been shipped to his Mechanicville warehouse for storage.
>
> The cheese is dipped in melted parafine, boxed and taken to a room cooled to 35 degrees above zero. The boxes are of different weights, running from 35 to 84 pounds each. It will all be exported via Boston, during the winter months.

Another substantial freight item was crushed stone and cut stone. As early as April 4, 1882 the LITTLE FALLS JOURNAL & COURIER reported as a Newport item that there was a large force of men at work in the quarry of Waldo Sherman. The stones were to be shipped to Herkimer, where there was a ready market for them. The Adirondack & St. Lawrence Time Table No. 1, August 31, 1891 listed Sherman Quarry as a flag stop on the railroad. Crushed stone from the Newport Quarries also was shipped in huge quantities through the years that the railroad operated in the Kuyahoora Valley.

The depot in Newport was located at the Bridge Street crossing of the railroad. This building was demolished in 1970.

Just north of the depot was the Michigan Condensed Milk Company plant. The Borden Company took over this plant in 1916. Borden continued the condensed milk operation but later manufactured caramels and fortified malted milk powder. In 1942 the company turned to the manufacture of instant coffee. In 1971 the plant was closed down because newer processes had been developed for use in the instant coffee field and it was not feasible to convert the Newport plant. Previous to the time of its closing, the plant produced 7,000,000 pounds of instant coffee per year. It is evident that the loss of this freight business was a severe blow to the Herkimer-Poland branch line.

POLAND

Poland was the terminal of the narrow gauge railroad which reached there on May 29, 1882. At that time it was a busy little village and much manufacturing was done there and at Cold Brook, two miles distant. The manufactures consisted of wagons, carriages, chair seats, veneering, wooden buttons and saw handles. A considerable amount of butter, cheese and farm produce was also shipped away from this point.

When the narrow gauge was changed to standard gauge it was all done in one day and that was Sunday, June 7, 1891. An engine and two coaches arrived in the village on Monday, June 8th and was ushered in with the firing of cannon and the blowing of whistles.

Speaking of whistles, it has been told that on Armistice Day, November 11, 1918 that Daniel O'Donnell was the engineer on the train that brought the news to Poland and he started his whistle at the edge of town and continued to blow it until he ran out of steam. Mr. O'Donnell was an employee for 47 years and an engineer for many, many years on the Herkimer-Poland line. He was a resident of Herkimer.

Lumber and other forest products long remained the most important freight shipped from Poland. When on May 30, 1972 the operation of the railroad was permanently suspended by a washout north of Herkimer, it was the final blow to the wood products industry located there and the last of these establishments was closed and the equipment dismantled.

The passenger station at Poland remains as a landmark. It is in fair condition. It contained a freight house, baggage room, waiting room and ticket and telegraph office. A few years ago it was proposed to renovate the building and use it for a Veterans of Foreign Wars Post but the plan was not carried out to a successful conclusion.

NORTH OF POLAND

When the Herkimer, Newport and Poland Extension Railway or Adirondack & St. Lawrence Railway if you prefer, was built north of Poland in 1891, a substantial change was made in the channel of the West Canada Creek. What was a peninsula on the Charles W. Bowen farm was cut off by a new channel 1600 feet in length. This eliminated bridging the creek. Nevertheless it kept the roadbed in close proximity to the West Canada Creek and on September 9, 1905 the Utica SATURDAY GLOBE reported that earlier in the week there had been a cloudburst at Poland. There were several washouts on the Mohawk and Malone with resultant damage to bridges and culverts. The Adirondack Division of the M&M railroad between Herkimer and Remsen was "abandoned." (The use of the word "abandoned" was rather an overstatement.)

On February 15, 1908 another bad washout occurred and a contemporary newspaper reported that at ten o'clock that morning the West Canada Creek washed out about 100 feet of the roadbed of the Mohawk and Malone Railroad just north of Poland. The passenger train leaving Herkimer at 12:40 was compelled to transfer its passengers to a freight which was on the north side of the washout. The passenger train was in charge of conductor Harry Crandall and the freight conductor was Charles Lansing, both of Herkimer.

This area was the last place the railroad was bothered by a flooding West Canada Creek. There was a gradual ascent from Poland north. The right-of-way swung away from the creek towards Gravesville. The last contact with the creek was when the railroad crossed the Trenton Chasm at Trenton Falls and was then 75 feet above the waters of the West Canada.

BEAUTY AND GRACE ARE ITS PRAISES

Trenton Falls had been a mecca for sight-seers from the first quarter of the 19th century on. It was a famous resort with visitors coming from far distances to enjoy the beauty of the water falls and the chasm. It had been developed for the enjoyment of its visitors with a dancing pavilion for use of excursionists and picnickers. Among its paeans were those of Mr. George William Curtis who said: "Trenton is the summer song of rest * * * Beauty and grace are its praises," and Mr. N. P. Willis gave expression to his views in this wise: "The most enjoyable beautiful spot among the resorts of romantic scenery in our country is Trenton Falls."

The West Canada Creek fell over 300 feet within three miles

Northbound train crossing Gravesville Bridge. Circa 1892. Box car carries lettering Adirondack & St. Lawrence Ry. (Helen Schermerhorn)

Beecher Trestle north of Poland. The trestle was in the process of being filled in. Today it is a solid embankment. (Helen Schermerhorn)

Southbound passenger train crossing the bridge at Trenton Falls over the West Canada Creek. Circa 1900. (Railway Historical Society of Northern New York)

Dam and R. R. Bridge, Trenton Falls, N. Y.

A full view of the great bridge 75 feet over the West Canada Creek at Trenton Falls. The power company dam has now been built and this date the picture about 1910. When erected this bridge was supposed to have been the largest solid floor bridge in the world. It was 350 feet long with the middle span of 200 feet. (Harter collection)

forming a combination of six cascades, passing through a deep, narrow ravine, with dark limestone walls varying from 70 to 250 feet in height. A path had been made by which the chasm might be explored nearly its entire length.

From the time that the Black River and Utica Railroad was opened in 1855, Trenton Falls was its premier scenic attraction. When the Adirondack & St. Lawrence Railway began operating in 1892, Trenton Falls was served by a second railroad. At first thought one might think that this meant an upsurge in the Trenton Falls attraction. In fact the opposite occurred. Howard Thomas in his TRENTON FALLS, YESTERDAY & TODAY pointed this out:

> Though Trenton Falls was now blessed with two railroads, it found that most of the passengers merely gawked out of the windows to divert themselves before enjoying the newer pleasures that lay to the north.

Charles Moore, the proprietor of the Trenton Falls Hotel tried to stem the flow but the attractions and pleasures to be had in the North Woods was too great a competition to overcome. The erection of power stations in the gorge after 1900 terminated the lure of Trenton Falls for sight-seers.

Following abandonment of railroad service between Poland and Remsen in the 1930's the great bridge remained across the chasm until the World War II era when the bridge was dropped to the creek bottom and the steel salvaged for the war effort.

MILK

Milk and milk products amounted to a great deal of business for the railroad. In 1905, for instance, there were six creameries on the Mohawk and Malone Railway. They were located at: Kast Bridge, Middleville, Newport, Poland, Gravesville and Prospect. It is interesting to note that on the same list that provided the above information there were fifty-seven creameries listed on the Rome, Watertown and Ogdensburg Division, north of Utica and Rome.

In 1976 the author was fortunate in being able to talk with Albert A. Hess, a retired New York Central conductor, who then resided in Chadwicks, N. Y. Albert had started working for the Central in Utica in 1919 as a call boy.

In 1928 or 1929 he worked on the Adirondack Division north out of Herkimer. He said that he and other members of the crew would go by trolley, over the New York State Railways line, from Utica to Herkimer. They would then take their train north from the Herkimer yards. This was listed as a mixed train, carrying passengers as well as express but primarily a milk train. He recalled that there were two milk plants in Middleville at that time. The train crew did quite a little loading by hand and the maximum number of cars they could handle was five. This was all they could take and make their meet with the down freight train on account of the length of the sidings. If they got into Remsen in time to make a meet, they would transfer their loaded cars to the RW&O so that they could be taken directly to Utica and the New York milk train would not have to stop at Herkimer and pick up the cars.

THE LAST DAYS FROM POLAND TO REMSEN

The last day of passenger service from Herkimer to Remsen was on October 31, 1934. The next year the time tables listed freight service only from Poland to Herkimer. The rails northward from Poland were abandoned in due time and were torn up except for a short spur that was left from Remsen to the gravel pit near Prospect.

The old right-of-way is very easy to locate in many places. The underpass of the Beecher Road north of Poland is in first class condition and is a fine example of stone work. However, it is almost impossible to locate, from the highway, where the great bridge at Gravesville is located. It is now so overgrown with trees and brush that little remains to show where this fine piece of engineering work crossed the Mill Creek at Gravesville.

UTICA AS A TERMINAL

The changing of the terminal of the Adirondack and St. Lawrence Line of the Mohawk and Malone Railway from Herkimer to Utica in 1893 presented a rather strage situation. The Herkimer-Remsen road continued to be part of the Adirondack Division of the New York Central even after it was severed between Remsen and Poland. Adirondack Division trains left Utica over the St. Lawrence Division of the former Utica and Black River section of the Rome, Watertown and Ogdensburg Railroad. The Adirondack Division trains were switched over to their own division at Remsen for the run north to Tupper Lake, Lake Placid, Malone and Montreal.

The time tables issued for public use gave the mileage from Herkimer at the start but as soon as the terminal change was made, the distance shown on public time tables was from Utica. Employee's time tables continued to show the distance from Herkimer. This undoubtedly was due to the fact that the mileposts, then and now, show the distance from Herkimer. In the mid 1940's the employee's time tables were revised to give the distance from Remsen north.

No documentation in this history has been attempted on the railroad from Utica to Remsen as this is part of the St. Lawrence Division. There were some incidents that took place between Utica and Remsen that concerned Adirondack Division trains but they were for the most part of a relatively minor nature. While these occurrences were of major import to those directly concerned, they had little effect on the Mohawk and Malone Railway.

In the strange way that destiny works, it now appears that the revival of the Remsen-Lake Placid segment of the old Adirondack Division is going to force the upgrading of the Utica-Remsen branch line. The same course of events will apply to the Union Station in Utica.

REMSEN

Remsen was suddenly thrown into prominence in the railroad world when Dr. W. Seward Webb decided it would be a junction point between his proposed Adirondack and St. Lawrence Railway and the older and well established Rome, Watertown and Ogdensurg Division of the New York Central. Remsen became the scene of great activity as surveying parties descended on the community, followed soon after by hordes of workmen.

Construction was started in 1891 on the road to Prospect as well as to the north. Engineers working out of Remsen finally decided that the road would follow the RW&O track for two miles north of the village and then strike eastward towards Forestport.

The workmen livened things up around Remsen while they were located there. The village was happy when the time came that the workmen moved on and the village could return to its customary pace of life.

The new railroad from Herkimer came into Remsen on the east side of the village in proximity to the existing RW&O right-of-way and that road's depot was used. This station building lost its roof on July 14, 1892 when a severe storm passed through the area. The building burned in 1903 when a lantern exploded starting a fire. A coach served as a station until the station could be replaced. There are several pictures extant showing the depot at Remsen. It is interesting to note that in the earlier pictures the station board shows the milage as:

U (Utica) 21. — REMSEN — C (Carthage) 53

Later the station board read:

H (Herkimer) 27.7 — REMSEN — M (Montreal) 210.3

The Remsen junction provided the necessary change point for passengers on the RW&O division who wanted to travel towards the Fulton Chain area and north from there. The nearby Junction House was a popular place to spend time while waiting for the trains. In later years it became run down and eventually it burned down.

A turntable was installed in the Remsen yards. This probably was used for turning the engines on the Herkimer trains. In winter time the engines running between Remsen and Tupper Lake, etc., on snow fighting trains could also be turned around. The RW&O probably used the turntable in a like manner.

In 1916 an overhead bridge was built to carry the highway over the tracks of the two railroads about eight-tenths of a mile north of the Remsen station. This bridge was removed in 1977 as the main highway now went north by a different route and the bridge needed rebuilding.

A DOZEN EACH WAY

A study of the time tables during the summer periods of 1913 and 1914 shows that at least a dozen passenger trains arrived in Remsen from the south each day. A like number departed from Remsen southward. The trains were on the three lines running into Remsen; The Rome, Watertown and Ogdensburg; The Mohawk and Malone; and the Herkimer-Remsen line. Adding the freight trains to the passenger train traffic made Remsen a busy rail point.

The teen years were the high points of rail passenger traffic. Competition from bus lines and private automobiles was developing and it wasn't long before the passenger traffic was in its steady decline.

THE GENERAL'S MONUMENT

In 1907 the Village of Herkimer decided to erect a monument in memory of General Nicholas Herkimer. The General Herkimer Chapter, Daughters of the American Revolution, provided the granite pedestal which supports the large bronze statue of the General. The boulder used for the pedestal was found near Remsen on the Pirnie farm. It was loaded on a flat car and transported to Herkimer where the General Herkimer Monument now stands in Myers Park.

SNOW

A bizarre anecdote has been passed along concerning the ill-starred engineer, Jim Kelley. On one occasion he was the engineer on

Snow plow X-606 in the yard at Malone on April 30, 1937. (McKnight collection)

Engine 4712 headed for Utica with a consist of sleepers being deadheaded back to Utica. (McKnight collection)

Flangers 732 and 764 waiting for the winter snows at Malone on April 16, 1938. (McKnight collection)

A deadhead Pullman extra, southbound with engines no. 4566 and 4741 at Saranac Inn, February 5, 1938. (McKnight collection)

On Sunday, February 25, 1940, train no. 11 did not have a mail car but did have a parlor car for Lake Placid in its consist. (McKnight collection)

Train no. 11 with the regular weekday consist is pictured at Saranac Inn on March 23, 1940. (McKnight collection)

NYC no. 4490 with train no. 3 at Saranac Inn on March 26, 1940. (McKnight collection)

Snow scenes at Lake Placid Station, February 18, 1963. (Albert Hess collection)

Snow jammed on front of diesel No. 8251 after a hard trip from Utica, February 18, 1963 at Lake Placid. The snow had to be shoveled away before engineer could leave the cab. (Albert Hess collection)

the "Owl" as the train going north at 2:00 A. M. was called. When he received his orders the dispatcher told the operator to tell Kelley to look out for drifts at Honnedaga. Later on Kelly was asked what that meant to him and he replied, "When I struck Honnedaga I had the wheels turning as fast as possible. I got through the drifts but my head light was gone and every window in the cab was broken but I had to run to Tupper Lake like that."

Snow was one of the constant foes of north country railroading. It could be expected from November till the end of March. The amount that fell varied from year to year but the real trouble-maker was the hard blowing storms that filled the drifts and cuts as fast as they were cleared. There was a rotary plow stationed at Malone.

The first winter that the Mohawk and Malone operated was the most severe winter in years. December 1892 and January 1893 were very cold and February was a "Howler."

On February 23, 1893 the BOONVILLE HERALD reported that a big blizzard had stalled a train on the Adirondack and St. Lawrence:

> On Monday morning, February 20, Train No. 47 left Herkimer for Malone with two theatrical companies on board. The train became stalled near Prospect in drifts that had formed in less than two hours. A relief engine was sent out and the train reached Remsen and the actors were fed at the Bristol Inn. After a short delay at Forestport the train made its way to Malone, although it was hard wheeling. The trains on the Rome, Watertown and Ogdensburg were also several hours late.

The story of another tussle with an Adirondack snowstorm was related to me by George Clark, a retired engineer, whose home is in downtown Tupper Lake near the former junction. This occurred more than a half century later than the preceding account of James Kelly's battle with the drifts at Honnedaga. But, this lapse of time merely proves what was stated previously, that snow fighting was a constant battle all through the years.

On the day in question in the early 1960's George Clark was the engineer on the Utica-Lake Placid passenger train. The weather was threatening and Mrs. Clark, who was a passenger on the train, asked the conductor before they left Utica if they would have any difficulty getting to Tupper Lake. The conductor told Mrs. Clark that she shouldn't worry about the snow, George would get them into Tupper Lake on time. George had overheard this conversation and he said, "After I heard that, I knew I would have to do it. It was quite a trip and I think that the fireman had all he wanted on that ride." They got into Tupper Lake Junction on time or reasonably close to it but the train had to on to Lake Placid. George said that when they did get to Lake Placid that the snow had to be shoveled off the diesel locomotive as it was packed so hard and deep that he couldn't get out of the cab until they had got the snow cleared off.

There was a moment of silence after George Clark finished telling the story of snow fighting. Then he said, "I can close my eyes and see the whole division." Mrs. Clark added, "Yes, and when the steamers were running George could tell the number of every engine that blowed for the Tupper Lake crossing by the way it sounded."

A former maintenance of way department employee once remarked to the author that of all the cold, windy, snowy and downright miserable places in an area that none could come up to a railroad yard during and after a blizzard. He said that you stood there, leaning against a bitter wind with a shovelful of snow and wondering what you were going to do with it. The difficulty in reopening a railroad yard after a major storm is an undertaking that is incomprehensible to the public.

But snow can be beautiful and exciting. Ray McKnight was born in a house right next to the Mountain View station. One time while discussing a photo of the cut just north of Mountain View Ray said, "Just over the top of the rise the track swung to the right towards Owl's Head. This cut was fairly deep, and now and then, a strong wind from the northwest would blow it full. It never caused any serious problem however, but I do recall when I was just a little fellow how excited I'd get watching No. 2 smash through the drift and send the snow flying!"

Owl's Head, the next station north of Mountain View was for many years the preeminent, if unofficial, weather reporting station of the north country. The newspapers would invariably give the temperature at Owl's Head during severe cold periods and this gave credence to the belief that it was the coldest place in the Adirondack area.

One of the quaint tales of the north country cold weather railroading comes from Albert Hess. In 1951 he was a freight conductor running between Utica and Malone. He said that they had their caboose fixed up real good with a storm door, electric heater, etc. When they arrived in Malone they would spot it at the freight station where they could plug into the electricity and use it for lights and a heater. Albert said that they stayed in the caboose during their layover time and were comfortable even when the outside temperature dropped to thirty-five degrees below zero.

It is certain that no one who ever worked on the Adirondack Division of the New York Central during the winter months ever forgot the experience and the rigorous physical punishment that had to be endured upon occasion.

ADIRONDACK EXPRESS WRECK AT REMSEN

On January 3, 1924, the Adirondack Express, Train No. 2, was wrecked coming into Remsen. The Utica SATURDAY GLOBE has an account of the disaster:

> The life of a Utica engineer was crushed out Thursday afternoon when the Adirondack Express due in Utica at 4:30 was derailed when the train hit an open or defective switch near the Remsen station. The victim was James D. Kelly of Utica.
>
> The engine and four cars of the express were derailed when the train hit an open or defective switch and the engine and the cars tipped over on one side. James Daley, the fireman, was injured but not critically. Scores of passengers were shaken up and bruised and a couple received more serious injuries.
>
> Engineer Kelley was found beneath the locomotive. He was placed on another train and reached the Faxton Hospital at Utica where he expired.
>
> James Kelley was the third member of his family to meet death on the railroad. A brother, Daniel Kelly, was killed in a wreck at North Herkimer on December 10, 1920. He was an engineer on a passenger train on the Mohawk and Malone Railroad and he lost his life when his train was derailed because workmen had removed a rail and were working on it and overlooked the passenger train schedule. Another brother, Thomas, was killed in a train wreck at Carter, N. Y. 22 years ago, while acting as a fireman on a passenger train.

The author has spent much time trying to find information about the accident involving Thomas Kelley. During this period, the New York State Railroad Commissioners investigated or requested information from the involved railroad on every accident. There is no record of the "Thomas Kelley" accident in the commissioners' report for 1901 or 1902. Microfilms of the contemporary newspapers have been examined at length but no reference was ever found concerning the death of Thomas Kelly in a wreck near Carter in 1902.

FORESTPORT STATION

The details on the Adirondack and St. Lawrence Railway bridge over the Black River were reported by the BOONVILLE HERALD on January 21, 1892. It was 240 feet long with a center span of 100 feet. The rails were 49 feet above the water. The bridge proper was 25 feet in height and it rested on granite piers.

REMSEN. N.Y. DEPOT.
SHOWING THREE RAILROADS.
UTICA & BLACK RIVER.
MOHAWK & MALONE. AND
HERKIMER. BRANCH.

A favorite picture at Remsen. The three railroads make a striking photo. The former Utica & Black River is on the left, the center train is headed into Utica from the Adirondack Division and the train on the right is headed for Prospect & Herkimer. Date would be approximately 1910. (Denio collection)

REMSEN DEPOT   PHOTO BY THOMAS
                      REMSEN, N.Y.

A pair of 10 wheelers heading north into the Adirondacks. Circa 1912. (Harter collection)

Headed north crossing Main Street in Remsen. Date about 1912 or earlier as a highway bridge was erected over the railroad in 1913. This bridge was demolished in 1978. (Margaret P. Davis collection)

Breaking the drifts at Remsen in 1912. Not certain which NYC branch is shown. (Margaret P. Davis collection)

Loading the huge granite boulder at Remsen for the General Herkimer monument in the park at Herkimer. The date was July 21, 1907 and the engine is No. 1669. (Margaret P. Davis collection)

No. 2114, 4-6-0 heading for Herkimer from Remsen. Probably in the 1920's. (Margaret P. Davis collection)

An aerial view of the Dairylea plant at Remsen. The Herkimer branch is at the top and the connecting spur shows directly in back of the milk plant. Note turntable. Date is uncertain but the motor vehicles in picture would date it in the late 30's or early 40's. (Margaret P. Davis collection)

Forestport Station was established about two miles north of the bridge and it was about one and one half miles east of the settlement of Forestport. The station at Forestport is in a good state of repair and is being used for commercial purposes.

Across the highway from the station is the dining establishment known as the Buffalo Head, so named from the days that hotelman Donovan had the preserved head of a buffalo reposing on the porch. The entire little hamlet around the station is sometimes referred to as Buffalo Head.

Although Forestport was an important lumber town a great deal of its finished products were shipped via a feeder canal to the Black River Canal and only a small part was shipped over the railroad.

The Utica OBSERVER-DISPATCH MAGAZINE on June 4, 1939 gave an amusing report of George R. Ainsworth's recruiting a logging crew for the Forestport Lumber Company:

> One year Ainsworth went up "Webb's Railroad" to Tupper Lake to gather a gang of log drivers. He put 40 men on the train to Forestport and they got drunk. They had a rousing party. They kicked the oil lamps off the ceiling. They broke the windows and let in the air. They fetched the emergency ax out of the glass box and laughed at the "hatchet." They hurled it through one of the remaining windows.
>
> "I'm going to take this bunch down to Herkimer," the conductor told Ainsworth. "That's all right with me," replied Ainsworth, "but my ticket says Forestport, and that's where I get off." "You can get off," said the conductor, "but your men go down to the law in Herkimer."
>
> So the train stopped at Forestport and the conductor, letting Ainsworth pass, stepped in front of 40 lumberjacks. The jolly crew climbed right over the conductor and tumbled out after Ainsworth. Not a man went to Herkimer. They went up Black River and drove logs.

THE FOREST PRESERVE

The so-called "Blue Line" of the Adirondack State Park is just north of White Lake Station. However, the Adirondack Division of the New York Central considered the Forest Preserve as extending from Forestport to Whippleville. The Public Service Commission orders relative to the operation of coal burning locomotives were observed within these limits.

WHITE LAKE

Ice was harvested on White Lake as well as from the Fulton Chain and Raquette Lakes. Dewey R. Hill and Elliott R. Hughes in their monograph ICE HARVESTING IN EARLY AMERICA state

The shelter at Kayuta was typical of the shelters provided at the flag stations on the Mohawk & Malone. Kayuta was about 6 miles north of Remsen. (Margaret P. Davis collection)

A busy day at Forestport station about 1918. (Sheldon S. King collection)

Former Forestport station in 1974. This is a fine example of the preservation of a depot by commercial interests. (Harter collection)

The "Necessary" was an important part of the railroad stations in the old days. (Harter collection)

Southbound passenger train in the siding at White Lake Station awaiting a northbound train. Date is about 1910. (Railway Historical Society of Northern New York)

An interesting picture from the engineering standpoint of the Kayuta trestle. (William Huther)

that George C. Wood established an ice company in Utica in 1910. In 1911 he built one of the largest ice houses in the United States at White Lake. This ice house was made of wood and held 46,000 tons of ice. It was 380 feet long, 220 feet wide and 55 feet high. The plant was equipped with a car conveyor capable of loading 100 cars a day for winter shipment.

The Public Service Commission, 2nd District, reports for the year 1911 and the following years have several references to special tariffs on ice from White Lake to various locations in New York State.

On July 4, 1928 the ice house at White Lake was struck by lightning and the ensuing fire destroyed it. The gradual decline of the natural ice business had already started so the building was not replaced.

WOODGATE

The last year that White Lake was listed as a station on the Mohawk and Malone Railway was in the 1923 time tables. The change from White Lake to Woodgate was effective June 24, 1924 and Woodgate was listed thereafter.

DERAILMENT NORTH OF WHITE LAKE

On June 21, 1901, Train No. 655, the northbound Montreal Express, left Utica at 1:05 A. M. Shortly before 3:00 A. M. it ran into a washout between White Lake and Otter Lake. The engine, baggage car and two passenger coaches were derailed but no one was injured. The conductor was Mr. Lighthall and the engineer was Mr. Plato. It was reported that Train No. 654 had passed over the spot at 1:40 A. M. without trouble.

ACCIDENT AT PURGATORY

Construction was approaching the final stages between Remsen and Fulton Chain when on Tuesday, May 31, 1892, a serious accident occurred about three miles south of the Moose River Crossing at a place called Purgatory. A short piece of track had been reballasted there and it was not solid enough to hold one of the monstrous engines, No. 33, a 4-6-0 ten-wheeler type, recently received by the railroad.

As the engine was backing on the newly laid track, the sand was forced from under the ties and the huge locomotive toppled over and went down an embankment twenty feet and came to rest upside down.

The fireman jumped and was not injured but the unlucky engineer, Michael McDonald, was caught between the cab and the tank. He was extricated by chopping the cab away but lived only a minute after being released.

A wrecking crane was sent out from Utica and the engine was put back on the rails and it was not seriously damaged.

McKEEVER

In 1892 the Adirondack and St. Lawrence Railway reached the Moose River and place where it bridged the stream became known as McKeever. This was about four miles upstream from the Moose River Settlement, the terminal of the Fulton Chain Railroad better known as the "Peg Leg Railroad." Rev. Frank A. Reed, the "Lumberjack Sky Pilot," attributes the name McKeever as a memorial to a Mr. McKeever who was a superintendent on the construction of the railroad and who was killed in an accident on the Moose River. There was also a R. Townsend McKeever who was first identified as a private secretary to Dr. Webb. Later in 1892 this McKeever was a trainmaster with headquarters at Herkimer and eventually became an assistant superintendent of the Adirondack & St. Lawrence. He went on to be the general manager of the Fonda, Johnstown and Gloversville Railroad and subsequently was the president of a western railroad.

The New York Central and Hudson River Railroad pointed out in the next edition of its railroad excursion book, HEALTH AND PLEASURE that the natural advantages of McKeever would seem to insure its early development as a manufacturing point. This forecast was not long in realization.

Retired New York State Governor John A. Dix was active in the leadership of the Moose River Lumber Company which operated the Iroquois Paper Company and a big hardwood sawmill. A Moose River logging railroad extended a number of miles to the east from McKeever. This was built by the Moose River Lumber Company for the purpose of transporting logs to the mills. The road originally ran on iron straps fastened to wooden rails. John A. Dix was one of the organizers of the Raquette Lake Railway and was interested in that project as a means of getting several millions of board feet of timber which he had in the Rondaxe area to his mill at McKeever. He later sold out to the Gould Paper Company and the Moose River logging railroad was abandoned in 1914 or 1915.

This is a good example of what happened to some of the depots on the Mohawk and Malone after the road was shut down. Inside the building is just as bad as the outside. Picture taken in 1974 of the Woodgate, formerly the White Lake depot. (Woodgate)

The station at Otter Lake is in back of the northbound train standing at Otter Lake. The Otter Lake Hotel is to the left of the picture just a few hundred feet away from the depot. Circa 1920. (Harter collection)

Train 2 and Train 3 meeting at McKeever Station about 1908. (Harter collection)

The Moose River bridge, 1978. (Larry Lowenthal)

PURGATORY AND BIG MOOSE HILLS

Purgatory Hill is a 1.87% grade located between mileposts 44 and 46. It has been located at various other places on the railroad by some writers but the Adirondack Branch profile map locates it as above, between Woodgate and Otter Lake.

Conductor Albert Hess said that when they reached Purgatory Hill they could tell if they were going to experience any difficulty with the Big Moose Hill which was a much longer grade. This was a 1.11% grade, for about five miles from Carter (Clearwater) to Big Moose. Conductor Hess said that if they had had difficulty at Purgatory Hill they would stop at Carter and leave part of the train there to avoid doubling while on the hill. Doubling on a hill was always a dangerous operation and was avoided when possible.

As a word of explanation, doubling a hill means uncoupling and leaving the rear part of a train while taking the front part over the top of the hill to the next siding. Then the engine returns and takes the rear part up and over the hill. The two sections are then re-coupled and the train proceeds on its way.

THE HEAD-ON COLLISION AT NELSON LAKE

The most severe collision that ever occurred on the Mohawk and Malone happened at 3:06 P. M. on Saturday, May 9, 1903. It happened one thousand feet south of the south switch at Nelson Siding, which was located between McKeever and Minnehaha.

The collision was between southbound regular Train No. 650 and the Northbound regular Train No. 651. When Train No. 651 left Utica it carried signals for engine No. 29, occupied by Assistant Superintendent W. J. Fripp and other New York Central Officials. Engine 29 was an inspection type locomotive and was running north as Second No. 651. The inspection engine and train No. 651 were ordered to meet train No. 650 at the Nelson Lake Siding. Nelson Lake was not a telegraph station but was a regular meeting point for trains No. 650 and No. 651. However, Second No. 651, inspection engine No. 29, lost so much time that a second order was issued calling for train No. 650 to meet Second No. 651 at McKeever instead of Nelson Lake. Engineer Edward J. Neville misread his orders and believed he was to meet both sections of train No. 651 at McKeever overlooking the fact that the meet with First No. 651 at Nelson Lake had never been changed.

Train No. 650 was running between fifty and sixty miles an hour when it went through Nelson Lake. Train No. 651 was approach Nelson Lake at a reduced speed prepared to stop at Nelson Lake and await train No. 650, if it had not arrived. Conductor John O'Connor of train No. 650 realized that Engineman Neville had overlooked the meet and applied the emergency brake but the train was running so fast that the speed was only slightly reduced when the collision occurred approximately 1000 feet south of the expected meeting point. The trains met on a four degree curve and the trains when first sighted must have been very near each other.

At Tupper Lake, train No. 650 had added Pullman sleeper *FERNWOOD* to its consist. This was an empty car being deadheaded south and Conductor O'Connor had decided that it would be placed on the head end. This car was telescoped by the engine's tank but by its presence saved the lives of many passengers who would have otherwise been riding in the first car.

We must borrow the colorful prose of the SATURDAY GLOBE of May 16, 1903 for a description of what happened:

> On both trains thoughts of pleasure, business cares or domestic duties filled the minds of the travelers; no one was thinking of the proximity of death. In the clear atmosphere of the woods, sound travels far and those who heard them must have stood aghast as they listened to the two on-rushing trains, now drawing nearer and nearer, but the noise of his own drowning that of the other in the ears of each engineer and a great curve in the road hiding them from each other until it was too late. Suddenly there was a crash, the two great masses of energy-filled metal coming together with terrific force, and then a grinding, nerve-racking noise. Boiler imbedded in boiler, while the cars were piled on top of one another or torn into fragments. There were some groans and cries, but fewer than one might have expected. The heroic in men asserted itself and many of the injured demanded that somebody worse off be cared for.

There were nearly two scores of persons injured and some of them were very seriously wounded. John Best, a postal clerk in one of the mail cars was never able to work again. Those killed were Frank H. Foulkes, conductor of northbound train No. 651; William Yordan, fireman on southbound train No. 650 and newsboy John T. Glen (or Glynn) on train No. 650.

Engineman Edward Neville, after applying the brakes, managed to save himself by jumping from the cab but his fireman was not so fortunate.

The consist of train No. 651 and damages resulting were: Engine 2004, cab, truck, tank and all light work of engine demolished, frames bent and broken; baggage car NYC 2902, ends broken in;

baggage car NYC 2557, ends broken in; mail car NYC 2350, demolished; baggage car NYC 2748, telescoped by mail car 2350; smoker St. Lawrence & Adirondack 46, small damage; coach NYC 955, small damage; kitchen car NYC 947, small damage; Pullman dining room *TUPPER LAKE,* small damage.

The consist of train No. 650 and damages resulting were: Engine 2014, tank, truck, and all light work on engine demolished, left cylinder broke, frames bent and broken; deadhead Pullman sleeper *FERNWOOD,* telescoped by tank; mail car NYC 2374, demolished; baggage car NYC 2464, demolished; smoker NYC 1220, ends and sides torn out; coach St. Lawrence & Adirondack 45, small damage; kitchen car NYC 743, small damage; Pullman dining room *SARANAC LAKE,* small damage.

The accident was attributed entirely to Engineman Neville's misreading or overlooking his orders to meet train No. 651 at the Nelson Lake siding.

The disaster was in a desolate section with no houses from which to obtain assistance for the injured. Therefore the rescuers, who were the crewmen and uninjured passengers, were thrown upon their own resources. Among those who distinguished themselves in this humane work were four lady members of the Bandit King Dramatic Company. These women divested themselves of much of their wearing apparel, which they tore into strips to make bandages, rolled up their sleeves and worked like trained nurses to alleviate those groaning with pain. Their noble work saved more than one life and many of the injured would have suffered very much more but for these brave hearts. Not once did they flinch though the sights they were compelled to witness were too much for even a man short of the heroic kind to face.

A special train had to be sent from Utica with doctors and medical assistants to attend to the injured. Those treated were in due time taken to Utica to the Faxton and St. Luke's Hospitals for further attention.

FULTON CHAIN STATION — THENDARA

John Brown, a merchant of Providence, R. I., in about 1800 acquired title to the vast tract of land in and about the territory between the Black River Valley and the Fulton Chain of Lakes. He attempted to settle this area with farming people but the effort was unsuccessful. The only result of this endeavor was the rough wagon road he had laid out for the 25 miles between Remsen and the Fulton Chain of Lakes.

About 1811 Brown's son-in-law, Charles Frederick Herreshoff conceived the idea that iron could be mined successfully in the area south of the lakes. He opened a mine near what was later the Fulton Chain Station and built a forge near the foot of the first of the Fulton Chain Lakes. This venture was a dismal failure and to such a degree that Herreshoff ended his life because of it.

Herreschoff had replaced the Remson road of John Brown with a rough, little developed road from Boonville to Fulton Chain via the Moose River Settlement. This was the Brown Tract Road and as bad as it was, it was the main road to the Central Adirondacks for over three quarters of a century.

The Herreshoff mansion had remained unoccupied for some years after the iron mine failure, when Otis Arnold from the Boonville area looked the house over and decided to move in. He and his family lived there for many years and the map-makers finally initiated the use of Arnold's or Arnold's Clearing as a name for the region in and about the present Thendara. The Arnold family, eventually, all departed but there were a few hardy souls who continued to live in the neighborhood.

Arnold's Clearing became the first objective of Dr. Webb's engineering staff working north from Remsen. It proved to be impossible to route the new railroad all the way to the foot of the lakes at the Old Forge so Fulton Chain Station was located in Arnold's Clearing. The first scheduled train from Herkimer arrived on July 1, 1892.

For many years forestry products were produced in great volume here and were a source of substantial freight business for the railroad. On July 28, 1918 a serious fire destroyed the lumber mill and yards of the Brown's Tract Lumber Company and set fire to the freight station and Van Auken Hotel, but they were saved.

The Fulton Chain Station was important as the entry point to the Adirondacks via the Fulton Chain of Lakes. The short railroad to Old Forge was soon constructed and the volume of passengers through the Fulton Chain Station grew rapidly. (See the preceding chapter covering the Fulton Chain Railroad.)

Effective June 27, 1920 the New York Central changed the name on the time tables from Fulton Chain Station to Thendara. This change was made because Lyon DeCamp, who developed much of the region, thought that Thendara was a distinctive name for the area. The name change also eliminated any confusion with other places in the state using the name of Fulton or its derivatives.

The passenger station at Thendara still exists. It has been thoroughly renovated for use by the Adirondack Railroad and it will be a wonderful showplace for the newly restored line.

SIXTY MULES WITH HARNESS

When the railroad reached Arnold's Clearing and the station named Fulton Chain, the first complete segment of the route was in service. Although the country south of Fulton Chain was more open than that to the north, several bridges of considerable size had to be built between Poland and Fulton Chain. We should not underestimate the great engineering ability exhibited in the construction of these bridges particularly in view of the lack of some of the 20th century construction equipment. It would be interesting to see an account of how some of the steel for the bridges was transported through the wilderness and by what means the trusses or girders were set up.

The equipment used in grading the roadbed was primitive and when Thomas B. Redmond, one of the sub-contractors, ran into severe difficulties his outfit was purchased by a David Bukofzer. A copy of the Bill of Sale dated February 5, 1892 is enlightening. There were about sixty mules listed and they were variously described as: mouse colored mare mule, sorrel colored mare mule, black horse mule, gray horse mule, etc. Other items listed were: five dump carts; five lumber wagons with neck yokes and whiffletrees; thirty sets of double harness; five pairs of heavy double bobs with racks, boxes, whiffletrees and neck yokes; fifteen dump carts; twenty cart harnesses; railroad jobbing tools and implements together with any other equipment on the railroad job on the Adirondack and St. Lawrence line. This was the type of equipment used to build the railroad through the North Woods.

PAY SCALES

The examination of an 1893 time book reveals several facts about the working conditions on the Mohawk and Malone. The book available was in use at Big Moose, N. Y. for Road Division 1, Section 14, Section Gang from May 1893 to October 1896. Two books were used in alternating months. As one month ended the time was certified by the foreman and sent to the roadmaster for examination and approval and then the book was sent to the paymaster.

The foreman was paid $50 per month for a ten hour day. Laborers and track walkers received $1.35 per day for ten hours. In September 1893 the hours were reduced to nine per day and the hourly rate of 13½¢ was used. During the winter months the force was reduced to the foreman and one or two laborers. In July 1894 the foreman was replaced and the new man received only $40 per month and the other employees were reduced to 12½¢ per hour.

It would appear that a seven day week was the usual thing all through the period from 1893 to 1896.

A schedule of pay rates for agents and operators for the year of 1909 was avilable for study. The agents at the smaller stations received from $40 to $50 per month while the agents at Tupper Lake Junction and Malone received $90 and $110. However, at the smaller stations the agents income was increased by commissions on express, Pullman sales, Western Union, etc. The operators general salary was nearly the same as the agent, running from $40 to $50 per month.

A copy of AGREEMENT BETWEEN THE NEW YORK CENTRAL RAILROAD COMPANY AND THE ORDER OF RAIL-ROAD TELEGRAPHERS dated 1924 gives us an insight on the wage scales of that period. The rate of pay had been changed to an hourly rate and presuming the agent worked full time his income was now up to between $115 and $125 monthly. This was for a six day, 48 hour week. Sunday time was compensated for in addition. This was the start of the period in which Adirondack Division stations were being closed and abandoned. Improved communications and better highways permitted agents to supervise car loadings at adjacent places resulting in several consolidations covering compatible situations.

RIGHT-OF-WAY CONDITIONS ARE UNUSUAL

The inspection report on the Adirondack Division for the Public Service Commission in 1910 is well worth considering:

> A large portion of the division lies in the Adirondack mountains and its maintenance presents some features not met with to such an extent on the other divisions of the New York Central and Hudson River Railroad: the destructive effect of violent intersecting torrential streams, often carrying large masses of heavy material; the risk of slides, both earth and rock, which in many cases cannot be avoided, as well as those peculiar to treacherous loose formations which, though not tending to slip in masses, are constantly crumbling away; and the obstructions caused by heavy snowfalls. The difficulties caused by snow are usually taken care of by snow-fences, and those due to the running water by more or less developed systems of main drainage. The keeping of waterways free of obstructions to the passage of water is, then, one of the chief points to be observed in order to afford proper protection to the roadbed of this division. The clearance of the waterways is generally well attended to, though in some instances obstructions in the form of boulders were noticed at up-stream ends of such openings. It may be remarked, in passing, that the best method of protection against snow-drifts is afforded by woods, and that all risk of the occurrence of snow-drifts may be disregarded in a well wooded country. It is, perhaps,

needless to call attention to the fact that the preservation of the forest growth in the direction of the prevailing winds will always accrue to the benefit of the railroad.

CLEARWATER-CARTER

Clearwater appeared in the time tables of 1899. It was the junction of the Adirondack & St. Lawrence line with the Raquette Lake Railway.

Effective with the June 23, 1912 timetable the New York Central substituted the name of Carter for Clearwater for this station.

A MISFORTUNE AT CLEARWATER

It has been noted that Ex. Governor John A. Dix had a considerable amount of timber in the area near Rondaxe which he transported to his mills at McKeever.

On June 24, 1901 brakeman Nelson Avery died of injuries he received when he fell from a log train near Clearwater. The train was enroute to McKeever and was being shifted at the switch when Avery, who was the head brakeman, fell under the cars suffering injuries which proved fatal later that day. The newspaper account says that Nelson Avery was a general favorite.

The Raquette Lake Railway reported that an employee had been killed in 1901 but no details were available from official sources and it is therefore possible that Nelson Avery could have been the Raquette Lake employee referred to in the Raquette Lake Railway statistical report.

THE KELLEY BROTHERS

In the Remsen section of this book, there is a discussion of the three Kelley brothers who were killed in accidents on the Mohawk & Malone. Nothing definite has been discovered concerning the death of Thomas Kelley near Carter about 1902. His death was referred to by both the UTICA STATURDAY GLOBE and the UTICA DAILY PRESS in their articles about the wreck at Remsen on July 3, 1924 when James Kelley was killed.

ANOTHER MISHAP AT CARTER

F. Ray McNight spoke about another wreck at Carter:

. . . during the winter of 1914–15 Father (Orville K. McKnight) was working the second trick at Carter and he has told me that one night an "ice extra" (back then train loads of ice were shipped out) came out of the Raquette Lake and ran into some cars standing on the south leg of the wye. The coal boards broke in the tender and the fireman was buried under about two tons of coal.

No other details of this mishap have come to light including how badly the fireman might have been injured.

LOGGING NEAR CARTER

Rev. Frank A. Reed in his LUMBERJACK SKY PILOT says that the territory north of Old Forge was "alive with logging operations." This was about 1917. George Vincent had nine camps around Carter and Big Moose for the International Paper Company. George Harvey acted as superintendent for Mr. Vincent with headquarters at Carter.

WRECK NEAR CARTER TIES UP TRAFFIC

The LAKE PLACID NEWS of January 10, 1936 gave the following account of the wreck near Carter:

Michael Kelly, New York Central railroad freight engineer who was pinned beneath an overturned car of coal Sunday night when his locomotive and 12 cars were derailed, died Monday in Utica. The wreck caused delay of the northbound train Monday, making arrival of morning mail and passengers late by several hours in reaching Lake Placid.

Kelly and Everett Montana, fireman, were both hospitalized after the wreck near Carter, seven miles north of Old Forge, but Montana was found to have suffered only a broken nose. He was thrown clear when the cars left the tracks.

Wrecking crews were at work Monday attempting to restore order to the scene made dangerous by the spilling of four cars of coal and two tank cars of gasoline. Extreme precautions were being taken. All trackage for a distance of several hundred feet was ripped up by the crash, the cause of which remained undetermined.

Rail passenger service was maintained by running southbound trains as far as Carter and then transferring passengers to busses which transported them to Thendara. Kelly and Montana were on the second engine of the freight which was going north. Their locomotive, separated from the head engine by five cars, overturned on its side and rolled

The depot at Fulton Chain about 1910. The Fulton Chain Railway ran in back of buildings pictured being barely visible in right corner past the shed. (McKnight collection)

Trains 2 & 3 meeting at Thendara in August 1948. The depot is in back of train No. 3. (Railway Historical Society of Northern New York)

Big Moose, road from Eagle Bay crossing in foreground, Depot in distance at center. Note the two sidings. (Harter collection)

The station at Big Moose in 1974 while being used as a loggers' camp. (Harter collection)

July 1979, repainting the grade crossing signal at Big Moose getting ready for operation by the Adirondack Railway. (Richard F. Palmer)

At Beaver River, looking south along the Adirondack Division in September 1962. In foreground is the location of the derailment of the Montreal Express in 1925. (Dorothy Somers)

The Norridgewock Hotel and the depot at Beaver River. The Norridgewock burned in 1914 and the station in 1940. The family of Station Agent Partridge lived in the apartment upstairs over the depot for many years. The spur line in foreground ran to a gravel pit. (Leon Johnson)

Successful hunters getting ready to board the train at Beaver River. This was an annual event for many men and they would take their deer home via the railroad. Circa 1920. (Leon Johnson)

Raising the locomotive from the Stillwater Reservoir following the derailment of the Montreal Express on April 12, 1925. (Photograph courtesy of The Adirondack Museum, Blue Mountain Lake, N.Y.

down a shallow embankment followed by the four coal cars, two tank cars, two box cars and a flat car.

Other cars, though derailed, remained upright and were but slightly damaged. Two coal cars, however, were described as "hopelessly wrecked." The box cars were splintered and the tank cars cut open.

HIGH POINT

Big Moose is the highest point above sea level on the Mohawk and Malone Railway. The elevation at the station is 2034 but the grade continues for a short distance north of the station before the descent starts towards the St. Lawrence River many miles to the north. The Big Moose Hill was the controlling grade for northbound trains and the train tonnage was figured so that the grade could be made without doubling the hill. Whether one or two locomotives were used depended on the number of cars and this was decided before the train left Utica. Southbound trains sometimes required a helper for the Big Moose Hill also and this was usually supplied at Tupper Lake.

AN UNSCHEDULED MEET NEAR BIG MOOSE

January 30, 1904 was the date that a northbound way freight and a southbound extra freight tried to use the same track at the same time two miles north of the Big Moose station. The northbound train consisted of locomotive No. 1666, ten loaded cars, one empty car and a caboose. The southbound train was made up of locomotives No. 1721 and No. 1755, fifteen loaded freight cars, twenty-four empties and a caboose.

The trains met on a reverse curve and neither engineman could have seen the approach of the other train until they were very close together. Locomotive No. 1666 was turned around, headed south, and practically demolished. Engine No. 1721 was badly damaged and engine No. 1755 climbed up on the tank of No. 1721. Eight freight cars were demolished and eight others had their ends broken in.

The northbound train was running downgrade at about 25 miles per hour. The southbound train was traveling at a somewhat lesser speed but the force of the collision was very great nevertheless.

Fortunately, in all this chaos, no one was injured very seriously and all recovered. The accident was blamed on the conductor and engineman of the northbound train and the Big Moose station agent-operator.

BIG MOOSE STATION

After using a makeshift set up for a few years, a new passenger station was erected at Big Moose in 1900. Patrons of hotels and camps on Big Moose Lake, Twitchell Lake and Dart's Lake used this station. Private cars were often switched to the Big Moose siding while their owners were staying in the neighborhood.

The station building at Big Moose is standing, is in apparently good repair and is utilized as a loggers' camp.

WOODS LAKE DERAILMENT

Northbound train No. 655 consisting of locomotive No. 12, baggage car, mail car, seven coaches and two sleepers were derailed and wrecked about one and one half miles south of Woods Lake on April 3, 1902. The train was traveling at a speed of 20 to 25 miles per hour. The engine ran about 250 feet after being derailed and went down an embankment and turned on its side. The baggage car ran about its length beyond the engine and on the opposite side of the track. Three coaches were tilted but not turned over. The mail car and a fourth coach were off the track but the rest of the train remained on the track.

BEAVER RIVER

In the early 1900's, the Black River Regulating Board decided to create the Stillwater Reservoir where water could be stored for paper mills, electrical plants, factories and farmers down in the big valley between Boonville and Lowville. About 10,000 acres of woodland were involved.

The first operation consisted of clearing the land. Beaver River suddenly became a boom town. In due time the cut-off was completed and the dam was erected. The flooding of this area soon resulted in a reservoir with 70 miles of shoreline.

HUNTING AND FISHING AT BEAVER RIVER

The only access to the hamlet of Beaver River was the Mohawk and Malone Railway. This area was a favorite with hunters and fishermen and they would come in by train and stay at one of the various camps or at Hotel Norridgewock.

The author's uncle, Richard Harter, was one of those hunters who made an annual trek to Beaver River in the deer season. This was in the late teens and early twenties. Uncle "Rich" would tell of the great days of hunting in the area and it seemed that every year he would be able to add something to his store of anecdotes of deer-hunting at Beaver River. For instance, one year he was unsuccessful in bagging a deer while on his usual hunting trip. The day came when he must return to Herkimer and he arrived at the Beaver River station a little ahead of train time. To spend this excess time he took a walk along the railroad with his rifle and, Yes! you guessed it! He got his deer. Dressing it out immediately he toted it over his shoulder to the station and checked it out as baggage and went merrily on his way home. You will note in one of the accompanying photos that the shipment of deer carcasses was a usual thing. There are at least a dozen in the picture.

There was also excellent fishing to be had in the area. Leon Johnson, whose father and brother were W. H. & C. B. Johnson, proprietors of the Beaver River Camps for several years in the teens and twenties gave me a booklet on the Beaver River Camps. They were located about 1¼ miles from the Beaver River station. The booklet states that 2869 brook and lake trout were taken by guests of the Camps in the 1912 season.

In 1905 the New York Central Lines "Four Track Series, No. 20, THE ADIRONDACK MOUNTAINS" listed the Elliott Camp, Hotel Norridgewock and Stanton Camps at Beaver River with a combined capacity of 150 guests. It is well to remember that all of the patrons had to arrive and depart by the Mohawk and Malone.

There was a school at Beaver River and the CONSER-VATIONIST for June–July 1965 says:

> A school was started, running from grades one to nine with one teacher. At one time, it was the smallest high school in the United States. Enrollment totaled one student! Most of the pupils were Partridges, belonging to the station master and his wife. Their nine children passed through Beaver River's tiny schoolhouse and all turned out to be good citizens.

In later years the scholars from Beaver River attended school at Old Forge and went back and forth by train at the start and end of the school week.

FIRE AT BEAVER RIVER

Up until May 18, 1914 there was only one hotel in Beaver River. After that there was none. On that Monday noon fire was discovered in the Hotel Norridgewock and the flames spread rapidly and the entire structure, which was of wood, was soon in ashes. The fire spread to the railroad station and it was only after a hard fight that the safety of that building was ensured. The nearby woods caught fire and they too were extinguished after a struggle. The four-story hotel accommodated about 100 persons.

There was no fire department in Beaver River and once the fire started there was no chance of saving the hotel so the efforts were confined to saving the railway station and the school house and devoting what attention they could to the woods fire. A fire train was sent in from Nehasane and that helped tremendously in bringing the fire under control.

THE MONTREAL EXPRESS GOES SWIMMING

In 1924 there was a change made in the level of the Stillwater Reservoir. When the surveyors found that the new level of the reservoir would reach the Mohawk and Malone tracks, officials of the Black River Regulating Board recommended that the tracks be rerouted around the end of the pond. This would also straighten out a curve in the road but the railraod questioned its right to go over the State land. It was therefore decided to raise the tracks.

At 12:24 A. M. on Sunday, April 12, 1925 southbound Montreal Express, train No. 4, was proceeding under a "Slow order" across the newly raised fill when the embankment gave way and the locomotive slid off the embankment into Stillwater Reservoir in about 15 feet of water. The mail and baggage cars followed the locomotive but were not totally submerged. About 200 feet of track was washed out. The UTICA OBSERVER-DISPATCH said:

> During construction of the dam and the reservoir the New York Central was compelled to raise its tracks, so that the tracks would be many feet above the water level. Although no definite statement was given out it is thought by employees of the construction company that the materials used to bolster the tracks were not of sufficient strength.

The TUPPER LAKE HERALD reported:

> The fill cut across a mere corner of the reservoir and it is subjected only to standing water. The banks when made first were covered with heavy granite riprap to prevent washing. The work was done in the winter which might have been the cause of its defective character.

Engineer Elmer D. Kane and Fireman Charles Armstrong received minor injuries. They were pinned in the cab at first but worked their way free with Armstrong, a strong swimmer, practically rescuing Kane. They were assisted from the tank of the engine to safety by a rope fashioned from Pullman sheets. Mail Clerk Daniel W. Bensley reached safety by the same method.

Immediate steps were taken to pull the undamaged cars back to Tupper Lake where they would be rerouted over the Ottawa Division and sent down the Rome, Watertown and Ogdensburg to Utica. The train was composed of two New York Pullmans, two Buffalo Pullmans, a day coach, a combination coach and baggage car, a mail car and a baggage car. There were no reports of passenger injuries.

The TUPPER LAKE HERALD described the repairs made and also the details on a second washout:

> A pile driver and a steam crane were run out to the middle of the fill to repair the damage and while working a second slide occurred leaving this heavy machinery marooned in the middle of the fill. The powerful vibrations of the pile driver no doubt contributed to the second slide.
>
> The work of repairing the damage proceeded night and day at the most rapid rate possible, and regular passenger service was restored Thursday morning, April 16. This was at least 14 hours sooner than was thought possible. No further trouble is anticipated. The track will be gradually raised. The problem of salvaging the engine, imbedded in mud and entirely submerged was postponed until the fill had been repaired.
>
> Gates of the reservoir were opened to prevent further filling and slides and to permit the work to proceed, thus temporarily delaying the complete filling of the great artificial pond built to store water for the industrial interests of the Black River into which Beaver River flows.

The restoration of service in four days and ten hours was an extremely well done piece of work. Fill had to be brought in from a long distance. The total length of both washouts was approximately 800 feet.

The locomotive was raised from its watery bed in the next few days and was sent to the shops for rebuilding. The fill was strengthened and brought up to the required height, service was restored to normal and once again the hazards of railroad life were a matter of history. The night that the Montreal Express went swimming at Beaver River was soon a nearly forgotten memory.

LOGGING TRAIN MISHAP

On February 1, 1930 John S. Kivlen, a brakeman, was killed just north of Beaver River. There was a slight downgrade for southbound trains at that point. The two locomotives on the southbound logging train had to stop at Beaver River for water. Rather than stop for water on the upgrade towards Big Moose, the train was brought to a halt on the descending grade and the engines cut off and run on to Beaver River. Coming back to pick up the train, there was a collision. It was believed that the angle cock on the stopped train had not been properly "fixed" and it allowed the part of the train left on the grade to start and roll on down the grade and eventually come into collision with the returning engines from Beaver River. The brakeman, John S. Kivlen, was killed in the collision and the accident was attributed to his failure to properly "fix" the angle cock on the train that was left on the downgrade.

BRANDRETH

On April 26, 1912 the TUPPER LAKE HERALD carried a long story on a huge lumber contract with operations being set up by the Mac-A-Mac Corporation in the Brandreth Tract located in Herkimer and Hamilton Counties near Beaver River. John N. MacDonald of Tupper Lake, a well known lumberman, was in charge of this mammoth undertaking. It was estimated that the operation would cover a period of twenty years. All of the soft woods with the exception of part of the hemlock and pines were to be shipped by rail to the St. Regis Paper Company. The balance was to be sawed up into lumber at a sawmill to be constructed.

On January 24, 1979 Rev. Frank A. Reed wrote in the BOONVILLE HERALD about this operation in the year 1917. Note the amount of railroad traffic that was handled.

> The operating company on the Brandreth Tract was the Mac-A-Mac Corporation comprised of John MacDonald, General E. A. MacAlpine and Judge Abbott. The corporation built a logging railroad from Brandreth station to Brandreth Lake, nine miles, with branches leading to other loading areas . . . a train of logs or more went out to Brandreth Station every day and from there on the New York Central to the paper mill.

AN ACCIDENT AT BRANDRETH

A New York Central brakeman, O. Charles Sowinski, suffered fatal injuries at Brandreth on February 17, 1947. He was assisting in moving freight cars from the siding at Brandreth when he slipped or was caught and thrown under the train. Train No. 4 was held at Tupper Lake until a doctor could be put aboard. The doctor attended to Sowinski who was placed aboard train No. 4 enroute to

Brandreth about 1913. Depot in background and spur line leaving off to the Mac-A-Mac lumbering operations at Brandreth Lake. (Harter collection)

Engine No. 1 of the Mac-A-Mac Corporation which operated out of Brandreth. No. 1 was a Heisler geared locomotive and engines of this type or similar ones were used on logging railroads. (Railway Historical Society of Northern New York)

TRAIN LEAVING JACK WORKS BRANDRETH LAKE NY

"Jack Works" is where logs which had been floated down by water were hauled up and loaded on cars for transport to the saw mills. Picture is of the Mac-A-Mac operation at Brandreth Lake. No. 1679 was a conventional New York Central locomotive. (Leon Johnson)

Near the Twitchell Creek bridge the northern and southern construction crews met and "drove the last spike" completing the construction of the Adirondack & St. Lawrence Railway on October 12, 1892. (Richard F. Palmer)

Utica. He was admitted to Faxton Hospital but did not survive his serious injuries.

ANOTHER SPRINGTIME DERAILMENT

About May 1967 a freight train was derailed between Nehasane and Brandreth. Five or six cars of pulpwood which were part of a 25 to 30 car train were derailed. The washout was probably due to a beaver dam backing water up against the roadbed and it finally gave way when the train was passing over it. The engine had got by the danger point and was not derailed but a couple hundred feet of track, more or less, was torn up. No one was injured.

NE-HA-SA-NE

In 1891 Dr. W. Seward Webb reportedly made purchases which totaled as much as 250,000 acres of Adirondack woodlands and lakes. Much of this land he later disposed of but he kept upwards of 115,000 acres for a private park or preserve. Later on, following controversy about the flooding of his lands in the building of Stillwater Reservoir, he transferred 75,000 acres to the State of New York. This left 40,000 acres in Nehasane Park.

Dr. Webb enclosed about 8,000 acres of Nehasane Park with a nine-foot wire fence and stocked it with big game in addition to the native deer. Attempts were made to stock black-tail deer, elk and moose. Eventually the forest fires of 1903 destroyed a portion of the fence and the experiment was abandoned.

However, Dr. Webb always enjoyed Nehasane and spent five weeks there shortly before his death in 1926. A full story of Nehasane is in itself a subject worthy of considerable treatment. The main lodge on Lake Lila, the forest conservation projects and the wild animal preserve are all deserving objects of description that exceed the scope of this book.

There were three stations in the Nehasane Park: Partlow which was used entirely for the lumbering operations; Keepawa which was used by those connected with the park operation; and Nehasane which was Dr. Webb's private station. No tickets were sold to, baggage checked for, or trains stopped at Nehasane without special orders directing that it be done. Nehasane was listed in the public time tables with the restriction (Private Station). Keepawa was not usually listed in public time tables, only in employee time tables.

The name appears in various forms, hyphenated or non-hyphenated, all capital letters or with capitals and lower case, viz:

NE-HA-SA-NE, Ne-Ha-Sa-Ne, NEHASANE, NeHaSaNe, Nehasane. There appears to be no consistency in which form is used. Charles H. Burnett says it is an Indian term meaning "beaver crossing river on log." Nehasane seems to be the most common form but that may be because it is the easiest to write.

In 1978 the State of New York was acquiring nearly 15,000 acres of the Nehasane Park land. In a rather complicated proceeding the transfer was being worked out with those of the Webb heirs who still had an interest in the property. The main lodge on Lake Lila is to be removed and the State will make no improvements on the 1409-acre lake.

Dr. Webb retained his interests in railroads long after he transferred the Mohawk & Malone to the New York Central and Hudson River. He was president and afterwards chairman of the board of the Rutland Railroad; director of the Lake Shore and Michigan Southern Railway; Director of the Pullman Company; director of the Central Vermont Railroad; director and president of the Fulton Chain Railroad and the Raquette Lake Transportation Company. He retired as president of the Wagner Palace Car Company in 1899. He was also active in and an officer of many other organizations not related to railroad affairs.

Dr. Webb was a great proponent of private cars and private trains. His private cars *ELLSMERE* and *SUNSHINE SPECIAL'S ELLSMERE* were magnificent cars with beautiful interiors of rare woods and sumptuous furnishings.

Some of the journeys arranged by Dr. Webb were considered to be highly newsworthy. One for example was the special train in March 1899 for a trip to Mexico. Because of the news that there were Vanderbilts on the train it was thought it might be worthy of attention of train robbers or other lawless characters. To insure the safety of the distinguished passengers an electric bell system was installed that would permit the engineer to instantly alert those aboard the cars in case the engineer encountered what he deemed to be a dangerous situation. The men in the party and the attendants were heavily armed.

Another tour was deemed the most costly and luxurious trip that ever crossed the continent. It was comprised of Dr. Webb's private car *ELLSMERE;* the private car *IDLER;* the new observation car *NA-HA-SA-NE;* the private compartment car *DAPHNE,* a private diner car and a combination car to carry the help and the baggage. The entire Webb family along with some relatives and friends made this trip. It was routed to southern California then north to Vancouver

Dr. Webb. NeHaSaNe Lodge at left and Lake Lila in background. (Photograph courtesy of The Adirondack Museum, Blue Mountain Lake, N.Y.)

Dr. William Seward Webb at NeHaSaNe Lodge. (Photograph courtesy of The Adirondack Museum, Blue Mountain Lake, N.Y.)

Station at Ne-ha-sa-ne in its prime days. (Photograph courtesy of The Adirondack Museum. Blue Mountain Lake, N.Y.)

The station at Ne-ha-sa-ne in July 1979. (Richard F. Palmer)

Dr. Webb's Ne-Ha-Sa-Ne Lodge in 1979. This is slated for demolishment by the State of New York Department of Environmental Conservation following the take-over of this part of the Webb estates. (Richard F. Palmer)

The abandoned station at Sabattis in July 1979. (Richard F. Palmer)

and east to the World's Fair in Chicago. The tour departed from Grand Central Station in New York on March 29, 1893 and arrived back in Niagara Falls on June 14, 1893. Leaving Buffalo on the same date, the train came east to Herkimer and then was taken to Nehasane for a few days before the party went on to the Shelburne Farms in Vermont. The train had gone approximately 13,000 miles on this trip.

In 1896 and 1897 the NEW YORK TIMES describes Dr. Webb's trip to the Jackson Hole Valley in Wyoming. Over 100 men were involved in these hunting trips and they were annual expeditions for Dr. Webb and his associates. Of course, the journey was made by private train.

Dr. Webb had set the style and it was widely copied. On April 9, 1905 the NEW YORK TIMES ran a story on "House Parties on Wheels Newest Fad Deluxe." It described the Webb special which was then in the far west and that train was even carrying an automobile in a baggage car attached to the train. These certainly were the great days of railroad travel.

Another memorable train was the special run from Chicago to Buffalo on October 24, 1895. Previous to this date a train in Great Britain had completed a special run from London to Aberdeen at an average speed of 63.93 m.p.h. The New York Central and Hudson River Railroad decided to try and best this record and on September 11, 1895 a special train of four cars covered the distance from New York to Buffalo, 436 miles, at the rate of 64.26 m.p.h. Immediately after this run, Dr. W. Seward Webb, a director of the Lake Shore and Michigan Southern, suggested that a trial run be made from Chicago to Buffalo over that line. A three car special train, including Dr. Webb's heavy *ELLSMERE*, was set up for October 24, 1895. The last section of the trip put into use a new 4-6-0, ten-wheeler, while the first parts of the trip had been drawn by 4-4-0's. The ten-wheeler saved the day and the average speed was 64.8 m.p.h. for the 510 miles. This outcome highly pleased Dr. Webb who was one of the passengers on the special run.

When Dr. Webb left the presidency of the Wagner Palace Car Company in 1899 he was presented a magnificent silver loving cup by the 4,000 employees of the company. It was 14 inches high and the design appropriately symbolized the evolution of the palace car building as developed while Dr. Webb was the president. This cup is now at the Shelburne Museum.

There could be no finer way to remember Dr. Webb's accomplishments than the words of Charles H. Burnett:

Dr. Webb was one of the handsomest and most charming men I have ever known. He possessed a fine mind in a stalwart body. He was highly educated, and his culture was inherited and natural. He was intensely alive, and always full of animation and interest.

He had a genius for friendship. He bound his friends and associates to him by countless acts of consideration and generosity. He was most loved and admired by those who knew him best. He was idolized by his servants and employees.

His executive ability was of a high order. He kept in close touch with a number of important enterprises of which he was the directing head — The Wagner Palace Car Company, the Adirondack & St. Lawrence Railroad, Shelburne Farms, Nehasane Park, the Sons of the American Revolution, the American Hackney Horse Society and many others — and still found time for travel and healthful recreation. He put the utmost energy into everything he undertook. He followed the old trackmen's motto, "Crowd your work or your work will crowd you." To be on his staff was like belonging to a fire department — the calls were sudden and frequent, and always interesting. Major Burns used to say, "He has a dozen irons in the fire, and they're all red hot."

He had a singularly open mind. He was always ready to exchange an old idea for a better one, and was glad to consider suggestions from all with whom he came in contact. At the same time he was tenacious of his opinions when they were once fully formed, and was capable of carrying through a project against all opposition.

He had vision, and in many respects was far ahead of his time. Those who ridiculed and derided his Adirondack railway lived to acknowledge that his foresight was greater than theirs.

He was absolutely honest in thought and deed. He was just and fair and liberal. He respected the rights of others. He never knowingly did an injury to a living soul. If he had any enemies he regarded them as friends who did not understand him.

His friends were legion and their loyalty was unswerving. His magnetism drew them, and his thoughtfulness and genuine regard held their affection and interest. He loved to be surrounded by guests; he was the soul of hospitality.

Hon. E. C. Smith, former Governor of Vermont and for many years president of the Central Vermont Railroad also spoke of Dr. Webb saying:

Aside from wonderful qualities of mind and heart he possessed an exquisite artistic sense. In whatever direction his mind turned, whether to railroading, farming, architecture, flowers, fruit or trees, or even to organizing an excursion to Europe, Alaska or the West, a breadth of vision and perfection of detail were immediately manifest, and the consummation was flawless.

When he passed away the homage of affection and sorrow was rendered by a real multitude, comprising the highest and the lowest, who had grown to love and respect him sincerely as a friend.

NE-HA-SA-NE INCIDENTS

The 1907 ANNUAL REPORT OF THE PUBLIC SERVICE COMMISSION, SECOND DISTRICT records a wreck on November 5, 1907 at Ne-Ha-Sa-Ne. The report merely stated that the accident was investigated but gives no details. No other information has become available about this accident.

An account of the terrible forest fires which threatened Nehasane are to be found in the chapter on forest fires.

One October afternoon in the 1960's the engine crew of a passing freight train was startled to see a man hanging from the front of the station at Nehasane. The train was stopped and the crew notified the caretaker at Nehasane Lodge, a quarter of a mile away, and he called the police. At the time the man was not identified and how he had reached this out of the way place was not immediately determined.

A VIOLENT HEAD-ON COLLISION

On March 22, 1953 a violent collision occurred at Nehasane. At 9:59 P. M. a southbound freight train consisting of 42 loaded cars and 49 empty cars stopped at the station to await a northbound freight train which had eight cars of logs and one freight car. The northbound train which arrived at 10:03 P. M. was supposed to have stopped and entered the siding but it failed to do so and struck the standing train head-on.

The logs were cascaded over the area and as they flew caught Fireman Raymond L. Goppert and Brakeman Stanley S. Sielagowski of the northbound train as they were trying to jump from the engine, causing fatal injuries to both of them. Engineer Morris L. Capstraw of this train remained in the cab and was pinned in. Engineer James Daly of the southbound train was also pinned in but Fireman Simeon Cossette tried to jump off and he was hit and severely injured by flying debris. The remaining five members of the two crews escaped serious injury.

A wrecking crane reached the scene Monday morning and by 8:00 P. M. had succeeded in clearing the siding. Additional track was laid and regular traffic resumed. Up until that time trains had been rerouted over the St. Lawrence Division.

The engineer of the northbound train, Morris Capstraw, later sued the New York Central, alleging negligence on the part of the railroad, claiming the brakes on his train failed to hold on the downgrade entering Nehasane.

LONG LAKE WEST — SABATTIS

Long Lake West was the station for Long Lake which was located to the east. Stage lines connected it with Little Tupper Lake, four miles away, and with Long Lake, eighteen miles away. From Long Lake other stage connections could be made for Blue Mountain Lake, twelve miles away and Newcomb, fourteen miles distant.

The chapter on Forest Fires describes the destruction by fire of the hamlet of Long Lake West in October 1903. One of the establishments destroyed was listed as a livery stable which had accommodations for 200 horses, so it is evident how extensive the stage business was. There was some lumbering activity near Long Lake West.

The New York Central started using the name Sabattis instead of Long Lake West on June 26, 1923.

RAQUETTE RIVER RAILROAD
LONG LAKE RAILROAD

The Raquette River Railroad Company was chartered on April 25, 1895. It was projected to run about 10 miles eastward from Tupper Lake, N. Y. to the hamlet of Axton, N. Y. Axton was an old lumber settlement on the Raquette River about 13 miles by river from Tupper Lake but considerably closer by air line.

This hamlet was originally called Axetown according to Richard F. Palmer in his article on Brooklyn Cooperage operations in the NORTHERN LOGGER for March 1971. It was here that the Cornell College of Forestry established its field headquarters.

No sooner had the Raquette River Railroad's request for a certificate been approved by the Board of Railroad Commissioners than another application for a certificate for the Long Lake Railroad was presented. This railroad was projected to run from Long Lake to the hamlet of Axton. The directors were the same as those of the Raquette River Railroad Company.

The Board of Railroad Commissioners took a dim view of this method of extending a railroad, stating that nothing had been said about extending the railroad from Axton to Long Lake when the first certificate was issued. The Commission wondered just what the ultimate destination of this railroad might be. Its decision was to deny

Derailment near Na-ha-sa-ne May 1967. Water had backed up against roadbed from Beaver dams. When it broke through the roadbed it washed out the tracks. General view of derailment. Train had several cars of pulpwood in its consist. (Gordon R. Lyons)

Wrecking crew at work near Sabattis following derailment of train No. 5 on April 4, 1963. (Albert A. Hess collection)

Wrecking crew at work near Sabattis following derailment of train No. 5 on April 4, 1963. (Albert A. Hess collection)

THE R.R. STATION, PIERCEFIELD N.Y. Photo by H.M.Beach

Piercefield station around 1915. (Photograph courtesy of The Adirondack Museum, Blue Mountain Lake, N.Y.)

the application as not of sufficient public necessity. However, the case was appealed and the Appellate Division of the Supreme Court directed that the certificate be granted.

After all this legal hassle apparently neither railroad was ever constructed. The Brooklyn Cooperage Company later on built a logging railroad in the general area north of Axton.

WASHOUT DERAILS THE MONTREAL EXPRESS NEAR SABATTIS

Train No. 4, the Monteal to New York Express, southbound, ran into a washout a half mile south of Sabattis, near Milepost 94 at 9:10 P. M. on September 30, 1924.

The engine, three Pullmans and the baggage car left the rails and at least one car turned over. It was reported that the fireman was the only person injured although the passengers got a bad shaking up in their berths.

ANOTHER WASHOUT NEAR SABATTIS

The engine and four cars of Train No. 165 from Utica to Lake Placid was derailed but remained upright near Sabattis after it came upon a 200 foot washout caused by flooding streams. This was on April 4, 1963. No one was injured but service on the line was delayed until repairs could be made.

STILL ANOTHER WASHOUT NEAR SABATTIS

By now the Adirondack Division was part of the Penn-Central and the weekly Utica to Saranac Lake freight train derailed Saturday, April 19, 1969 near Sabattis. Engineer Gordon Lyons had been warned to look out for washouts near milepost 94 but he had reduced speed earlier and was traveling about 31 miles per hour in a 35 m.p.h. section when the train hit the washout. The engine was derailed but not overturned and stopped right at milepost 93. Five cars of the fourteen car freight train jumped the tracks and a couple of these turned over on their side.

The crew said their radio was not able to transmit a report of the derailment and it was necessary to walk six miles to report the accident. In the two hour walk to get help eight or ten more washouts were observed.

In a newspaper account of the wreck the crewmen were reported as saying that, "Judging by past experience it should take about three to four weeks to clear the track." It was also reported that the railroad sent out scouting vehicles ahead of the weekly train but it was too far ahead with situations changing during the time between the scout's passing and the train.

A HEAD-ON MEET AT HORSESHOE POND STATION

For a concise report of this tragic accident we will turn to the account in the 1896 REPORT OF THE RAILROAD COMMIS-SIONERS:

> On the morning of December 20, 1895, Engineer Hart, with engine No. 547, and freight train was given orders to run from Tupper's Lake Junction to Fulton Chain at a rate of speed not exceeding 20 miles per hour. The train left Tupper's Lake Junction at 2:55 a.m. Passenger train No. 623, known as the Montreal Express, northbound was due at Horseshoe Pond station, where the freight train was expected to side track, at 3:56 a. m., thus allowing 56 minutes for the freight train to run 13.7 miles. Owing to slippery rails, heavy grades and inability to make steam, it became apparent when near Childwold station, 6.5 miles south of Tupper's Lake Junction that the freight train would not be able to reach Horseshoe Pond station in time. The conductor thereupon placed one of his brakemen on the engine and ordered the engineer to proceed with his engine southerly as far as it was safe, leave the brakeman to flag the approaching passenger train and then return with his engine to the freight train. In accordance with these instructions, the engineer proceeded toward Horseshoe Pond, near which point his engine collided with that of the Montreal Express, killing the engineers of both trains and Fireman Myers of the freight train, and seriously injuring Brakeman Gray of the freight train. An investigation of the accident was made by the Inspector of this Board, and from his report it appears that there was gross negligence on the part of the conductor in not holding the engine at Childwold Station where there was a siding, or on the part of the engineer in miscalculating the distance and time on his southbound run to flag the approaching train.

William C. Brassel was the engineer of the northbound express train and A. P. Lam was his fireman. John Hart was the engineer of the southbound train and John Myers was the fireman. Brassell, Hart and Myers were killed and the brakeman riding with Hart and Myers was seriously injured. Fireman Lam was able to jump from his engine prior to the crash and was not hurt. None of the passengers were injured either. Engineer Brassell had been in the employ of the Adirondack & St. Lawrence since it opened and prior to that he was employed on the narrow gauge road running from Herkimer to Poland.

LOGGING RAILROADS NEAR HORSE SHOE

A. Augustus Low had logging interests in the vicinity of Horse Shoe Station. He built a logging railroad eastward from there and this was known as the Wake Robin Railroad and was about four miles in length. To the westward, Low built another logging railroad known as the Maple Valley Railroad. Maps of the era show a third branch running to the northwest but this was probably only a spur from the Maple Valley Road. According to information available, the Low roads existed from 1897 until 1915.

HORSESHOE — HORSE SHOE — AMERICAN LEGION

The name of this station on the railroad appears as both Horseshoe and Horse Shoe without much regularity but the New York Central LIST OF PASSENGER STATIONS shows that the railroad changed the name from Horseshoe to Horse Shoe on June 1, 1931.

About 1922 the American Legion established its Veterans Mountain Camp on Big Tupper Lake on property formerly belonging to the Barbour estate. The only access to this camp at that time was by water from Tupper Lake Village or by a five mile dirt road from Horseshoe Station. Later another road was built into the camp from the Tupper Lake highway. However in 1947 the timetables of the New York Central begin to list this station as American Legion instead of Horse Shoe.

DERAILMENT NEAR CHILDWOLD

About 100 passengers were shaken up, some of them suffering slight bruises when the New York-Montreal express, northbound, was derailed near Childwold at 5:30 A. M. on July 4, 1922. Six of the twelve cars left the tracks, turning over on their sides. The two locomotives hauling the train dragged the cars several hundred feet before they, too, left the tracks.

Relief trains were rushed to the scene and the passengers were taken on to their destination and the officials estimated that regular traffic would be resumed on the following day.

PIERCEFIELD

From Piercefield Station a spur track ran into the little village of Piercefield where the Piercefield Paper and Manufacturing Company was located. Later this company was transferred to the International Paper Company. The transfer of cars from Piercefield Station to the mill at Piecefield was handled by the company who had a couple of locomotives that they used for this purpose. On occasion there was a derailment on this short line and the New York Central would go in and take care of the trouble. Like many of the other forestry product companies, operations were curtailed by the depression of the 1930's and they were eventually suspended.

On July 3, 1912 there was a serious head-on collison directly in front of the Piercefield Station. A work train consisting of an oil-burning locomotive and a caboose running at the speed of about 15 m.p.h. ran head-on into a northbound freight train which was standing in front of the Piercefield Station. The work train locomotive was demolished and the engineer, fireman and conductor were severely injured and were taken to a Utica hospital by the Montreal-Utica express a little later in the morning. The cause of the accident was attributed to the failure of the work train to take the siding at Piercefield.

CHRISTMAS TRAFFIC DISRUPTED

On December 24, 1943 a train of coaches being deadheaded south derailed between Tupper Lake and Piercefield. The train had come north to Lake Placid during the morning bringing vacationers and many servicemen who had obtained leave to visit their homes over the holiday. The cause of the accident was believed to be caused by upheaved tracks. The severe cold of the preceding week, it was thought, caused the ground under the tracks to crack and upheave, breaking the rails. Two empty sleeping cars, the engine and a passenger car left the rails but remained upright. No one was injured.

The disruption of train schedules was more than just an inconvenience because there were many servicemen on the following trains who were trying to get home for the holiday. In some cases the men had to return to their bases without seeing their families and in other cases they had to start back within hours from the time they had finally reached home. Passengers due in Lake Placid on Christmas morning spent their holiday the best they could on the train which did not reach its destination until 5 P. M.

UNDERWOOD

In 1899 the New York Central installed a sidetrack a little more than a mile south of Tupper Lake Junction and established a freight station known as Underwood. The station had been established because of a sawmill at that location. However, after 1911 there was no rail traffic from this point because the timber had been exhausted and the sawmill demolished. The station was discontinued in 1914.

On March 8, 1902 there was a serious accident at Underwood. An extra log train, southbound, consisted of locomotive No. 2027, 7 empty flat cars and a caboose with the locomotive attached to the front end of the train but running backwards. The train was running from 18 to 20 m.p.h. about a half mile south of Underwood at 8:15 A. M. when the tank of the locomotive left the rails followed by the engine and the train.

Fireman J. R. Cummings was fatally injured and Engineman D. Kelly had his foot and hip severely bruised. The investigation showed that the cause of the derailment was uneven track caused by upheaval from frost and that the tank of the locomotive got swaying and jumped the rails. The running of the locomotive backwards was the direct cause but it was felt that this practice could not be avoided at times when a train was sent out to handle log cars at various sidings and mills.

TUPPER LAKE

Tupper Lake became an important railroad terminal the day that John Hurd brought his first Northern Adirondack Railroad train into the settlement on July 1, 1890. The first effect was the touching off of a building boom. The transportation of materials by rail decreased the cost of all goods and business rapidly expanded.

When Dr. Webb started planning on a railroad through the wilderness he first had the idea that he could purchase the Hurd road and reach his desired destination of the St. Lawrence River and Canada by that route. In a much told story, Hurd reneged on a deal he had made with Dr. Webb and gave an option to another lumberman for a higher amount than the Webb deal would bring. When the new potential owner offered the road to Dr. Webb at a higher figure than he had paid, Dr. Webb rejected the whole proposition and made a decision to build through Tupper Lake to Malone by a new route.

Because the Adirondack and St. Lawrence approached the Tupper Lake area on the west side of Raquette Pond, no attempt was made to reach the settlement of Tupper Lake and the Northern Adirondack Railroad was crossed at a point that became known as Tupper Lake Junction. This was a little over a mile and one-half from the uptown part of Tupper Lake. The area near the junction became known as Faust.

Louis J. Simmons in his admirable MOSTLY SPRUCE AND HEMLOCK says:

> As the junction point for Hurd's and Webb's railroads, downtown Tupper was the Adirondacks' leading rail center, with a sprawling

freight shed and offices, extensive yard facilities, water tower and coal chutes, and a roundhouse where upwards of 40 men were kept busy on maintenance and service work on the locomotives operating over the Utica-Montreal and Tupper-Ottawa lines. Webb Row was built to accommodate the families of railroaders.

Downtown Tupper Lake was known as Faust for more than 60 years. By the mid-1890's enough people had settled there and were sufficiently weary of traveling uptown for their mail that they petitioned for and got their own postoffice. The selection of its name was left up to the Junction residents and the name selection was decided by lots drawn to decide who would name the new post office. Mrs. Frank Pelsue won the drawing and chose the name Faust, thereby ensuring confusion for a couple of generations of strangers who took Faust to be a separate village from Tupper Lake.

Faust post office existed from 1898 to 1959 when the present main post office was opened and the name has now fallen pretty much into disuse.

From the start of the construction of the Adirondack & St. Lawrence Railway, Tupper Lake Junction was a very busy place. Dr. Webb had a great mountain of materials sent into the Junction over the Northern Adirondack Railroad and construction crews worked both north and south from there.

The history of the Northern Adirondack Railroad, later the Northern New York Railroad, later the New York and Ottawa Railroad, later the New York and Ottawa Railway and the Ottawa and New York Railway are beyond the scope of this book. These railroads were taken over and operated by the New York Central and Hudson River Railroad as its Ottawa Division until May 6, 1937 when it was abandoned and dismantled. However, during the years of operation it contributed much traffic to the Adirondack Division, nearly all of which was forest products of some description.

The grade crossing of the two railroads at Tupper Lake Junction was protected by semaphore signals with neither division having precedence over the other.

The uptown station or what was originally the Northern Adirondack Railroad station on Martin Street existed until 1932 when it was destroyed by fire. All through the years there had been controversy between the New York Central and the Village concerning rail service between Tupper Lake Junction and uptown Tupper Lake a distance of 1.7 miles.

From time to time agitation developed over a new station to be built at the Junction but the proposition never gained sufficient momentum to be carried out. The reason for this is probably con-

Depot and yards at Tupper Lake. Grade crossing with New York & Ottawa Railroad just beyond station, governed by semaphores. Yards are visible to the left. Circa 1908. (Harter collection)

(Photograph courtesy of The Adirondack Museum, Blue Mountain Lake, N.Y.)

(Photograph courtesy of The Adirondack Museum, Blue Mountain Lake, N.Y.)

(Photograph courtesy of The Adirondack Museum, Blue Mountain Lake, N.Y.)

Train #2 swinging through Blue Rock Curve near milepost 125 during the summer of 1939. (McKnight collection)

Ernest W. Blue at milepost 129 near Saranac Inn about 1915. He was later a District Forest Ranger and Herkimer and Hamilton Counties were part of his district. (Mildred Blue collection)

Saranac Inn station in the summer and in the winter. This was a very busy station. (McKnight collection)

The daily meet between trains 2 and 11 at Saranac Inn. Train 11 is headed towards photographer. (McKnight Collection)

Train No. 2 with engine 4507 leaving Saranac Inn March 26, 1940. (McKnight collection)

Lake Clear Junction approximately 1913. Canopy was later removed. (McKnight collection)

tained in the following item from the TUPPER LAKE HERALD of
May 1, 1925.

> It was thought that with the building of a big Federal hospital that a
> new and modern depot would be built but it was announced that a
> decision had been made to improve the old station.
>
> One reason attributed to this was the New York Central was ready
> and glad to erect a new and up-to-date station for Tupper Lake, but as
> the railroad committee representing the village and railroad officials
> could not agree as to the location of the new station, the project was
> dropped for (maybe) another ten years.

A BIZARRE MISHAP

Probably the weirdest accident ever to occur to a passenger was
reported by the TUPPER LAKE HERALD on September 1, 1911.
The first part of the newspaper story described a circus that played at
Tupper Lake and then the story continued:

> A circus man walked into the Tupper Lake Junction station, severely
> injured, and said he had fallen through an open window of the Pullman
> sleeping car which carried the employees from Tupper Lake to Fulton
> Chain. It was a miracle that he didn't get killed. The train left the Junc-
> tion Friday morning, made up of 10 circus cars. It must have been
> going 30 miles an hour at the curve just this side of Underwood Bridge
> when the accident happened. When he rolled out he knew nothing of
> the accident until he regained consciousness some hours later. After
> receiving medical attention he was considered capable of taking care of
> himself and he was placed aboard a train and joined the show at Fulton
> Chain.

AN UNUSUAL COLLISION

In a terse item under JUNCTION NOTES, the TUPPER LAKE
HERALD reported on May 1, 1912 that while changing engines on
the southbound passenger train Saturday morning, the engine just
detached from the train collided with the engine about to be attached,
hitting the cab and pinning Engineer McGraw. After several mo-
ments one of the engines backed off and the injured man was placed
under a physician's care.

TUPPER LAKE ENGINEHOUSE SWEPT BY FIRE

A spectacular early morning fire on Sunday, May 20, 1951, completely destroyed the New York Central landmark along with a
locomotive. The TUPPER LAKE FREE PRESS AND HERALD on
May 24, described the conflagration:

Fire which broke out about 12:50 Sunday morning and raged unchecked for hours, completely destroyed the New York Central enginehouse here and left one oil-burning locomotive, engine No. 4452, a flame-seared wreck. The engine and building were valued at between $100,000 and $150,000.

Of the enginehouse, a Tupper Lake landmark for more than 50 years, nothing remained Sunday morning except the brick out-walls. Saved from destruction by the combined protection of the enginehouse brick wall and streams of water played on it by local firemen was the railroad office situated only about 8 feet from the blazing building. It contained railroad records and a few drums of oil and minor railroad equipment.

Cause of the blaze is not known. Elmer Farmer an enginehouse employee for the past 32 years said that oil-burning engine No. 4452 was fired up about 10:30 and shut off at 10:45. He signed off duty at 11:30 and left for home shortly before the fire broke out. A hostler, the only employee on duty was working in the boiler room when the flames flared along the roof above engine 4452 and began spreading rapidly. He had barely time to climb to the cab of engine No. 4587 and back it out to safety, blasting an alarm on its whistle. Driven off by the flames in an attempt to save the other locomotive he called local firemen and the uptown and Faust truck were on the scene within a few minutes.

By the time they arrived, however, the interior of the building was a mass of flames, and because of the imminent danger of an explosion of the burning locomotive's fuel tank or the large stationary boiler in the boiler room, no attempt was made to extinguish the engine house blaze.

Hundreds of cars filled every available space in the area as spectators thronged to the scene. Throughout the fire an eerie high-pitched whistling sound filled the night, which railroaders identified as steam escaping from the burning locomotive.

At 1:45 A.M. fire cascaded high into the night as an acetylene kit went up. At 1:55 A. M. the rescued engine, 4587, with Louis Malerba at the throttle made the first of several runs past the blazing enginehouse to shunt a coal-laden gondola and strings of loaded freight cars. Spectators distanced earlier in the blaze had begun to move in closer when a four inch pipe from the stationary boiler used to supply steam heat to the nearby railroad clubhouse and station burst at 2:15 A.M. and steam under 100 pounds pressure blasted out from the boiler room, again scattering onlookers.

At the height of the blaze fire roared more than 100 feet into the night sky from the tank of the burning locomotive and a pall of heavy smoke drifted sluggishly over downtown Tupper Lake.

Not only was the loss of the enginehouse a serious blow to the Junction but within two years the New York Central wrecking crew moved in and tore down the fire-blackened walls of the roundhouse and at the same time obliterated several other Junction buildings and structures. The Central was then in the process of changing from steam motive power to diesel. Therefore, the coaling plant, which towered 40 feet above the railroad yards, was no longer needed and was razed. It had been built in 1929 to replace the original inclined coal chute. At the same time two 10,000 gallon tanks which had held heavy bunker oil for the old steam locomotives were demolished and the huge 100,000 gallon capacity steel water tank near the railroad station was torn down.

TIE-UP ON THE CENTRAL

On February 10, 1952 the NEW YORK TIMES reported that a coupling snapped on a freight car sending three cars off the rails and tying up the Adirondack Division of the New York Central near Tupper Lake. One car was thrown about forty feet from the tracks and the other two went down an embankment just off the tracks. Railroad officials said that no one was reported hurt.

THE DOWNHILL SLIDE

Things were pretty much on the downhill at Tupper Lake from this time on. With the arrival of the diesels, engines were no longer serviced at the Junction and passenger service north of Lake Clear Junction was soon to be discontinued. The passenger trains for the few remaining years ran directly to Lake Placid. The freight service dwindled accordingly and the importance of Tupper Lake as a railroad terminal faded away.

LAKE CLEAR JUNCTION

This junction was the connecting point for the branch line to Saranac Lake and Lake Placid. In 1906 Paul Smith's electric railroad also was brought into Lake Clear Junction. This was a very busy place in its heyday. Some trains were run directly into Saranac Lake but usually the Pullmans were shifted from the Malone or Montreal express trains and run over the branch line to Lake Placid.

In 1960 the railroad north of Lake Clear Junction was abandoned and the rails were removed a couple of years later. The right-of-way was sold to the Niagara Mohawk Power Corporation. Thereafter all trains running north of Tupper Lake terminated in either Saranac Lake or Lake Placid.

Lake Clear Junction about 1910. The Montreal Express, engine No. 2004, is in the center. Saranac Lake local at left with engine No. 942. Paul Smith's Electric Railroad's car is at right. (Photograph courtesy of The Adirondack Museum, Blue Mountain Lake, N.Y.)

A busy minute at Lake Clear Junction on Sunday, April 4, 1938. Left to right, train No. 22 to Utica, No. 148 to Saranac Lake and No. 13 to Malone. (McKnight collection)

What the Adirondack Railway was faced with at Lake Clear Junction. Looking north from highway bridge and south from same vantage point on June 24, 1976. (Harter collection)

BALSAM?

Ernest W. Blue wrote an amusing little story which was published in the April–May 1961 issue of the CONSERVATIONIST:

> During the years 1912–1916, the State planted about five million trees on Forest Preserve land in the vicinity of Paul Smith's, Saranac Lake and Lake Placid. The trees were raised from the seed in a garden located in the hamlet of Lake Clear, lying between the highway and the railroad. These seed beds were fertilized with horse manure shipped from a livery stable in Montreal and loaded in gondola railroad cars which were unloaded at Lake Clear Junction. It smelled to Heaven! One fine spring day, when the New York train stopped to discharge passengers bound for Saranac Lake and Lake Placid, I was approached by a well dressed man with a worried look. He had apparently come to the Adirondacks for the first time to enjoy the scenery and the aroma of the Great North Woods. "Pardon Me," he said. "Do I smell balsam?"

LAKE CLEAR JUNCTION DEPOT

A new station was built at Lake Clear Junction in 1910. The original station was a two-storied building which was jacked up and moved about fifty feet north and made into a freight station. The station at Lake Clear Junction still exists.

GABRIELS

The hamlet of Gabriels sprang up with the building of the Adirondack & St. Lawrence Railway in 1892. Until Paul Smith built his electric railroad into Lake Clear Junction, Gabriels was listed on the timetables as Paul Smith's Station. The change to Gabriels was made in 1906.

After regular service was abandoned north of Lake Clear Junction all indications are that the rails to Gabriels were left in service for a year or two but the definite date of final removal of these rails has not been determined.

CHAMPAGNE

Reference has been made previously to the "Prohibition" amendment and one of the more humorous incidents resulting from this amendment occurred on September 4, 1931. The NEW YORK TIMES in an unusually facetious manner headlined the story:

> Train Hits Champagne Auto; Engine is Sent to Round House —

Gabriels, N. Y., Sept. 4 — A passenger train locomotive met a load of champagne today and had to go to the roundhouse to recover.

It happened this way:

A rum runner was hurrying with his carload of liquor; he reached a railroad crossing here at the same time a southbound passenger train started across; the locomotive was disabled; the driver jumped out and fled, and Federal agents seized what was left of the load.

DERAILMENT ON GOOD FRIDAY

Lake Kushaqua disappeared from the time tables at the end of 1953 and Stonywold was used in 1954.

On Good Friday, April 16, 1954 train No. 5 was northbound with three diesels on the head-end. The leading engine only was being used, the two following units were being deadheaded north to Malone for servicing. At a point about 3 miles north of Stonywold and a mile south of Loon Lake, the second and third diesel units left the track probably because the roadbed had softened up with the frost coming out. The lead unit was derailed but did not tip over as the other two units did. A mail car, an express car, a combination baggage and passenger car and a coach were derailed but no one was reported injured.

Six hundred feet of track were ripped up. The two units of the engines, the mail and express cars flopped on their sides but the other cars remained upright. There were about 20 passengers on the train.

Freight trains from Utica were rerouted through Watertown and cranes and work crews were sent from Watertown and Utica.

A REPEAT PERFORMANCE

The MALONE EVENING TELEGRAM gives the following account of the second derailment in the Stonywold area within two weeks:

Thirteen cars of a 95-car New York Central freight train were derailed last night on the Adirondack Division, about two and a half miles north of Stonywold. No one was injured but traffic on the line is blocked.

The accident is in the same vicinity where a passenger train derailed on April 16. No reason could be given for the derailment, which occurred about 10:30 P.M. The train was southbound and had left Malone shortly before the accident.

Telephone service in the area was disrupted when one or more of the derailed cars struck and toppled a pole near the tracks.

Engineer on the train was Ray Barber of Malone and Ernest W. Kelly was conductor.

The derailed cars were in the middle of the train and they remained upright. The front part of the train went on to Tupper Lake and the rear cars were removed to allow wrecking crews from Watertown and Utica to clear the tracks.

It is expected that passengers and baggage and express will be carried to Lake Clear this evening by motor car to catch the evening passenger train that is normally scheduled to leave here about 9 P. M. for Utica. The track is expected to be blocked until tomorrow.

MOUNTAIN VIEW

Orville K. McKnight went to Mountain View as the agent in 1916. He stayed there until the job was abolished in 1932. His son, F. Ray McNight was born in the agent's dwelling at the north of the station.

WATER OVER THE DAM At Mountain View in the Adirondacks by Dr. Floy S. Hyde contains an excellent story by Station Agent McKnight. The entire article is very interesting and is recommended as a source of information on this station.

MALONE

Malone's railroad history seems to be more or less predicated on the Rutland Railroad and its predecessors. Ironically it is the New York Central's line that is Malone's remaining rail link. The 10.3 mile Malone secondary line extends from Malone in Franklin County to the Canadian border, where it becomes a Conrail branch to Huntingdon, Quebec. This line has been operated by Conrail under contract, with state subsidy.

We have had an account in the chapter "South from Malone" as to how quickly the citizens of Malone responded when Dr. Webb told them that if they would subscribe $30,000 within a week, he would bring a railroad into Malone from the south. Both propositions were successful, we know.

Many people from Malone found work on the Mohawk and Malone Railway or Adirondack Division of the New York Central. Engine crews and train crews, maintenance workers and shop men all found employment. Several attained positions of importance and among those was Mr. E. R. Tattershall who became the Superintendent of Bridges and Buildings on the Division.

F. Ray McKnight was born in the agent's dwelling at Mountain View and he lived near and worked for the New York Central all of

Two 4-6-2's headed north on the fill separating Rainbow Lake from Lake Kushaqua. Lead engine is an oil burner and second engine is a coal burner. Circa 1951. (Bing Tormey photo, Michael Kudish collection)

Train No. 5 derailed near Stony-wold on Good Friday, April 16, 1954. The second and third diesel units were being transported to Malone for servicing and these units and the mail and baggage cars turned on their sides. (Albert A. Hess collection)

An early station at Mountain View. (Robideau Studio, Malone)

Southbound freight No. 90 with a pair of H5 class 2-8-2's charging through Mountain View on an August morning in 1916. F. Ray McKnight was born in station agent's cottage which is between the lead engine and the depot. (C. C. Badger, photo — McKnight collection)

On this postcard mailed in 1915, Ernest Blue had written, "Just landed here at Owls Head. Its an awful drear place." (Mildred Blue collection)

Train No. 5 leaving Mountain View for Malone about 1928 is reflected in the outlet of Mountain View Lake. (McKnight collection)

St. Lawrence and Adirondack engine No. 2, a 2-6-0, pushing Grand Trunk snowplow No. 15 north past the Malone Junction Depot. Note Signal device. When the red ball or red light was displayed, New York Central trains were clear to cross the Rutland Railroad. Circa 1894. One must admire the perseverance of the photographer in the foreground. (Helen Schermerhorn collection)

Snow plow train apparently getting turned around on the wye at Malone Junction before starting north. Circa 1894. (Helen Schermerhorn collection)

Station at Malone Junction. Rutland Railroad crosses from right to left. Circa 1909. (Harter collection)

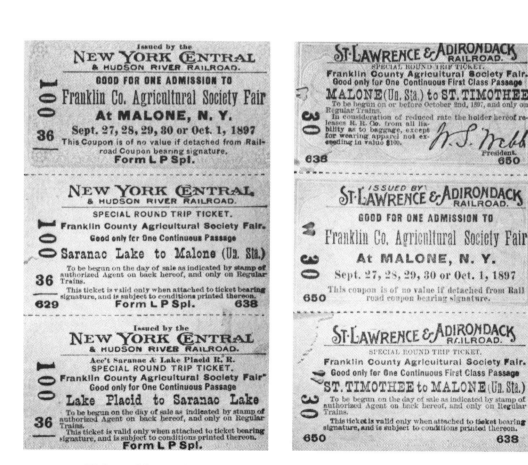

Tickets sold to Malone Fair which was held September 27 to October 1, 1897. (McKnight collection)

New York Central train headed south at Malone Junction. Circa 1910. (Harter collection)

Engine No. 1881, 2-8-2 Mikado, pulling freight train through the station, headed south. June 19, 1937. (McKnight collection)

Train No. 11 with engine 4471, 4-6-2 Pacific, northbound for Montreal. June 19, 1937. (McKnight collection)

Malone Junction station — November 1975. Rutland Railroad formerly crossed the New York Central in the foreground. (Harter collection)

A bird's eye view of the New York Central yards at Malone Junction on June 19, 1937. The picture was taken from the top of the coaling station and the view is to the south. In the distance the card shop is on the right and the engine house on the left. (McKnight collection)

Looking north from Malone Junction. Spur now serves the Malone concerns which still have freight service. The building still standing was the old freight station. There are a few hundred feet of track in back of the photographer and the tracks in the distance lead off to Huntingdon, Que. (Harter collection)

This chair came from the private car of Commodore Vanderbilt. It is now in the museum at Malone. (Franklin County Historical and Museum Society)

his working years. His description of Malone as a railroad town is an indispensable and highly informative part of this history.

Malone, of course, was quite a railroad town. It all started when the old Northern road, later the Ogdensburg and Lake Champlain, then the Rutland, built into Malone in 1850. They constructed a huge enginehouse, shops and other buildings of that nature. The village became a true "railroad center" when the Adirondack & St. Lawrence-St. Lawrence and Adirondack were built.

Several things dictated why the new roads were laid out as they were. One reason was having ample space to construct a yard. The area around downtown Malone lies in rather a broken terrain and by 1890 the town had grown enough so about the only available area left was to the east. Here, about a mile from the downtown area, Dr. Webb found the room he needed for a "terminal."

The Rutland Railroad was crossed at this point and the grade crossing was protected by a signal of the ball type. This governing signal was a red ball by day or a red light by night when displayed at the top of the signal mast indicated that the Adirondack Division trains had the right to cross, and when no signal was displayed from the top of the mast the Rutland trains had the right to cross. There was no interlocking in use.

The one building that has remained the same down through the years was the passenger station, located right at the southwest corner of the "diamond." Initially it was the headquarters for the Adirondack & St. Lawrence and for a few years the St. Lawrence & Adirondack. It housed the freight and passenger accounting departments and offices for the officials. It also contained the ticket office, waiting room and baggage room. It was the operational point for the railroad.

I understand that the first enginehouse was a wooden affair but I was never able to verify this. The brick enginehouse was started after the New York Central & Hudson River Railroad took over. This was a six stall house with stalls 78' long. Later 3 stalls 92' long were added and finally two of 115' length. It was the biggest on the division. Tupper Lake Junction had one of five stalls 72' long. There was a one stall 90' house at Saranac Yard. The Valleyfield house of two stalls 87' long. At Herkimer there was a four stall house of 78' length. The old New York and Ottawa house at Tupper Lake was a two stall affair of 70' and the one at Raquette Lake was a single stall of 64'. These were the enginehouses on the division about 1920.

At Malone was the only car repair shop. The division's only steam wrecking crane which had a forty ton capacity, was also stationed there and it had an assigned wrecking crew.

There was an ice house that would hold 630 tons of ice. Also a track scale rated at 150 tons was installed. There were times that these facilities were taxed to their maximum but they proved to be adequate.

I have drawn a map of the yard at Malone as near as I can remember

St. Lawrence and Adirondack wreck on the bridge over the Trout River near Constable. Circa 1897. (Robideau Studio, Malone)

A 2-8-0 crossing the Trout River on the Constable Hill about 1912. (C. C. Badger, photo. McKnight collection)

around 1935. My draftsmanship is far from excellent but this will give one a fair idea of the layout. The distance from one end of the yard to the other was about one mile. From Yard Limit to Yard Limit it was about two miles. To avoid having trains standing on the diamond while loading or unloading passengers, mail and head-end work; also to avoid blocking the Elm Street crossing, a canopy was constructed about fifty feet south of the station where all trains made their station stop. There were exceptions to this at times. Train No. 12 that departed south-bound late in the afternoon usually loaded on the north side of the diamond. Trains from Montreal usually discharged passengers on the north side.

Because Malone was an "International point" there was a lot of United States Customs and Immigration work. All less than carload lot freight was transferred moving into Canada and the freight house was a pretty active place. I have been told that at one time a track ran along the west side of the freight house and l.c.l. freight could be taken from the cars on the east side house track, trucked into the house, inspected, declared and then loaded into cars on the west side for Canada or for the Rutland.

As a rule, engines were very seldom turned on the wye at Malone. The turntable was of sufficient length to handle the largest engines working into Malone, the H-6a class 2-8-2's. In addition it was a rather involved operation to turn an engine on the wye in that permission had to be obtained from the Rutland dispatcher and it would be necessary to get the "block" from the Rutland operators at Malone and Chateaugay since the move required using the Rutland main. Chances are that a cost would also be involved.

In the last years of steam, the New York Central started using some L-1 and L-2 class 4-8-2's on UM-1 and WS-8 between Malone and the "Hojack" (St. Lawrence Division). These trains ran over the Rutland between Malone Junction and Norwood. The L-1 or L-2's would have to be turned on the wye because they were too long to fit the turntable.

After the Rutland closed their enginehouse at Malone, they transferred this operation to the New York Central house at the Junction, about 1933. However, the Rutland engines were only coaled, watered and sanded. They did not use the turntable nor the enginehouse. Whenever they had to turn an engine it was done on the wye but this was very seldom as the only engines they had in Malone were the yard engine and the one off the local freight.

Following the abandonment of both the Rutland and the Adirondack Division there is little left at Malone Junction except the passenger station. The yards have been totally dismantled along with all the structures. The lone track leading off to the north to Huntingdon is the sole indication of that great railroad center once located at Malone Junction.

CHAPTER XVI
The Later Years

THE HERKIMER, NEWPORT & POLAND
(EXTENSION) RAILWAY

With the decrease of rail passenger traffic affecting the Adirondack Division as it did all others, the passenger service between Herkimer and Remsen ended on October 31, 1934. A bus service had been running between Herkimer and Cold Brook, a mile east of Poland, for many years and this line had taken care of what passengers there were between the West Canada Valley points. Incidentally, the bus service only lasted a decade after the rail passenger service was discontinued.

Apparently the freight service north of Poland ended at the same time that the passenger service did as the April 28, 1935 Employees' Time Table lists freight only, as far as Poland. Following timetables show the road as existing between Poland and Remsen until 1945 when the termination is at Poland. This is in keeping with the reports that the rails gathered rust from 1934 until they were torn up during World War II. The great bridges at Gravesville and Trenton Falls were demolished at the same time.

Diesels took over the Herkimer-Poland run in the 1950's. Leo O'Connor wrote a delightful story for the UTICA OBSERVER-DISPATCH of September 22, 1957. Before we take our reluctant leave of the former Herkimer, Newport and Poland, let us enjoy Mr. O'Connor's nostalgic tale of the run to Poland and return in the early fall of 1957:

> Herkimer — Leaden skies held the promise of rain as No. 895 backed slowly toward the caboose near the Herkimer freight station at State and Caroline Streets. There was a chill in the air and the ripe richness of autumn. It was 7:10 A. M., EST.
>
> The caboose lurched slightly as the locomotive and six cars coupled on. Brakeman L. M. Manion checked the coupling and climbed into the caboose.

"We're just about ready to go, I guess," Conductor Daniel P. Breheny explained as he checked through his waybills for the last time before the start of the run.

The caboose lurched again and No. 895, the Herkimer-Poland traveling switcher was underway. It picked up speed as it rolled out of the yard toward the main New York Central line. "We have to travel a short distance on the main line to reach the Poland spur," explained Agent Griffin Bogan who was on the train. While the train rolled along, he pointed out the fact that it was carrying four carloads of green coffee for the Bordon Company Manufactured Products Division at Newport. "That's where they make the instant coffee," he said. "We're also carrying an empty car to be loaded with baled hair at the Haight and Company tannery in Middleville," Breheny put in.

Meanwhile the train was switching to the Poland Adirondack Division track. It moved cautiously along the right-of-way toward Middleville. Sitting in the elevated deck of the caboose, you got a breathtaking view of some of the finest scenery in the foot hills of the Adirondacks. The locomotive and caboose nearly met on several S-curves along the banks of the bubbling West Canda Creek.

On the other side, a herd of cows grazed near the river. One stood stolidly in the stream, placidly lapping at the water.

At Kast Bridge, the train slowed for the crossing. Along the Dugway, you felt as if you could reach out and touch the few cars moving along the highway near the track. Again the train moved along the banks of the West Canada. On a boulder in the river, an ingenious businessman had painted the name of his firm. "That creek really moves along," Bogan commented.

Middleville was a brief stop, Brakemen Manion and R. D. Jones, an extra man on the run for the day, left the caboose with Breheny, who supervised the switching operation. The empty car for baled hair was dropped off at the tannery storehouse. The men returned to the caboose after the train re-coupled.

Again it moved along the banks of the West Canada, past a calm area where the glass-like water reflected the brightening day. What seemed like minutes later, Newport came in sight. There the switching operation was more complicated. At the Borden Plant, the four cars of green coffee were dropped off together with two empties, one of which had been picked up in Middleville. Two loaded cars were picked up. They contained instant coffee for Cleveland and New York. While the train was switching the foreman of the shipping department talked to Breheny, asking for the additional car. Originally he had requested a single car. "We can do it," Breheny said.

Soon the train rolled on to Poland. There, it dropped two empties and took out two loads of lumber from the Northern Lumber Company plant. It was time for coffee, too, in Poland. Engineer H. D. Ruess reminisced as he sat waiting for his coffee and hamburg. "At one time, this was a pretty big railroad, you know," he said. "It went to Montreal by way of Malone. It also stopped at Trenton Chasm which used to be quite a tourist resort."

"As a matter of fact," Ruess continued, "they were running four passenger trains a day when I came on the Central in 1912. North of here, the old St. Lawrence and Adirondack took over at Malone for the trip to Montreal. They used to run a big milk train over this route," he concluded.

Soon it was time to return to the train — this time to ride in the cab of the locomotive for the return trip to Herkimer.

There was a crisp odor of autumn in the air as the sun broke through the clouds and the train rolled along the banks of the West Canada Creek. "There sure is some pretty country along this line," Fireman Andrew Kinsinger said as the train rolled between the ridges of the Adirondack's foothills. "Yes," Ruess agreed, "You should have a movie camera and take shots from start to finish."

Two and one-half miles south of Newport, the train halted for a picture. It stopped again at the Dugway where the track, train, highway and river were tucked into the billowing hills.

In Herkimer, the engine rolled into the Standard Furniture Company spur to pick up a loaded car, destined for San Francisco.

At 1:30 P.M. EST, the train pulled into the yards near the Herkimer freight house. Ruess shut off the diesel and climbed from the cab with his coat in his hand. The trip was over. He smiled with satisfaction as he walked into the freight house to check out before going home.

The Herkimer-Poland branch remained a part of the Adirondack Division and as the work force on the Utica-Malone-Montreal run decreased, the displaced men still had rights that could be used on the Herkimer Branch and several first line railroaders ended their railroad careers running between Herkimer and Poland.

On October 27, 1972 the Penn Central Transportation Company was petitioning the Public Service Commission for permission to abandon the railroad. Permission was not obtained that time but in May 1973 the track was damaged in a flash flood and it was never put back in operation.

Despite much talk and promise of help from politicians nothing ever resulted and in 1979 the dismantlement of the line started in earnest with the rails north from Herkimer being rapidly torn up.

The fate of the right-of-way has not been determined. Herkimer County officials have been investigating the possibility of turning it into a recreational trail, mainly for snowmobiles. However, the Penn Central has been asking $10,000 per mile and this is considered to be an exhorbitant figure and may prevent the recreational plans from being carried out. Not mentioned is the provision in many old deeds that when and if the property ceased to be used for railroad purposes the land would be subject to reversion.

THE MOHAWK AND MALONE RAILWAY
(The Adirondack Division of the New York Central Railroad)

It is always a sad time when one or another of our railroads withers away and finally comes to the end of its time. So it was with the Mohawk and Malone Railway which so gaily started out in life as the Adirondack & St. Lawrence Railway. By the time it was 30 years old the decline had set in. New and improved highways had siphoned off great blocks of passenger and freight business.

The days of ostentatious living were changing rapidly and private railroad cars were becoming passé. The forest lands under private ownership were being depleted. Mechanical refrigeration was replacing ice cut on the northern lakes. Internal combustion engines were replacing the horses in what was left of the lumbering industry and this did away with two sources of railroad traffic, hay for feed and the by-product of the stalls which was shipped out to be used as fertilizer. On the Herkimer-Remsen line the milk stations began to close as other methods of handling this product were developed.

Attempts were made to bolster passenger revenues with excursions, both to and from places on the Adirondack Division but these events could not match the day-to-day loss of revenue.

The number of daily trains was gradually decreased through the years. The Fulton Chain Railroad was shut down in 1932 and the Raquette Lake Railway in 1933. The Poland-Remsen line was closed down in 1934.

As might be expected World War II changed the pattern of the rail service on the Adirondack Division as it did to so many other railroads. However, following the war the lack of freight loadings again became critical. Heavy trains were sent north over the Adirondack Division but actually most of this traffic was diverted from the St. Lawrence Division and the New York Central gained nothing by the diversion except, in some cases, it improved the service to Canadian points. The route through the mountains was shorter but there were some heavier grades to be encountered. During the research work for this book, one engineer stated that he had started from Utica with five diesels units ahead of 193 cars. He arrived at Malone with 192, the drawbar of a car loaded with coal had pulled out on the Barneveld hill and had to be set out. The same engineer made the observation that one of the difficulties encountered in the later years was the increased length and carrying capacity of freight cars and this

ADIRONDACK DIVISION

SUBURBAN SERVICE — SERVICE SUBURBAIN

Corrected to June 16th, 1946 — Corrigé le 16 Juin 1946

TRAINS ARRIVE AT AND DEPART FROM WINDSOR STREET STATION, MONTREAL
L'ARRIVÉE ET LE DEPART DES TRAINS S'EFFECTUENT A LA GARE WINDSOR, MONTREAL

Read Down—Lire de Haut en Bas — SOUTHBOUND—VERS LE SUD   **Read Up—Lire de Bas en Haut — NORTHBOUND—VERS LE NORD**

2 Daily Quot.	26 Sat. Only	32 Daily ex Sun.	4 Daily Quot.	Miles from Montreal	STATIONS / GARES	25 Daily Ex Sun.	5 Daily Quot.	27 Sat. Only	31 Sun. Only	3 Daily Ex Sun.
AM	PM	PM	PM			AM	AM	PM	PM	PM
7 00	12 35	4 25	5 25	0	Lv. MONTREAL ... Que.	Ar. 7 20	11 00	3 22	7 40	9 00
h 7 06	h12 41	h 4 31	h 5 31	2	Westmount	i 7 12	i10 52	3 15	7 32	i 8 52
h 7 12	h12 47	h 4 37	h 5 37	5	Montreal West	i 7 05	10 45	3 08	7 25	8 45
h 7 17	12 52	4 42	5 42	8	LaSalle	6 55	10 38	3 05	7 18	8 38
h 7 20	12 55	4 45	5 45	9	Adirondack Jct.	6 45	10 35	3 03	7 15	8 35
h 7 22	f12 59	f 4 47	f 5 52	10	Kanawaki	6 42	.....	.....	.....	8 33
7 28	1 04	4 53	5 56	14	The Heights	6 36	f10 22	2 57	7 01	8 27
f 7 32	1 07	4 58	6 00	15	Chateauguay	6 31	10 17	2 54	6 56	8 24
7 36	1 11	5 03	6 04	17	Woodlands	6 27	10 11	2 49	6 51	8 18
f 7 41	f 1 17	5 08	6 07	19	Bellevue	6 24	10 06	2 44	6 46	8 13
7 46	1 22	5 13	6 11	20	Maple Grove	6 17	10 02	2 40	6 42	8 08
7 50	1 26	5 18	.....	22	Beauharnois	6 10	9 59	2 37	6 38	8 04
.....	f 1 32	5 24	f 6 23	26	Melocheville	6 03	9 45	2 30	6 31	7 56
8 02	f 1 39	5 31	g 6 30	31	St. Timothée	6 00	9 39	2 24	6 23	7 49
.....	1 43	5 38	6 36	34	Cecile Jct.	5 50	9 34	2 18	6 17	7 41
8 14	1 46	5 45	f 6 44	36	Valleyfield	5 38	9 22	2 15	6 14	7 37
8 22	1 50	5 54	6 48	41	St. Stanislas	.....	9 15	.....	6 04	7 26
8 35	.....	5 58	f 6 58	43	New Erin	.....	9 08	.....	5 55	7 21
8 43	.....	6 07	7 05	48	Huntingdon	f 5 10	8 43	.....	5 40	7 15
8 58	.....	6 15	.....	52	Athelstan	.....	8 16	.....	5 21	7 05
.....	.....	6 30	g 7 18	60	Constable ... N.Y.	.....	.....	.....	.....	6 30
9 10	.....	6 50	7 30	66	Ar. MALONE	Lv. 5 00	8 05	.....	5 10	6 19
AM	PM	PM	PM			AM	AM	PM	PM	PM

Buffet Lounge Car   **Trains Nos. 4 and 5**   **Between Malone and Montreal**

REFERENCE MARKS AND NOTES

Light face figures denote A.M. time; Dark face figures P.M. time.

a   Stop on signal Saturdays only.
f   Trains stop on signal to land or receive passengers.
g   Stop on signal Sunday only.
h   Stop to pick up passengers for south of Adirondack Jct. only.
i   Stop to land passengers from south of Adirondack Jct. only.

MARQUES ET NOTES EXPLICATIVES

Les chiffres légers indiquent A.M.; les chiffres noirs P.M.

a   Arrêtant sur signal les Samedis seulement.
f   Trains arrêtant au signal, pour faire descendre et laisser monter les passagers.
g   Arrêtant sur signal des Dimanches seulement.
h   Arrêtant pour laisser monter les passagers pour le Sud de la Jonction Adirondack seulement.
i   Arrêtant Sud de laisser descendre les passagers venant du Sud de la Jonction Adirondack.

The Suburban service between Malone and Montreal was discontinued in 1957.

NEW YORK STATE AREA TIME TABLE

IMPORTANT

Time shown herein is Daylight Saving Time

EFFECTIVE APRIL 26, 1964

NEW YORK—THENDARA—SARANAC LAKE—LAKE PLACID

Main Line

READ UP 6 Daily	READ UP 28	Main Line Nos.	Miles	READ DOWN 35 Daily	READ DOWN 27
AM				PM	
Ar 7 55		Lv NEW YORK (G.C.T.) (EDT)	0	10 40	
6 55		Lv Croton-Harmon	33	11 31	
6 05		Lv Poughkeepsie	73	12 27	
4 55		Ar ALBANY (EDT)	142	1 56	
	12 25	Lv BOSTON (South Station) (EDT)	0		3 15
	10 58	Lv Worcester	44		4 24
	9 42	Lv Springfield	98		5 35
	7 27	Ar ALBANY	200		7 55
	4 30	Lv ALBANY (EDT)	0		2 55
	3 00	Ar UTICA	95		4 34

Adirondack Division

READ UP 164 Daily	Adirondack Division Nos.	Miles	READ DOWN 165 Daily
AM			AM
Lv 2 10	Lv UTICA (EDT)	0	4 55
12 25	Ar Thendara (Old Forge)	52	6 32
11 57	Ar Big Moose	63	6 55
11 40	Ar Beaver River (NCB)	72	f 7 10
11 33	Ar Brandreth (NCB)	76	f 7 17
11 21	Ar Ne-ha-sa-ne (Priv. Sta.) (NCB)	82	f 7 29
11 08	Ar Sabattis (NCB)	89	f 7 45
10 57	Ar American Legion (NCB)	94	f 7 55
10 32	Ar Tupper Lake	108	8 30
9 50	Ar Lake Clear Jct. (Saranac Inn) (NCB)	126	9 05
9 33	Ar SARANAC LAKE	132	9 30
9 15	Ar Ray Brook (NCB)	136	f 9 40
9 00 PM	Ar LAKE PLACID (EDT)	142	10 0_ AM

Typical of the last time tables issued for the Adirondack Division was this one of April 26, 1964 showing trains 164 and 165. The scheduled time changed little through the years. In 1914 the time was 28 minutes more but probably this was all used in making the additional station stops that were made in those days, as well as handling mail and express.

caused difficulty with the sharp curves and the type of roadbed on the Adirondack Division.

In 1951 preparations were being made to completely change over from steam to diesel operation. The last steam locomotive to arrive at and depart from Malone was faithfully reported on by the UTICA OBSERVER DISPATCH on March 28, 1952.

> The final curtain on the use of the "Iron Horse" on the St. Lawrence and Adirondack Divisions of the New York Central has been rung down.
>
> The last steam locomotive to puff into Malone Junction from Montreal was No. 2971, pulling a fast freight.
>
> Trainmaster Jack Davis of the Adirondack Division said the departure of the 2971 from the North Country also means the end of the roundhouse at Malone Junction. The 2971 is the last of 25 steam locomotives that were operating out of Malone when the first diesel-electric unit was put into service about three years ago. Since then diesel units have increased steadily and by so doing have gradually edged the steam locomotives out of the picture. Diesels replaced the steamers on the Utica to Lake Placid runs about six months ago. The next roundhouse vacated of steamers was at Tupper Lake, and now the Malone-Montreal Division becomes totally dieselized.
>
> Today two more steam units, small surplus engines, left the Malone Junction yards, probably enroute to scrap yards in West Albany. The big L-2's (2971 class) are being shunted to other divisions, possibly the Michigan Central.
>
> The Mohawk and Hudson Divisions of the New York Central are practically 90 percent dieselized with Utica established as one of the principal diesel servicing installations.
>
> Diesel switching units have replaced all of the steam "yard goats" in the Utica yards, and all freight trains operating from the Utica transfer terminal are now being pulled by diesel units.

In the NEW YORK CENTRAL HEADLIGHT of October 1952 an announcement was made that the St. Lawrence and Adirondack Divisions were operating entirely on diesel motive power, making it unnecessary to maintain coal servicing facilities.

Passenger service revenue had continued to decline and by September 1952 the New York Central was requesting permission from the Public Service Commission to discontinue the daylight train to Lake Placid. The request was withdrawn but by 1953 it was again active but the Public Service Commission ordered the railroad to continue the two daily trains to Lake Placid.

In August 1957 the Public Service Commission ordered the New York Central to continue passenger service between Lake Clear Junction and Malone for at least 90 days but December 13, 1957 was the last day trains No. 5 & 4 operated north of Lake Clear Junction. The Public Service Commission pointed out that the number of men in the train crews outnumbered the passengers.

In 1959 the New York Central was again requesting permission to drop Lake Placid passenger service. Again permission was refused. The Central persisted and in December 1960 it was again petitioning for permission to end passenger service on its St. Lawrence and Adirondack Divisions. "Beeliners" or Budd cars were now being used but they were not able to overcome what the New York Central termed as "huge losses." The road north of Lake Clear Junction had been entirely discontinued by this time.

There was a constant series of petitions to the Public Service Commission, hearings and findings for the next few years but finally in 1965 the New York Central received permission to discontinue passenger service to Lake Placid. The effective date was April 24th and this in effect was to discontinue all passenger service on the division.

Owen VanBuskirk wrote the railroad's epitaph in the April 24, 1965 UTICA OBSERVER DISPATCH:

> Passengers bound for Minnehaha, Big Moose, Beaver River or Horse Shoe on the New York Central run to Lake Placid couldn't afford to miss the train today. There wouldn't be another.
>
> There'll be trains. They'll still pull out of the Utica yards and tunnel along the leafy route through the Adirondacks. But they'll not be the same. The freights won't be met as passenger trains once were, by stages and private hotel limousines. There won't be holiday-bound families on them, filling baggage cars with the paraphernalia for a season in the mountains.
>
> Despite the once-great popularity of the run, and the nostalgia, it was ended at 5 A. M. today when engine No. 165 left Utica for the five-hour trip. The decision to end service was reached by the Central when patronage declined to what they called impossible levels.
>
> Sapped of its riders by the automobile, hard roads and even the plane, the line that once knew private cars and prestigious sleepers was reduced to carrying four or five riders a day.

On September 25, 1965 the Central New York Chapter of the National Railway Historical Society ran a memorable Fan Trip from Utica to Tupper Lake. The special trip actually started in Syracuse and ran to Utica but the Remsen-Tupper Lake trip was the real treat. About 950 enthusiasts made the trip on a train consisting of 16 coaches, 2 baggage cars and 2 gondolas drawn by 3 EMD diesel locomotives.

320 Miles, Round Trip

DIESEL POWERED, Air Conditioned Train.

EXCURSION TRAIN!

ALL DAY, SAT., SEPT. 25, 1965

ADIRONDACK FALL COLOR TRIP

FROM SYRACUSE, N.Y., AND UTICA, N.Y., TO TUPPER LAKE & RETURN

Bring Your Camera!

NUMEROUS PHOTO STOPS WILL BE MADE AT SCENIC POINTS.

TWO OPEN GONDOLA CARS WILL BE PROVIDED FOR YOUR **MAXIMUM ENJOYMENT** OF THE **BEAUTIFUL ADIRONDACK FALL SCENERY.** THIS WILL BE THE LAST PASSENGER TRAIN TO RUN ON THE ADIRONDACK LINE

BRING YOUR OWN PICNIC LUNCH

AND SUPPER

OR BUY SANDWICHES AND SOFT

DRINKS AVAILABLE ON TRAIN.

TRAIN LEAVES EAST SYRACUSE STA. **9:00 a.m.** LEAVES UTICA: **10:10 a.m.**

FARE

ADULTS: $9.50

CHILDREN 5 - 11 yrs. **$4.75**

$1. Surcharge on Tickets Purchased After Sept. 19.

FOR TICKETS AND INFORMATION, CONTACT: N. R. H. S. c/o MR. HOWARD WALKER 109 CAMILLUS PARK DRIVE CAMILLUS, NEW YORK (Phone: 672 - 3443)

OR: GRUBE'S HOBBY SHOP, MILTON AVE., SOLVAY, N.Y.

OR: TICKET AGENT, NEW YORK CENTRAL R.R., EAST SYRACUSE, N.Y. OR UTICA, N.Y.

TRIP SPONSORED BY CENTRAL NEW YORK CHAPTER, NATIONAL RAILWAY HISTORICAL SOCIETY

ANTIQUE 2-8-0 TYPE STEAM LOCOMOTIVE WILL BE ON DISPLAY FOR PASSENGERS AT TUPPER LAKE.

TRAIN WILL RUN VIA MAIN LINE TO UTICA AND VIA ADIRONDACK BRANCH TO OLD FORGE, BIG MOOSE, NE-HA-SA-NE, SABATTIS, TUPPER LAKE AND RETURN TO UTICA & SYRACUSE.

ORDER BLANK

Please send me the following Excursion Tickets for the **Sept. 25, 1965** fan trip.

.... Adults at **$9.50** each.

.... Children 5 - 11 yrs. at **$4.75** each.

$.............. Payment is enclosed.

I will board the train at: ☐ E. Syracuse. (PLEASE CHECK ONE) ☐ Utica.

Name..................................

Street..................................

City & State..........................

TOTAL REMITTANCE REQUIRED!

POSTER DESIGNED BY W. A. MORRISON

The last scheduled passenger train on the Adirondack Division of the New York Central was the fan trip sponsored by the Central New York Chapter of the National Railway Historical Society on September 25, 1965. It was a sell-out!

And then in 1971 it started all over again. By now the Penn Central Transportation Company had taken over the New York Central System but the pattern was the same. The railroad was petitioning the Public Service Commission to permit abandonment of the 118 mile Remsen-Lake Placid rail line. Service was down to about one train a week and then a washout occurred and service was halted.

On August 19, 1972 the Interstate Commerce Commission issued an order that allowed the Penn Central Company to abandon the Remsen-Lake Placid line. The washout on the line was not repaired and what rolling stock remained on the north end was eventually taken out over the state highway on heavy trailers. It was duly reported that more than one motorist got quite a thrill when meeting a railroad box car coming up the highway.

This for all intents and purposes was the end of the operation of the Mohawk and Malone Railway except for the Herkimer-Poland line which was still in operation.

THE ADIRONDACK RAILWAY

In 1973 the voters of the State of New York defeated a $3.5 billion transportation bond issue. Part of this was to have been used to purchase the Remsen-Lake Placid line and restore freight service on it. Failure of the bond issue proposition apparently doomed the railroad and the Penn Central Transportation Company awarded contracts for dismantling the rails and bridges on the Lake Placid line.

Considerable litigation developed when efforts were made to preserve the road, at least temporarily. A recital of all the legal actions that took place in the next year or two would hardly prove of interest to the average reader.

In January 1974 the newspapers were reporting that the dismantling was taking place as weather permitted. In April 1974 Governor Malcolm Wilson ordered state acquisition of the abandoned rail line in the first use of funds provided in a new $670 million mass transportation package. This effectively stopped the salvage by the Penn Central Company. Some rails were removed, especially in the Raybrook area but not a great deal of dismantlement had taken place.

A physical inspection by State Department of Transportation officials was made in the Spring of 1974. The matter of the State of New York taking over the railroad returned to the courts many times in the next months and years but it was definitely established that the road was under the control of New York State and would be paid for at a price to be finally determined at a latter date. Perhaps the complications of all the legal difficulties could be explained by the quotation from the SYRACUSE HERALD AMERICAN on August 18, 1974:

> The Remsen-Lake Placid line involves a complex legal situation since the rails and right-of-way the state wants to purchase are owned by the bankrupt Penn Central, under the control of Federal Courts in Pennsylvania.

During the years 1974–76 the State Department of Transportation had the matter of re-opening the Remsen-Lake Placid line under study.

In March 1975 the State Department of Transportation released a thirty page REPORT ON THE RESTORATION OF RAIL SERVICE ON THE ABANDONED RAIL RIGHT-OF-WAY BETWEEN REMSEN, ONEIDA COUNTY, AND LAKE PLACID, ESSEX COUNTY. Parts of the summary of this report are quoted:

> Because the abandoned rail right-of-way between Remsen and Lake Placid is a unique and valuable resource, the decision has been made to acquire the right-of-way and to determine its best use. The option of restoring conventional rail service was given particular attention and was closely examined to determine its economic ramifications. . . . Having now actually acquired the right-of-way and forestalled any option for other use of that right-of-way being preempted as a result of a precipitous liquidation by the Penn Central, the State has assured the preservation of the land and trackage until a decision on use is made. The opportunity now exists for all responsible interests to develop schemes for the use of the right-of-way which are beneficial to the public interest.

In April 1975 the State Department of Transportation issued a SPECIAL REPORT ON RAILROADS and made the statement:

> The Department of Transportation has moved swiftly to preserve an essential transportation corridor between Remsen and Lake Placid in the heart of the Adirondack Park. The State took title to the right-of-way early in February.
>
> This 120-mile corridor, because of its location and length, provides various opportunities for present or future public use. Acting now to preserve this corridor will make it possible for the State to examine all possibilities for further development in the area.
>
> The importance of decisions to be made is seen in the fact that a 30-member Advisory Committee, representing various interests, has been appointed to assist the Department in studying and recommending future steps to be taken.

In July 1975, the Technical Assistance Center, State University of New York, Plattsburgh, N. Y., preepared A STUDY OF THE ECO-

NOMIC FEASIBILITY AND ECONOMIC IMPACT OF RESTOR-
ING SELECTED SERVICES ON THE REMSEN-LAKE PLACID
RAILROAD. The 4th paragraph of the summary of this report is
quoted:

> The report also concludes that the railroad is not economically viable
> without excursion and winter charter service to sustain a large part of
> the maintenance of way. . . . In fact, no conventional freight or sched-
> uled passenger service can support the burden of expenses and remain
> viable. However, break-even operation can be achieved with both if the
> railroad is operated for excursion and charter trains.

Although seemingly up against a stone wall at times, James Ellis
of Tupper Lake, Chairman of the Remsen-Lake Placid Advisory
Committee and his associates persisted in their endeavor to see the
railroad rehabilitated.

In October 1976 the SYRACUSE HERALD JOURNAL stated:

> James Ellis and some other Adirondack residents are joining with the
> owners of a Pennsylvania-based railroad firm to form the Adirondack
> Railroad Corporation to operate the proposed line.

On February 25, 1977, Lt. Gov. Mary Anne Krupsak announced
that rail service between Utica and Lake Placid could be restored.
Under contract with the State, the newly formed Adirondack Railway
Corporation was to make the repairs to the rail line. A lease arrangement would then enable the railway to run recreational trains on the
Utica and Lake Placid route. The state's portion of the project was to
cost $1.721 millions, Krupsak said.

Frank Menair, president of the Adirondack Railway Corporation
said at the Krupsak press conference that two types of trains would be
used. His line will run recreational trains based on old-time steam
engines and trains using up-to-date modern equipment.

It was hoped to have the newly restored railroad in operation by
the fall of 1977 but the amount of work involved prevented this.

The Union Station at Utica also underwent renovation and it is
hoped that this work will be completed at the time that the Adirondack Railway Corporation is opened for business.

Work on restoring the line was resumed in the Spring of 1978
and continued throughout the year when weather permitted. By the
Summer of 1979 the railroad was in condition so that work trains
could be run to Lake Placid. It is planned that the Adirondack Railway will be opened to the public at the end of September 1979. This
will give the employees and the railroad itself a chance to settle down

and become accustomed to steady traffic prior to the demands expected to be made by the 1980 Olympics at Lake Placid.

Isn't that a nice way to end a book on the history of a railroad? I think so.

Henry A. Harter
Hamilton, N. Y. July 1979

CHAPTER XVII

An Album of

Adirondack Division pictures
from the collection of F. Ray McKnight

Eastbound Rutland No. 8, a milk train, hauled by Rutland No. 48, 4-6-0, crossing over New York Central track at Malone Junction, July 10, 1935. (McKnight collection)

NYC No. 1920, 2-6-0 Mogul, at Tupper Lake, August 7, 1937. (McKnight collection)

NYC 1818, 2-8-2 Mikado, at Malone, December 5, 1936. (McKnight collection)

NYC 5192, 2-8-2 Mikado at Malone, July 1, 1935. This engine was later renumbered 1892. (McKnight collection)

NYC 1821 was one of the heavy United States Rail Administration 2-8-2 Mikados built in 1918 while the USRA controlled the nation's railroads. This was a very successful type of engine and was in service many years. On turntable at Malone, April 20, 1937. (McKnight collection)

Inspection engine "Mohawk" No. 29, was a familiar sight on the Adirondack Division for many years. Built in 1892 it was retired in 1925. Photo date circa 1910. (McKnight collection)

NYC 1881, 2-8-2, coming into Malone yards on June 19, 1937. (McKnight collection)

Engine 876, 4-6-0 Ten-wheeler, on the Malone turntable April 25, 1937. This class of engine was usually used on the Valleyfield-Montreal suburban trains. (McKnight collection)

This photo of 2088 was taken just north of the Rutland crossing at Malone Junction. The ten-wheelers were the heaviest passenger engines north of Malone for years due to a weight restriction over the St. Lawrence River at Lacine. C. C. Badger took the picture at Malone in 1916. (McKnight collection)

Pacific 4-6-2, K11c class, at Lake Clear Junction, July 30, 1938. (McKnight collection)

Oil-burning No. 3092 at the oil storage tanks in Malone yards on July 1, 1935. (McKnight collection)

NYC 3057, Class K11c Pacific, at Malone on January 22, 1936. The only K11 on the Adirondack Division with a booster exhaust in front of the stack. (McKnight collection)

No. 3121, Pacific type, standing south of Malone Junction station on December 23, 1935. (McKnight collection)

Engine 4479, formerly No. 3079, Pacific type 4-6-2, was the first engine in the United States to be equipped with the Franklin truck booster for added traction force to start heavy trains. At Malone Junction on April 24, 1938. (McKnight collection)

At the oil storage tanks in Malone Junction on May 2, 1937, No. 4570 has just been refueled. (McKnight collection)

Train No. 1 approaching Mountain View about 1923. (McKnight collection)

Of this photo Ray McKnight said, "By the dawn's early light, third section of train No. 5 with 8 cars, bringing in the crowd for Labor Day Weekend on Saturday, September 4, 1937." Passing through Saranac Inn, the first section of No. 5 had double-headed through with 14 Pullmans. (McKnight collection)

Train No. 2 coming into Thendara, with engine 4483 hauling express, mail, baggage & smoker, 2 coaches, 2 chair cars. Circa March 1952. (McKnight collection)

*No. 4566 with 1 coach and 6 sleepers headed for Lake
Placid. An extra train, passing through Saranac Inn
on August 20, 1938.* (McKnight collection)

*Train No. 17 at Saranac Inn, with engine No. 4570 headed north with 7
cars on August 20, 1938.* (McKnight collection)

APPENDIX I
Component Companies

ORGANIZATION OF COMPANIES

Several companies by name or action were involved in the construction of the railroad through to Montreal. Charles H. Burnett makes mention of this by stating:

> A number of companies were organized, covering different portions of the line.

In one of the appendices of CONQUERING THE WILDERNESS he gives a "list of Officers and Supervisory Personnel of Adirondack Enterprises." This list contains only "Adirondack & St. Lawrence Railroad 1891–1892" and "St. Lawrence and Adirondack Railway 1895–1896."

THE NEW YORK TIMES published an article on May 18, 1891 entitled THE ADIRONDACK RAILROAD. This article said in part:

> So many companies were found to be necessary because as surveys were made routes were changed, and original charters added to cover all of the territory through which it is now intended to pass.

It does appear that some of the companies seem to overlap each other and either of the two explanations above would seem to adequately explain the reasons for their organization. It should also be noted that there has been a tendency by various writers not to be too careful in the correct use of railroad or railway when referring to the corporate name of the various companies. A brief history of the various companies follows.

THE HERKIMER AND TRENTON RAILROAD
This company was formed in 1836 and a survey made in 1837. There was no construction.

THE HERKIMER, POLAND AND JOCK'S LAKE RAILROAD
The NEW YORK TIMES reported on September 17, 1890 that this company was to take over the Herkimer, Newport and Poland Narrow Gauge Railway on October 1, 1890. No further mention of this company has been found.

THE HERKIMER, NEWPORT & POLAND
NARROW GAUGE RAILWAY

Chartered on June 29, 1880, construction was completed to Poland in 1882. This was reincorporated as the Herkimer, Newport and Poland Railway Company and changed to standard gauge on March 16, 1891. It was also, on April 30, 1891 consolidated with the Mohawk Valley and Northern Railway Company under the latter name.

THE HERKIMER, NEWPORT AND POLAND RAILWAY

On March 16, 1891 the change of name from Herkimer, Newport and Poland Narrow Gauge Railway Company to the Herkimer, Newport and Poland Railway Company was authorized by passage of Chapter 78 of the Laws of 1891. The change of gauge from 3 feet 6 inches to 4 feet 8½ inches was authorized also as this was the reason for the change of name. In 1892 this company was one of those consolidated into the Mohawk and Malone Railway Company.

THE HERKIMER, NEWPORT AND POLAND
EXTENSION RAILWAY COMPANY

Incorporated on September 10, 1891 the purpose of this company was to build a standard gauge railroad from a point of intersection with the Herkimer, Newport and Poland Narrow Gauge Railway, at or near the village of Poland, in Herkimer County, New York and running thence in a northerly direction to the village of Remsen, in Oneida County. A branch line from Prospect, Oneida County, to Northwood (Hinckley) in Herkimer County was to be built. According to the BOONVILLE HERALD of May 7, 1891 the railroad from Poland to Remsen was already being built by the Mohawk Valley and Northern Railway. Inasmuch as the MV&N had its northern terminus listed as Nobleborough it apparently was found necessary to organize the Herkimer, Newport and Poland Extension Railway when the terminus was changed to Remsen.

On June 23, 1892 the HN&P Extension Railway was one of those consolidated into the Mohawk and Malone Railway. In its history of the organization of the Mohawk and Malone Railway Company, the Railroad Commissioners of the State of New York in their 1894 report made the statement:

> The Herkimer, Newport and Poland Extension railroad between Poland and Remsen, and the St. Lawrence and Adirondack railroad between Remsen and Malone, were organized October 1, 1891, by a reorganization in two divisions of the Mohawk and Adirondack railroad extending from Poland to Malone.

This is one of the perplexing occurrences in trying to trace the various companies. Apparently the HN&P Extension Railway became part of the Mohawk and Adirondack Railroad in some period but when it came time to consolidate into the Mohawk and Malone, the HN&P Extension Railway was one of the primary companies and any other affiliations were disregarded at the time of the consolidation.

THE MOHAWK VALLEY AND NORTHERN RAILWAY

This company was chartered on October 31, 1890, and was to have as its termini the Village of Poland and a place called Nobleborough both in Herkimer County. On April 30, 1891 this company was consolidated with the Herkimer, Newport and Poland Narrow Gauge Railway under the name of Mohawk Valley and Northern Railway Company. In June 1891, the MV&N was the company that applied to and received permission from the Supreme Court to construct and operate a standard gauge railway upon the roadbed of the former HN&PNG. The Herkimer, Newport and Poland Narrow Gauge Railway had already been given the right to change its name from HN&PNG to HN&P and to change to standard gauge on March 16, 1891. Why the Mohawk Valley and Northern should have been consolidated with the Herkimer, Newport and Poland Narrow Gauge Railway Company and not with the Herkimer, Newport and Poland Railway Company is a question to which the answer has not been found.

The BOONVILLE HERALD on May 7, 1891 reported that the MV&N was constructing the railroad north from Poland to Remsen. On September 10, 1891 the Herkimer, Newport and Poland Extension Railway was incorporated to construct or operate a railroad from Poland to Remsen, and apparently it took over from the Mohawk Valley and Northern at that time.

On June 18, 1891, the BOONVILLE HERALD reported:

> At a meeting in New York June 10 of the stockholders of the Mohawk Valley and Northern railway and the Mohawk and Adirondack railroad the articles consolidating the two roads with the Adirondack & St. Lawrence were approved.

No further mention of the Mohawk Valley and Northern has been found. For several years the Railroad Commissioners' annual reports stated that the Mohawk Valley and Northern Railway Company never made a report.

THE MOHAWK AND ST. LAWRENCE RAILROAD

Formed in 1890, the Mohawk and St. Lawrence Railroad was proposed to be built from Rome northward to Gouverneur and to Watertown and Clayton. An enterprise of the New York Central, the road was laid out to compete with the Rome, Watertown and Ogdensburg and all activity on the M&StL ceased when the RW&O was leased to the New York Central on March 14, 1891. That Dr. Webb intended his railroad to connect with the Mohawk and St. Lawrence is possible but was not the prime objective of Dr. Webb's line.

THE MOHAWK AND ADIRONDACK RAILROAD

The Mohawk and Adirondack Railroad was chartered on May 5, 1891 to build a railroad from Poland, Herkimer County to Malone, Franklin County. The BOONVILLE HERALD on June 18, 1891 reported that the Mohawk Valley and Northern Railroad and the Mohawk and Adirondack Railroad were consolidated with the Adirondack and St. Lawrence. However, according to the 1894 report of the Railroad Commissioners, the Mohawk and Adirondack was reorganized on October 1, 1891 into two divisions, the Herkimer, Newport and Poland Extension Railway between Poland and Remsen and the St. Lawrence and Adirondack between Remsen and Malone. Later reports of the Railroad Commissioners state that the Mohawk and Adirondack never made a report.

THE ADIRONDACK AND ST. LAWRENCE RAILROAD

The articles of Association of the Adirondack and St. Lawrence Railroad Company were filed with the State of New York Secretary of State on December 11, 1890. The company was formed to build a railroad from the town of Constable, or Burke, in Franklin County through Malone and to terminate in Schenectady.

The names of the directors are not familiar and do not appear to be any of those appearing in any of Dr. Webb's later companies. The name of Edson J. Chamberlin of St. Albans, Vt., was listed as a director and the holder of 1500 shares of stock in the company. Mr. Chamberlin was later identified on May 18, 1891 in a NEW YORK TIMES article as the manager of the Canada and Atlantic Railway. The same TIMES article also stated that Dr. W. S. Webb had entered into an agreement with Mr. Chamberlin regarding the railroad north from Malone to connect with the Canada and Atlantic at Valleyfield, Que. Dr. Webb may have assumed control over the Adirondack and St. Lawrence Railroad at this time. However, on May 6, 1892 the name of the A&StL was changed to the Malone and Schenectady. There does not seem to be any transfer of ownership of property of this road to any of Dr. Webb's roads. The change of name may have been made to free the Adirondack and St. Lawrence name.

THE ADIRONDACK AND ST. LAWRENCE RAILWAY

As far as can be learned this company was never chartered or incorporated as an operating railroad. It may have very well been a holding company under which construction and equipment purchases were made and the operation of a railroad carried out over other companies' rights and properties. The Secretary of State has no record of this company according to an inquiry made in January 1979.

Charles H. Burnett lists officers of the Adirondack and St. Lawrence Railroad for 1891–1892 only and this would cover the period up to the formation of the Mohawk and Malone Railway Company on June 23, 1892.

But when the Mohawk and Malone was formed it was made up of the Herkimer, Newport and Poland Railway Company, the Herkimer, Newport and Poland Extension Railway Company and the St. Lawrence and Adirondack Railroad Company. Early newspaper accounts all mention the Adirondack and St. Lawrence Railroad when discussing the Herkimer to Malone proposed railroad.

On September 11, 1891 the NEW YORK TIMES reported that Certificates of Incorporation were filed on that date for the St. Lawrence and Adirondack Railroad Company, the Herkimer, Newport and Poland Extension Railway Company and the Malone and St. Lawrence Railroad Company. The TIMES, in part, said:

> The certificates were filed by Henry L. Sprague. M. E. McKay of Malone, the attorney for the Adirondack and St. Lawrence Railway Company (Dr. Webb's) stated tonight that these new companies were to take the place of the Adirondack and St. Lawrence and were formed simply to perfect matters so that operations could be carried on without trouble. The old company "straddled" the old and the new laws and it was thought best to get the system under one law.

It has been assumed that the Adirondack and St. Lawrence operated south of Malone and the St. Lawrence and Adirondack operated north of Malone. This may be how it worked out but apparently the St. Lawrence and Adirondack was the underlying company south of Malone also. This does not mean that the same St. Lawrence and Adirondack company operated both south and north, which is also a matter of some confusion.

The early time tables were issued in the name of the Adirondack and St. Lawrence Railway (No. 1 — August 31, 1891) (unnumbered — July 15, 1892). Time Table No. 4, September 11, 1892 was issued by the Mohawk and Malone Railway Company but it was indicated in much larger type that it was the Adirondack and St. Lawrence *Line.* The use of Adirondack and St. Lawrence Line, apparently continued up until the New York Central took possession of the Mohawk and Malone and thereafter operated it as the Adirondack Division.

Bringing to light exactly what the Adirondack and St. Lawrence Railway Company owned in the way of real estate, trackage rights, buildings, locomotives and rolling stock would require an inordinate amount of research. This research was not attempted at this time. Many articles have been written about the locomotives of the Adirondack and St. Lawrence Railroad while all pictures of these same locomotives show that they carried the name Adirondack and St. Lawrence Railway. Rolling stock was also similarly identified according to all accounts. In view of all this, perhaps we can rightfully assume that the Adirondack and St. Lawrence Railway was more or less a holding company and never actually possessed the properties which were eventually to become part of the Mohawk and Malone Railway Company and in due course transferred to the New York Central Railroad.

THE ADIRONDACK AND ST. LAWRENCE RAILROAD

Just why it was felt necessary to name the four mile long railroad from DeKalb Junction to Hermon the Adirondack and St. Lawrence Railroad is not known. It was incorporated on April 19, 1906 as a common carrier and was discontinued in 1921. The corporation was dissolved on September 23, 1927. It had no physical or financial connection with the earlier Adirondack and St. Lawrence Railroad or the Adirondack and St. Lawrence Railway nor with the Adirondack Division of the New York Central Railroad.

THE ST. LAWRENCE AND ADIRONDACK RAILROAD
(South from Malone)

Chartered on September 11, 1891 this company according to the NEW YORK TIMES of the same date intended to:

> Operate a standard gauge steam railroad from a point at or near the Village of Remsen, in Oneida County, northerly to the Village of Malone, in Franklin County, which two points will be its terminals with branch roads running from its main line to the Village of Saranac, Franklin County, and to Cranberry Lake, St. Lawrence County, and to such other branches as shall hereafter be determined by its directors.

On June 23, 1892 the Herkimer, Newport and Poland; Herkimer, Newport and Poland Extension Railway Companies, and the St. Lawrence and Adirondack Railroad Companies were consolidated with the name changed to the Mohawk and Malone Railway Company.

Alvin F. Harlow in THE ROAD OF THE CENTURY states that Dr. Webb bought the Herkimer, Newport and Poland Narrow Gauge road, changed it to standard gauge and extended it as the St. Lawrence and Adirondack to Malone "from which another St. Lawrence and Adirondack was building to Montreal."

However, all construction after September 11, 1891 and after June 23, 1892 still seems to have been carried out in the name of the Adirondack and St. Lawrence Railway. Reference should be made to the short history of this railroad. Apparently at this time the Adirondack and St. Lawrence was set up to handle all construction and operations of the railroad built on the proposed St. Lawrence and Adirondack route.

THE MOHAWK AND MALONE RAILWAY

On June 23, 1892, Dr. W. Seward Webb consolidated the different railroads that made up his Adirondack system into one corporation. The joint agreement of consolidation of the Herkimer, Newport and Poland Railway Company; the Herkimer, Newport and Poland Extension Railway Company and the St. Lawrence and Adirondack Railroad Company forming the Mohawk and Malone Railroad Company was filed on June 23, 1892 in Albany. The RAILROAD GAZETTE on July 1, 1892, referring to the consolidation, made the observation that:

Several other joint agreements have been filed by these roads under different names since Dr. W. S. Webb began building his Adirondack railroad, these charters cover part of these lines.

On October 12, 1892 the last spike was driven near the Twitchell Creek bridge and the road from Remsen to Malone was open all the way. The formation of the Mohawk and Malone did not preclude the use of Adirondack and St. Lawrence in newspaper and other reports of progress in construction of the railroad. Various printed forms of the Adirondack and St. Lawrence Railway continued to be used for the next year or more but by September 11, 1892, the Mohawk and Malone Railway Company was issuing time tables but they carried the inscription "The Adirondack and St. Lawrence Line."

On March 1, 1893 the Mohawk and Malone Railway Company was leased to the New York Central and Hudson River Railroad Company and that company took over operations of the railroad. The lease to the New York Central and Hudson River Railroad was renewed in 1902. On February 26, 1913 the Public Service Commission permitted and approved the merger of the Mohawk and Malone Railway into the New York Central and Hudson River Railroad Company as the latter company held all of the stock of the former. As far is known there were never any locomotives or pieces of rolling stock that were lettered as Mohawk and Malone equipment.

In January 1979 the Penn Central Corporation was attempting to settle with the last of the M&M bondholders.

MALONE AND ST. LAWRENCE RAILWAY

The Malone and St. Lawrence was incorporated on September 11, 1891. It was to operate from Malone northerly and join the St. Lawrence and Adirondack in the Town of Burke, a distance of approximately twelve miles. It was leased for a short time to the Central Vermont Railroad Company. This was while the Montreal trains were being routed through Valley Field, Coteau Junction on the Canada Atlantic Railway and on the Grand Trunk Railway. On November 17, 1895 articles of consolidation of the Malone and St. Lawrence Railway Company and the St. Lawrence and Adirondack Railway Company were filed in Albany, the St. Lawrence and Adirondack to be the surviving company name. The Malone and St. Lawrence had no locomotives or rolling stock operating under its name.

SOUTHWESTERN RAILWAY

The Southwestern Railway was incorporated by Act of Parliament, passed in the fifty-first year of Her Majesty's Reign, Chapter 52. (May 22, 1888). In 1896 it was built from Beauharnois to Chaughnawaga (Adirondack Junction), a little over 13 miles. It also leased from the Grand Trunk Railway about 13 miles from Valleyfield to Beauharnois. On July 2, 1896 the Southwestern Railway Company was consolidated with the St. Lawrence and Adirondack Railway Company under the latter name.

THE ST. LAWRENCE AND ADIRONDACK RAILWAY
(North from Malone)

According to the ARGUS of April 22, 1888, the St. Lawrence and Adirondack Railroad Company was incorporated by the Canadian Parliament. This seems to be the first of the St. Lawrence and Adirondack Roads. The ARGUS used "railroad" but it seems that "railway" would have been correct. It was authorized to build from Valleyfield to the New York line in the direction of Lyon Mountain but there was nothing definite as to whether the line would go through Chateaugay or Malone.

The Malone and St. Lawrence having been built north from Malone joined the St. Lawrence and Adirondack Railway at Valleyfield. In 1896 the report of the New York State Railroad Commissioners gave the following history:

> The St. Lawrence and Adirondack Railway Company was organized November 18, 1895, by the consolidation of the Malone and St. Lawrence Railway Company and the St. Lawrence and Adirondack Railway Company, a corporation of the Dominion of Canada. The Malone and St. Lawrence Railway Company had been organized under the laws of the State of New York, September 11, 1891. The new St. Lawrence and Adirondack Railway Company absorbed by consolidation, on May 1, 1896, the Southwestern Railway Company, the latter having been incorporated by act of Parliament, passed in the fifty-first year of Her Majesty's Reign, Chapter 52 (1888).

The Southwestern Railway Company organized by Dr. Webb built approximately thirteen miles of railroad from Beauharnois to Caughnawaga (Adirondack Junction). The Southwestern Railway Company also leased from the Grand Trunk the Beauharnois Junction Railway, extending from Valleyfield to Beauharnois, a distance of nearly thirteen miles. Dr. Webb obtained a permanent trackage agreement with the Canadian Pacific Company, enabling him to run his own trains into the Canadian Pacific Station in Montreal. The entire distance from Malone to the Windsor Station was listed as a little over 65 miles.

The St. Lawrence and Adirondack Railway was operated by the New York Central and Hudson River Railroad Company under an agreement dated June 1, 1898, by which the operating company was simply the agent of the St. Lawrence and Adirondack Railway Company, and did not participate in the profits nor share the expenses of the line thus operated. In 1905 the New York Central acquired the entire capital stock and in 1915 the A&StL was leased to the New York Central for 21 years, this lease being renewed in 1936 for 99 years. The last through Utica-Montreal passenger service ended in 1953 and commuter service from Malone to Montreal stopped in 1957. With the abandonment and removal of tracks south of Malone in 1960, Malone freight service was continued from Huntingdon south to Malone on a weekly basis. This limited service is under constant study as to whether it shall be continued or not.

APPENDIX II
Stations, Places and Sidings

GEOGRAPHICAL LIST

of

STATIONS, PLACES and SIDINGS

on the

MOHAWK and MALONE RAILWAY

(The ADIRONDACK DIVISION,
NEW YORK CENTRAL and HUDSON RIVER RAILROAD)

Herkimer — Remsen
Remsen — Montreal

including

BRANCH LINES

and

CONNECTING LINES

(with references)

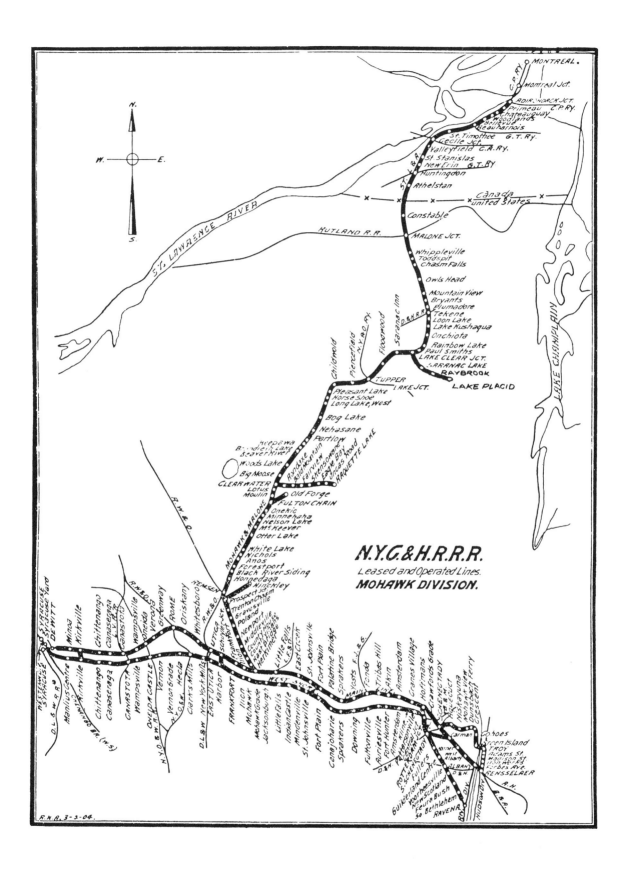

N.Y.C.&H.R.R.R.

Leased and Operated Lines.

MOHAWK DIVISION.

LIST OF BRANCH, FEEDER AND CONNECTING LINES TO
ACCOMPANY ALPHABETICAL LIST OF STATIONS,
PLACES AND SIDINGS ON THE MOHAWK AND MALONE RAILWAY
(The Adirondack Division of The New York Central
and Hudson River Railroad)

A   – Adirondack and St. Lawrence Railway

C   – Canadian Pacific Railway

CA   – Canada Atlantic Railway

CH   – Chateaugay Railway

D   – Delaware and Hudson Company

FC   – Fulton Chain Railway
FCRR   – Fulton Chain Railroad (Peg-leg Railroad)
FN   – Fulton Navigation Company

G   – Grasse River Railroad

GT   – Grand Trunk Railway

H   – Herkimer, Newport and Poland Narrow Gauge Railway
         Herkimer, Newport and Poland Railway

HB   – Hinckley Branch, Herkimer, Newport and Poland Extension
         Railway

HX   – Herkimer, Newport and Poland Extension Railway

MR   – Marion River Carry Railway

N   – New York Central and Hudson River Railroad

NO   – New York and Ottawa Railroad

P   – Paul Smith's Electric Light and Power and Railroad Company

PL   – Partlow Lake Railway

RL   – Raquette Lake Railway

RLT   – Raquette Lake Transportation Company

RU   – Rutland Railroad

S   – St. Lawrence and Adirondack Railway

SB   – Saranac Branch, Adirondack and St. Lawrence Railroad

SL   – Saranac and Lake Placid Railroad

U   – Utica and Black River Railroad

ALPHABETICAL LIST OF STATIONS, PLACES AND SIDINGS
ON THE MOHAWK AND MALONE RAILWAY
INCLUDING MAIN, BRANCH AND FEEDER LINES

Adirondack Jctn (S) (C)
Alms House (H)
American Legion (A)

Ames Mills (SL)

Anos (A)
Anos Siding (A)

Arnold's Clearing (A)

Athelstan (A)

Atwater (C)

Bald Mountain (RL)

Barneveld (U)

Beauharnois (GT)

Beaver River (A)

Bellevue (S)

Big Moose (A)
Black River Siding (A)
Blue Mtn. Lake (RLT)

Bog Lake (A)

Boisbriand (S)

Boonville Sand (A)

Brandreth (A)
Brandreth Lake (A)

Brandy Brook (G)

Brooklyn Cooperage (A)

Bryant's (A)

Buffalo Head (A)

Canadian Light & Power (C)

Carter (A) (RL)

Caughnawaga Jctn (S) (C)

Cecile Jctn (GT)

Chasm Falls (A)

Chateaugay (S)

Childwold (A) (G)
Childwold Station (A) (G)

Clark's (G)
Clarks (G)

Clearwater (A) (RL)

Conifer (G)

Constable (S)

Coteau Jctn (GT) (CA)

Cote des Neiges (C)

Cote St. Paul (C)

Countryman's (H)
Countrymans (H)

County Home (H)
County House (H)

Cranberry Lake (G)

Delevan (A)

Dempster's (H)

Desmonds (A)

Duquettes Pit (A)

Durant (RL)

Durante (RL)

Eagle Bay (RL)

Fair View (RL)
Fairview (RL)

Faust (A) (NO)

Fenners Grove (H)

Floodwood (A)

Forestport (A)
Forestport Station (A)

Fulton Chain (A) (FC)

Gabriels (A)
Gang Mills (HB)
Grasse River Club (G)

Gravesville (HX)

The Heights (S)

Herkimer (H) (N)

Herkimer Quarries (H)

Highlands (C)

Hinckley (HB)

Holland Patent (U)

Honnedaga (A)

Horse Shoe (A)
Horseshoe (A)
Horse Shoe Pond (A)
Horseshoe Pond (A)

Huntington (S) (GT)

Inman (A)

Johnson Siding (A)
Johnston Siding (A)

Jones' Camp (FCRR)
Jones' Crossing (H)

Kanawaki (S)

Kast Bridge (H)
Kast's Bridge (H)
Kayuta (A)
Kayuta Lake (A)

Keepawa (A)

Lake Clear Jctn (A) (SB) (P)

Lake Kushaqua (A)

Lake Lila (A)

Lake Placid (SL)
Lake Placid Station (SL)

LaSalle (C)

Little Rapids (A)

Long Lake West Station (A)
Long Lake Eest Station (A)

Loon Lake (A)
Loon Lake Station (A)

Lotus Siding (A)

Lyons (SL)

Malone (A) (RU) (S)
Malone Junction (A) (RU) (S)

Maple Grove (S)

Marcy (U)

Marion River (MR) (RLT)
Marion River Carry
  (MR) (RLT)

McCoy Siding (A)

McKeever (A)
McKeever Station (A)

Meekerville (A)

Melocheville (GT)

Middleville (H)

Minnehaha (A)

Minnow Brook (RL)
Minnowbrook (RL)

Montreal (Windsor) (C)

Montreal Junction (C)

Montreal West (C)

Morgans (A)

Morgan's Mills (A)

Mountain View (A)

Moulin (A)

Mount Arab (A)
Mount Arab Station (A)

Nehasane (A)
Ne-Ha-Sa-Ne (A)

Nelson (A)

Nelson Lake (A)

New Erin (S)

Newman (SL)

Newport (H)

Newport Crushed Stone (H)

Nichols Mills (A)

North Herkimer (H)
Northwood (HB)
Old Forge (FC)

Onchiota (A)

Onekio (A)

Otter (A)

Otter Lake (A)

Outremont (C)

Owl's Head (A)
Owls Head (A)

Partlow (A) (PL)

Paul Smith's (P)

Paul Smith's Station (A)

Piercefield (A)
Piercefield Station (A)

Pine Park (A)

Pit Four (A)

Pleasant Lake (A)

Plumadore (A)

Poland (H)

Primeau (S)

Prospect (U)
Prospect Junction (HX)

Pulpwood (A) (PL)

Racket Falls (A)

Rainbow (A)

Rainbow Lake (A)

Raquette Lake (RL)

Raybrook (SL)

Remsen (A) (HX) (U)

Ringville (A)

Robinwood (A)

Rondaxe (RL)

Sabattis (A)

St. Henry (C)

St. Luc Jctn (C)

St. Stanislaus (S)

St. Timothee (GT)

Saranac Inn (A)

Saranac Junction (A) (SB)

Saranac Lake
  (CH) (D) (SB) (SL)

Saranac Lake Junction (SB)

Saranac Village (SB)

Saranac Yard (SB)

Sherman Quarry (H)

Shurtleffs (G)

Silver Brook Jctn (G)

Skensowane (RL)

Sorten (C)

Smith Paper (GT)

Standcliff (A)

State Dam (A)

Stittville (U)

Stonywold (A)

Summit (RL)

Sylvan Lake (PL)

Tekene (A)

The Heights (S)

Thendara (A) (FC)

Titusville (A)

Todd's Pit (A)

Tracy's Spur (A)

Trenton (U)

Trenton Chasm (HX)

Trenton Falls (HX)

Tupper Lake Jctn (A)
  (NO)

Uncas Road (RL)

Underwood (A)

Utica (N) (U)

Utica City Ice (A)

Valleyfield (S) (GT) (CA)

Vaudreuil (GT)

Westmount (C)

Whippleville (A)

White Lake (A)

White Lake Sand Pit (A)

White Lake Station (A)

Woodgate (A)

Woodlands (S)

Woods (A)

Woods Lake (A)

Elevation above sea level	Mileage from Herkimer	Mileage from Utica	Branch or connection mileage	MAIN LINE	Branch or Connecting Line
				HERKIMER, NEWPORT AND POLAND NARROW GAUGE RAILWAY	
				HERKIMER, NEWPORT AND POLAND RAILWAY	
c 415	0.	. . . .	. . . .	Herkimer	
	2.	. . . .	. . . .	North Herkimer	
c 460	3.26	. . . .	. . . .	Kast Bridge	
				Kast's Bridge	
	4.	. . . .	. . . .	Dempster's	

Elevation above sea level	Mileage from Herkimer	Mileage from Utica	Branch or connection mileage	MAIN LINE	Branch or Connecting Line
c 490	5.21	....	....	Countrymans Countryman's	
	7.	....	....	County Home County House Country Home Alms House	
c 570	8.74	....	....	Middleville	
	10.	....	....	Jones' Crossing	
	11.	....	....	Fenners Grove Fenner's Grove	
c 650	13.06	....	....	Newport	
		....	....	Newport Crushed Stone	
		....	....	Herkimer Quarries	
	15.	....	....	Sherman Quarry	
c 720	16.52	....	....	Poland	

HERKIMER, NEWPORT AND POLAND EXTENSION RAILWAY

c 870	20.49	....	....	Gravesville	
	23.68	....	....	Trenton Chasm Trenton Falls	
c 1120	25.60	....	....	Prospect Junction	

HINCKLEY BRANCH

c 1120	25.60	....	0.	....	Prospect Junction
c 1140	....	....	1.02	....	Summit Street
c 1170	....	....	2.65	....	Hinckley Gang Mills
	....	....	(10.4)	....	Northwood
1200	27.67	....	....	Remsen	

Elevation above sea level	Mileage from Herkimer	Mileage from Utica	Branch or connection mileage	MAIN LINE	Branch or Connecting Line
				UTICA & BLACK RIVER RAILROAD	
				ROME, WATERTOWN & OGDENSBURG RAILROAD	
405		0.	. . . .	Utica	
		5.9	. . . .	Marcy	
		10.2	. . . .	Stittville	
		12.2	. . . .	Holland Patent	
		16.1	. . . .	Barneveld Trenton	
		17.4	. . . .	Trenton Falls	
		18.4	. . . .	Prospect	
1200		21.4	. . . .	Remsen	
				ADIRONDACK & ST. LAWRENCE RAILWAY	
1200	27.67	21.3	. . . .	Remsen	
1255	31.66	25.2	. . . .	Honnedaga	
		25.4	. . . .	Delevan Desmond	
			. . . .	Tracy's Spur	
			. . . .	Black River Siding	
	33.45	27.1	. . . .	Kayuta Lake Kayuta	
1215	35.57	29.3	. . . .	Forestport Forestport Station Buffalo Head	
c 1200		c 30.	. . . .	Meekerville	
1300	38.03		. . . .	Anos Siding	
			. . . .	Anos	
			. . . .	Boonville Sand	
	39.70	33.4	. . . .	Pit Four	
	39.81		. . . .	Johnston Siding Johnson Siding	
1347	39.94		. . . .	Nichols Mills	

Elevation above sea level	Mileage from Herkimer	Mileage from Utica	Branch or connection mileage	MAIN LINE	Branch or Connecting Line
1430	42.50	36.2	....	White Lake White Lake Station Woodgate	
			....	Utica City Ice	
			....	White Lake Sand Pit	
1565	47.57	41.3	....	Otter Lake Otter	
1540	49.15	42.9	....	McKeever McKeever Station	
1585	52.19	45.9	....	Nelson Lake Nelson	
1705	53.75	47.5	....	Minnehaha Jones' Camp	
1740	55.01	48.7	....	Onekio	
1712	57.93	51.6	....	Arnold's Clearing Fulton Chain Fulton Chain Station Thendara	

FULTON CHAIN RAILWAY

Elevation above sea level	Mileage from Herkimer	Mileage from Utica	Branch or connection mileage	MAIN LINE	Branch or Connecting Line
1712			0.	....	Fulton Chain — Thendara
1715			2.21	....	Old Forge
	60.66	54.4	....	Moulin	
			....	Lotus Siding	
1752	64.12	57.8	....	Clearwater	
			....	Carter	

RAQUETTE LAKE RAILWAY

Elevation above sea level	Mileage from Herkimer	Mileage from Utica	Branch or connection mileage	MAIN LINE	Branch or Connecting Line
1752			0.	....	Clearwater — Carter
1720			2.49	....	Rondaxe
			4.48	....	Summit
			5.55	....	Minnowbrook Minnow Brook

	Elevation above sea level	Mileage from Herkimer	Mileage from Utica	Branch or connection mileage	MAIN LINE	Branch or Connecting Line
	1800			5.7	. . . .	Bald Mountain
				7.2	. . . .	Fair View Fairview
				8.06	. . . .	Skensowane
c	1750			9.14	. . . .	Eagle Bay
				12.14	. . . .	Uncas Road
c	1762			17.89	. . . .	Raquette Lake Durante Durant

RAQUETTE LAKE TRANSPORTATION COMPANY

	Elevation above sea level	Mileage from Herkimer	Mileage from Utica	Branch or connection mileage	MAIN LINE	Branch or Connecting Line
c	1762				. . . .	Raquette Lake
c	1762			Boat	. . . .	Marion River Carry, Lower End

MARION RIVER CARRY RAILWAY

	Elevation above sea level	Mileage from Herkimer	Mileage from Utica	Branch or connection mileage	MAIN LINE	Branch or Connecting Line
c	1762			0.	. . . .	Marion River Carry, Lower End
	1789			.87	. . . .	Marion River Carry, Upper End

RAQUETTE LAKE TRANSPORTATION COMPANY

	Elevation above sea level	Mileage from Herkimer	Mileage from Utica	Branch or connection mileage	MAIN LINE	Branch or Connecting Line
	1789				. . . .	Marion River Carry, Upper End
	1789			Boat	. . . .	Blue Mountain Lake
	2034	69.31	63.0	. . . .	Big Moose	
	1875	73.47	67.2	. . . .	Woods Wood's Lake	
	1692	77.69	71.4	. . . .	Beaver River	
	1685	80.24	c 74.	. . . .	Little Rapids	
	1721	81.37	75.1	. . . .	Brandreth Lake Brandreth	
		82.77	76.5	. . . .	Keepawa	
c	1750	84.27	78.0	. . . .	Partlow Pulpwood P. O.	

Elevation above sea level	Mileage from Herkimer	Mileage from Utica	Branch or connection mileage	MAIN LINE	Branch or Connecting Line
				PARTLOW LAKE RAILWAY	
c 1750			0.	. . . .	Partlow
			5.0	. . . .	Sylvan Lake
1787	87.82	81.5	. . . .	Nehasane Ne-Ha-Sa-Ne NE-HA-SA-NE Lake Lila	
1760	90.7	84.4	. . . .	Bog Lake	
1760	90.89	84.6	. . . .	Robinwood	
1785	94.78	88.5	. . . .	Long Lake West Long Lake West Station Sabattis	
1738	99.91	93.6	. . . .	Horse Shoe Horse Shoe Pond Horseshoe Horseshoe Pond American Legion	
	103.14		. . . .	McCoy Siding	
1722	104.01	97.7	. . . .	Pleasant Lake Mount Arab Mount Arab Station	
1720	106.75	100.5	. . . .	Childwold Childwold Station	
				GRASSE RIVER RAILROAD CORPORATION	
1720			0.	. . . .	Childwold Station Childwold
			1.2	. . . .	Conifer
			4.0	. . . .	Grasse River Club
				. . . .	Silver Brook Junction
			9.0	. . . .	Shurtleff's
				. . . .	Brandy Brook
			12.0	. . . .	Clark's Clarks

Elevation above sea level	Mileage from Herkimer	Mileage from Utica	Branch or connection mileage	MAIN LINE	Branch or Connecting Line
c 1490			16.0	. . . .	Cranberry Lake
1674	109.23	102.9	. . . .	Piercefield	
			. . . .	Racket Falls	
		c 106.	. . . .	Underwood	
1556	113.64	107.3	. . . .	Tupper Lake Junction Tupper Lake Faust (Post Office)	
			. . . .	Brooklyn Cooperage	
1585	121.57	115.3	. . . .	Floodwood	
1615	128.56	122.3	. . . .	Saranac Inn	
1620	131.68	125.4	. . . .	Lake Clear Junction Saranac Junction	

SARANAC LAKE BRANCH

Elevation above sea level	Mileage from Herkimer	Mileage from Utica	Branch or connection mileage	MAIN LINE	Branch or Connecting Line
1620	133.68	125.4	0.	. . . .	Lake Clear Junction Saranac Junction
			5.82	. . . .	Saranac Village Saranac Yard Saranac Lake Junction
1560		131.6	6.23	. . . .	Saranac Lake

SARANAC AND LAKE PLACID RAILWAY
DELAWARE & HUDSON COMPANY

Elevation above sea level	Mileage from Herkimer	Mileage from Utica	Branch or connection mileage	MAIN LINE	Branch or Connecting Line
1560		131.6	0.	. . . .	Saranac Lake
			3.	. . . .	Ames Mills
c 1580		135.5	3.87	. . . .	Raybrook
			8.	. . . .	Lyons
1735		141.3	9.67	. . . .	Lake Placid Lake Placid Station Newman (Post Office)

PAUL SMITH'S ELECTRIC LIGHT AND POWER AND
RAILROAD COMPANY

Elevation above sea level	Mileage from Herkimer	Mileage from Utica	Branch or connection mileage	MAIN LINE	Branch or Connecting Line
1620			0.	. . . .	Lake Clear Junction

Elevation above sea level	Mileage from Herkimer	Mileage from Utica	Branch or connection mileage	MAIN LINE	Branch or Connecting Line
1617			7.13	. . . .	Paul Smith's
1695	136.69	130.4	. . . .	Paul Smith's Station Gabriels	
1695	139.19	132.9	. . . .	Rainbow Rainbow Lake	
1700	142.51	136.2	. . . .	Onchiota Pine Park	
1720	144.50	138.2	. . . .	Lake Kushaqua Stonywold	
	146.21		. . . .	Morgans Morgan's Mills	
1700	148.76	142.5	. . . .	Loon Lake Loon Lake Station Inman	
	150.13		. . . .	Takene	
	153.48	c 147.	. . . .	Plumadore	
		c 151.	. . . .	Little Bryant's	
		c 152.	. . . .	Bryant's	
1490	160.19	153.9	. . . .	Mountain View State Dam	
1510	162.83	156.5	. . . .	Owls Head Owl's Head Ringville	
1300	165.51	159.2	. . . .	Chasm Falls Standcliff Titusville	
	166.52		. . . .	Todd's Pit	
1055	169.28	163.0	. . . .	Whippleville	
		c 165.	. . . .	Duquette's Pit	
730	173.31	167.	. . . .	Malone Junction Malone	

Elevation above sea level	Mileage from Herkimer	Mileage from Utica	Branch or connection mileage	MAIN LINE	Branch or Connecting Line
				ST. LAWRENCE & ADIRONDACK RAILWAY (MALONE & ST. LAWRENCE RAILWAY)	
416	5.29	172.3	....	Constable	
c 275	10.23	177.2	....	International Boundary	
				ST. LAWRENCE & ADIRONDACK RAILWAY	
162	14.09	181.1	....	Athelstan	
155	17.93	194.9	....	Huntingdon	
	22.43	189.4	....	New Erin	
146	24.61	191.6	....	St. Stanislas	
145	30.19	197.2	....	Valleyfield	
				(This route used from 1892 to 1896 only) **CANADA ATLANTIC RAILWAY**	
			0.	Valleyfield	
c 35.5			5.3		Coteau Junction
				GRAND TRUNK RAILWAY	
c 48.9			18.7		Vaudreuil
c 74.9			44.7		Montreal (Central Station)
				GRAND TRUNK RAILWAY (Beauharnois Junction Railway)	
	32.07	199.1	....	Cecile Junction	
	35.34	202.3	....	St. Timothee	
			....	Canadian Light & Power Siding	
	40.55	207.6	....	Melocheville	
			....	Smith Paper Siding	
	43.99	210.5	....	Beauharnois	
				ST. LAWRENCE & ADIRONDACK RAILWAY (Southwestern Railway)	
	45.27	212.3	....	Maple Grove	

Elevation above sea level	Mileage from Herkimer	Mileage from Utica	Branch or connection mileage	MAIN LINE	Branch or Connecting Line
46.73	213.7	. . . .		Bellevue	
				Boisbriand	
48.86	215.9	. . . .		Woodlands	
50.92	217.9	. . . .		Chateugay	
51.82	218.8	. . . .		The Heights	
53.79	220.8	. . . .		Primeau	
55.48	222.5	. . . .		Kanawaki	
56.33	223.3	. . . .		Adirondack Junction	
				Caughnawaga Junction	

CANADIAN PACIFIC RAILWAY

	225.1	. . . .		Highlands	
59.		. . . .		LaSalle	
		. . . .		Sorten	
		. . . .		St. Luc Junction	
		. . . .		Cote Des Neiges	
60.50	227.5	. . . .		Montreal West	
				Montreal Junction	
62.36		. . . .		Cote St. Paul	
64.	230.	. . . .		Westmount	
64.53		. . . .		Atwater	
65.		. . . .		Outremont	
65.01		. . . .		St. Henry	
65.30	232.3	. . . .		Montreal (Windsor Station)	
				Montreal Wharf	
66.33		. . . .		Mile End	
68.37		. . . .		East End Cattle Market	
69.37		. . . .		Hochelaga	
71.37		. . . .		Montreal, Place Viger	
				Montreal Junction	

APPENDIX III
Chronology

1837 Feb.   1:   Timothy B. Jervis submits report on proposed Herkimer and Trenton Railroad

1879   :   Thomas W. Spencer commenced agitation to build narrow gauge railroad from Herkimer to Poland

1880 Jun. 29:   Herkimer, Newport and Poland Narrow Gauge Railroad Company organized

1880 Jul.   8:   Articles of Association filed by Herkimer, Newport and Poland Narrow Gauge Railroad Company

1880 Aug. 8:   Work on grading commenced on Herkimer, Newport and Poland Narrow Gauge Railroad

1881 Sept. 6:   Herkimer, Newport and Poland Narrow Gauge Railway completed to Middleville

1881 Dec. 31:   H.N.&P.N.G. Ry owned 1 locomotive. 1 passenger car, 8 freight & other cars

1882 Jan.   1:   Herkimer, Newport and Poland Narrow Gauge Railway completed to Newport

1882 May 29:   Herkimer, Newport and Poland Narrow Gauge Railway completed to Poland

1883 Sept.   :   H.N.&P.N.G. Ry owned 2 locomotives, 2 passenger cars and 19 freight, flat & gondola cars

1888 May   4:   St. Lawrence and Adirondack Railway Company incorporated by Canadian Parliament

287

1888   May 22:   South Western (sic) Railway Company incorporated by act of Canadian Parliament

1888   :   H.N.&P.N.G. Ry purchases locomotive No. 3

1889   :   Northern Adirondack Extension Railroad completed to Tupper Lake

1890   Oct. 31:   Mohawk Valley and Northern Railway Company Articles of Association filed

1890   Dec. 11:   Adirondack and St. Lawrence Articles of Association filed

1890   :   Canada Atlantic projected a railroad from Valleyfield, Que. to Malone, N.Y.

1891   Feb. 26:   Herkimer, Newport and Poland Narrow Gauge Railway purchased by Dr. W. Seward Webb

1891   Mar. 16:   Herkimer, Newport and Poland Narrow Gauge Railway change to standard gauge authorized by Chapter 78 of the Laws of 1891

1891   Mar.   :   Surveys started for line north of Poland

1891   May   5:   Mohawk and Adirondack Railroad chartered

1891   May 18:   Herkimer, Newport and Poland Narrow Gauge Railway change to standard gauge approved by Railroad Commissioners

1891
May 21, 22:   Town of Herkimer (21st) and Village of Herkimer (22nd) were served notice that the Mohawk Valley and Northern Railway Company was applying for leave to construct a standard gauge railway on the road bed of the Herkimer, Newport and Poland Narrow Gauge Railway

1891   Jun.   8:   Standard gauge train run on the Adirondack road

1891   Sept. 10:   Herkimer, Newport and Poland Extension Railway Company chartered

1891
Sept. 10, 11:   Malone and St. Lawrence Railway Company chartered (10th) and organized (11th). Leased to the Central Vermont Railroad Company

1891 Oct. 1: Herkimer, Newport and Poland Extension Railroad and the St. Lawrence and Adirondack Railroad organized

1891 Oct. 1: Herkimer, Newport and Poland Extension Railroad between Poland and Remsen, and the St. Lawrence and Adirondack Railroad between Remsen and Malone, were organized in two divisions of the Mohawk and Adirondack Railroad extending from Poland to Malone

1891 Oct. 31: Mohawk Valley and Northern Railway Company consolidated from Herkimer, Newport and Poland Narrow Gauge Railway and the Mohawk Valley and Northern Railway Companies, Articles of Association filed

1891 Dec. 8: Herkimer, Newport and Poland Railway Company certificate filed

1892 Jan. 11: First passenger train run from Malone to Valleyfield

1892 May 6: The name of the Adirondack and St. Lawrence Railroad Company by order of the Supreme Court changed to the Malone and Schenectady Railway Company. Certificate filed in office of Secretary of State

1892 Jun. : Malone and St. Lawrence under control of Dr. Webb turned over to Central Vermont Railway for operation

1892 Jun. 23: Certificate of Mohawk and Malone Railway Company filed. Herkimer, Newport and Poland Railway Company; Herkimer, Newport and Poland Extension Railway Company; St. Lawrence and Adirondack Railroad Companies consolidated to Mohawk and Malone Railroad Company

1892 Jul. 1: First train Herkimer to Fulton Chain

1892 Jul. 16: Opening date of the Adirondack & St. Lawrence Railway. Southern Division Via Herkimer to Fulton Chain. Northern Division — Utica to Norwood, R.W.&O.; Central Vermont to Malone; A.&St.L. to Childwold. First train from Malone to Saranac Lake

1892 Oct. 12: Last spike driven on the line between Childwold and Fulton Chain, half mile north of Twitchell Creek bridge

1892   Oct.   24:   Mohawk and Malone Railway, St. Lawrence Line, opened to public.
First solid train run through from New York to Montreal via Malone and Coteau Junction using Malone & St. Lawrence, Canada Atlantic and Grand Trunk

1893   Apr.   20:   Mohawk and Malone Railway Company leased to New York Central and Hudson River Railroad Company

1893   Aug.   1:   First train into Lake Placid over Saranac Lake & Lake Placid Railroad

1893   :   Mohawk and Malone Railway through trains routed north from Utica instead of Herkimer

1894   Mar.   1:   William Seward Webb assumed lease of Malone and St. Lawrence Railway Company. Road operated on his behalf after that date by New York Central and Hudson River Railroad Co.

1895   Nov.   18:   St. Lawrence and Adirondack Railway Company organized by the consolidation of the Malone and St. Lawrence Railway Company and the St. Lawrence and Adirondack Railway Company, a corporation of the Dominion of Canada

1896   Mar.   9:   Application of Fulton Chain Railroad Company for a certificate under Section 59 of the Railroad Law granted. Public convenience and necessity require the construction of such a railroad

1896   :   Construction of Fulton Chain Railroad completed

1896   May   1:   The new St. Lawrence and Adirondack Railway absorbed by consolidation the Southwestern Railway Company (incorporated by Act of Parliament in 51st year of her Majesty's reign Chapter 52 (May 22, 1888)

1896   Aug.   16:   Line from Beauharnois to Adirondack Junction completed. Through service established to Montreal via Canadian Pacific utilizing Windsor Station for passenger and Outremont Yard for freight trains

1899   Feb.   2:   Raquette Lake Railway Company incorporated with a capital of $250,000

1899 Feb. 7:   Raquette Lake Railway Company chartered

1899 Apr. 11:   Board of Railroad Commissioners approved certificate under Section 59 of Railroad Laws for the Raquette Lake Railway Co.

1899 Sept. 11: Collis P. Huntington left New York City in his private car and arrived in Raquette Lake Village over the Raquette Lake Railway

1900 Jul. 1:   Raquette Lake Railway opened

1900   :   Marion River Carry Railroad opened

1901 Jan. 1:   Operating department of the Raquette Lake Railway conducted by the New York Central and Hudson River Railroad Company

1902 Feb. 25:   Fulton Chain Railroad Company sold and reorganized as Fulton Chain Railway Company

1902 Apr. 16:   The Mohawk and Malone Railway Company was leased to the New York Central and Hudson River Railroad Company

1902 May 1:   W. Seward Webb assumed the presidency of the Rutland Railroad

1905 Jan. 1:   New York Central and Hudson River Railroad purchased the entire outstanding capital stock of the St. Lawrence and Adirondack Railway

1906 May 2:   Paul Smith's Electric Light and Power and Railroad Company certificate filed

1909 Jul. 13:   Adirondack Division starting using oil for fuel. First engine N.Y.C.&H.R. No. 2125

1913 Feb. 26:   Public Service Commission, 2nd District, authorized the merging of the Mohawk and Malone Railway Company into the New York Central and Hudson River Railroad Company

1913   :   Emporium Forestry Company constructed railroad from Childwold Station to Cranberry Lake

1914 Oct. 20:   Certificate of convenience and necessity for operation of an automobile stage route or bus line between Fulton Chain and Old Forge granted by Public Service Commission

1915 Jan. 9:   Grasse River Railroad incorporated

1915 Sep. 27:   St. Lawrence and Adirondack Railway leased to the New York Central Railroad Company

1916 May 15:   Grasse River Railroad commenced operation

1917 Mar. 14:   New York Central Railroad Company authorized to purchase entire capital stock of the Fulton Chain Railway Company and the Raquette Lake Railway Company by the Public Service Commission

1919   :   Old Forge-Utica Stage Coach in operation, revenue for 1919, $2763

1929 Sep. 15:   Last run of the Marion River Carry Railroad

1931   :   Hinckley Branch abandoned

1932 Jul. 11:   Fulton Chain Railway abandoned

1933 Sep. 30:   Raquette Lake Railway operations suspended

1934 Feb. 27:   Raquette Lake Railway abandoned

1934 Oct. 31:   Last day of passenger service on the Herkimer-Remsen line

1936   :   Paul Smith's Electric Railroad discontinued

1937 May 6:   New York and Ottawa Railroad abandoned from Tupper Lake to Moira. Dismantling started next day

1940   :   Delaware & Hudson secured trackage rights over Adirondack Division between Plumadore and Saranac Lake and the Delaware & Hudson line was abandoned between the same points

1940–41 circa: Tests conducted by Alco-GE with experimental diesels between Malone and Tupper Lake to determine effects of operation under extreme winter conditions

1943   circa: Poland-Prospect Junction tracks torn up during World War II. Trenton Chasm bridge demolished

1946   Aug. 29:   Interstate Commerce Commission authorized Delaware & Hudson to cease operations from Lyon Mountain to Lake Placid. New York Central Railroad Company authorized to acquire the line between Saranac Lake and Lake Placid.

1948   :   Grasse River Railroad Corp. tracks taken up except for 2 miles from Childwold Station to Conifer

1948   Apr.   7:   Big diesels permit hauling heavy freight trains, previously routed via St. Lawrence Division and the Rutland to Malone, direct from Utica to Malone. First train of 83 cars passed through Tupper Lake Junction

1951   Oct.   :   Diesels replaced steam locomotives on Utica-Lake Placid run

1952   Mar. 27:   Last steam locomotive, No. 2971 ran from Montreal to Utica

1953   Apr. 26:   Last Utica-Montreal through train

1957   May   :   Commuter service from Malone to Montreal discontinued

1958   Jan.   :   End of Lake Clear Junction to Malone passenger service

1960   :   Railroad abandoned between Lake Clear Junction and Malone

1961   :   Beeliner in use for round trip daily from Utica to Lake Placid

1963   :   Tracks removed between Lake Clear Junction and Malone

1965   Apr. 24:   Last scheduled passenger train on the Adirondack Division

1965   Sep. 25:   Last trip "Fan Trip" sponsored by Central New York Chapter of National Railway Historical Society

1971   May   :   Penn Central Transportation Company applied for abandonment of the Adirondack Division of the former New York Central System

1972   May 30:   Last day use of Herkimer to Poland Branch on account of bridge washout

1972   Aug. 19:   Interstate Commerce Commission order issued to permit abandonment of the 118 mile Adirondack Division

1972   Oct. 27:   Penn Central Transportation Company filed for abandonment of the Herkimer to Poland branch line

1975   Feb.   :   State of New York acquired the Remsen-Lake Placid line

1976   Feb. 27:   Penn Central Transportation Company's termination date on all rail service from Herkimer to Poland

APPENDIX IV

Incidents, Derailments and Accidents

other than at grade crossings

1881	Nov. 23:	Fatal accident while coupling cars at Middleville
1888	Feb. 14:	Fatal accident while narrow gauge trucks being placed under standard gauge freight car at Herkimer
1892	May 31:	Derailment near Purgatory Hill. Fatality
1893	Mar. 27:	Serious derailment one mile north of Kast Bridge. Train 4
1895	Dec. 20:	Head-on collision near Horseshoe Pond Station. Train 623 Montreal Express and freight train. Fatalities
1899	Jan. 6:	Trestle on "Y" at Herkimer collapsed. Fatality
1901	Jun. 21:	Train 655 derailed between White Lake and Otter Lake. Engine and 3 cars derailed. No injuries
1901	Jun. 24:	Log train brakeman fatally injured near Clearwater
1901	Aug. 19:	Round House explosion at Herkimer. Fatalities
1902	Mar. 17:	Log train derailment near Tupper Lake Junction. Fatality
1902	Apr. 3:	Train 655 derailed and wrecked near Woods Lake
1902	:	Wreck at Carter. (No details, incident not verified.) Fatality. Accident was referred to by two Utica newspapers in 1924.

1903   Jan. 30:   Derailment north of Herkimer

1903   May   9:   Head-on collision Nelson Siding between train 650 and train 651. Fatalities

1904   Jan. 30:   Head-on collision between way freight and extra near Big Moose

1907   Nov.   1:   Wreck at Ne-Ha-Sa-Ne

1908   Feb. 15:   Track washout north of Poland

1910   Feb. 28:   Flood at Herkimer covered yards and terminal area

1912   Feb. 24:   Locomotives collided while they were being changed on express train at Tupper Lake Junction

1912   Jul.   3:   Head-on collision at Piercefield Station between freight train and work train

1913   Mar. 26:   Washout at Dugway north of Kast Bridge

1913   Nov.   9:   Wreck on Raquette Lake Railway. Work train from Carter. Fatalities

1914–15 circa: Ice train from Raquette Lake collided with cars on south wye at Carter

1915   Sep. 18:   Rear-end collision between Delaware & Hudson freight train and New York Central passenger train near Raybrook

1916   May 30:   Switch engine derailed and tipped over in Malone Yards

1916   Oct.   :   Derailment of "Noon Train" from Lake Placid, south of Raybrook

1917   Jun. 11:   Montreal Express marooned near Holland Patent due to flooding conditions

1920   Dec. 20:   Derailment at North Herkimer. Fatality

1922   Jul.   4:   Montreal Express derailed near Childwold

1922   :   Way freight derailed at Mountain View

1924　Jan.　3:　　Adirondack Express Train 2 derailed at Remsen. Fatality

1924　Sep.　30:　　Train 4 derailed at Sabattis

1925　Apr.　12:　　Montreal Express Train 4 derailed and wrecked by washout near Beaver River Station

1928　circa:　　Freight train wrecked near Constable

1929　Sep.　:　　Engine 3092 exploded at Saranac Lake

1930　Feb.　1:　　Log train derailed by collision near Beaver River. Fatality

1936　Jan.　5:　　Freight train derailment near Carter. Fatality

1943　Dec.　24:　　Southbound train of empty passenger cars derailed south of Tupper Lake

1947　Feb.　17:　　Accident while cars being switched at Brandreth. Fatality

1951　May　20:　　Enginehouse at Tupper Lake destroyed by fire

1952　Feb.　10:　　Freight train derailed near Tupper Lake

1953　Mar.　22:　　Head-on collision between two freight trains at Ne-Ha-Sa-Ne. Fatalities

1954　Apr.　15:　　Derailment and wreck Train 5 near Stonywold

1954　Apr.　28:　　Derailment of freight train near Stonywold

1963　Apr.　4:　　Train 165 derailed and wrecked by washout near Sabattis

1967　:　　Derailment between Na-Ha-Sa-Ne and Brandreth

1969　Apr.　19:　　Freight train derailment near Sabattis

APPENDIX V
Rosters of Locomotives

ROSTERS OF LOCOMOTIVES
THE ADIRONDACK & ST. LAWRENCE RAILWAY
AND
THE ST. LAWRENCE & ADIRONDACK RAILWAY

The information and rosters of locomotives of the Adirondack & St. Lawrence Railway and the St. Lawrence and Adirondack Railway are used with the permission of the Railroad & Locomotive Historical Society, Inc., Boston, Massachusetts. This material appeared in the Society's Bulletin No. 90 published in May 1954.

LOCOMOTIVES OF THE ADIRONDACK
& ST. LAWRENCE RAILWAY
& ST. LAWRENCE & ADIRONDACK RAILWAY

The Herkimer, Newport and Poland R. R., forming the southern end of the A. & St. L., was chartered on June 29, 1880, and opened to traffic in 1881–2. Its gauge was 42″, and the line extended from Herkimer, east of Utica on the Mohawk River, in a northwesterly direction to Poland, N.Y. In 1892 the track gauge was changed to standard. At about this time, the N. H. & P. was continued to Remsen, 11 miles, through construction of the H. N. & P. Extension R. R.

In 1891–2, the A. & St. L. was built from the Remsen terminus to Malone, N.Y., and became part of the Mohawk & Malone R. R., by consolidation, in 1893, the M. & M. being a consolidation of the above three lines. The M. & M. was leased to the N. Y. C. & H. R., and was operated as part of that road's Mohawk Division. During its existence, the A. & St. L. had forty or more locomotives, on the tenders of which was lettered the road's name, and was painted the road's symbol, a "fleur-de-lis." Many of these locomotives were acquired by the Central Vermont, which assigned at least five of them to the Rutland Division, so-called, then under lease to the C. V.

For some time after the formation of the M. & M., tenders were lettered Adirondack & St. Lawrence *Line,* by which name the road was known. First Nos. 1, 2 and 3 of the A. & St. L. were originally the narrow gauge engines of the H. N. & P., which were rebuilt to standard gauge, and later Nos. 1 and 3 became C. V. Nos. 9 and 12.

In order to complete a rail route from Malone to Montreal, the Malone & St. Lawrence R. R. was built from Malone to the Canadian Line, where it connected with the St. Lawrence & Adirondack R. R., extending from there to Valleyfield, P. Q., and which was completed on January 11th, 1892. Dr. W. S. Webb acquired this line in June, 1892, and turned it over the the Central Vermont for operation, for a few years. Connection was made at Valleyfield to Ottawa, and, at Coteau, to Montreal via the Grand Trunk.

The line was returned to Dr. Webb, who (1) leased part of the Grand Trunk line from Valleyfield to Beauharnois, (2) built the Southwestern R. R. (chartered in Canada on Sept. 10th, 1891) from Beauharnois to Caughnawaga Jct. (now Adirondack Jct.), and (3) obtained trackage rights from there to Montreal, nine miles, over the Canadian Pacific. The St. L. & A., the M. & St. L., and the Southwestern Railroads were consolidated in 1896, to form a new St. L. & A., which was leased to the N.Y.C. & H. R. R. R. from June 1st, 1898, to January 1st, 1905, when the N. Y. C. bought all of the stock of the St. L. & A.

The St. L. & A. owned at least 30 locomotives, of which eight were acquired by the Rutland, and the others by the New York Central. Tenders of some of the engines were lettered with the road's full name, but, in later years, the single word "Adirondack" was painted instead.

To add to the confusion caused by the similarity of names of these two roads, there was another road bearing the name Adirondack & St. Lawrence. This was a short line (3.61 miles) in western New York, extending from Hermon village to DeKalb Jct., on the New York Central, and on which operations were suspended on February 12th, 1921. This road had three locomotives at the time of abandonment.

Adirondack & St. Lawrence, second No. 1. (H. K. Vollrath collection)

Adirondack & St. Lawrence, No. 11. (H. K. Vollrath collection)

St. Lawrence & Adirondack No. 7. This engine was transferred to the Rutland Railroad in 1900. (McKnight collection)

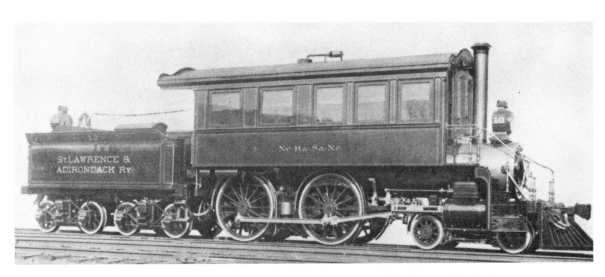

Dr. Webb's private engine, later transferred to the Rutland Railroad. (H. K. Vollrath collection)

Photograph of Dr. Webb's private engine, NE-HA-SA-NE, No. 10 at Tupper Lake in 1898. (Photograph courtesy of The Adirondack Museum, Blue Mountain Lake, N.Y.)

St. Lawrence & Adirondack No. 12, later transferred to the New York Central but was lettered "Adirondack" on tender for a period. (Harter collection)

THE LOCOMOTIVES OF THE ADIRONDACKS & ST. LAWRENCE R.R.

No.	Builder	C/N	Date	Type	Cyls.	DD	Date	Disposition To
1	Baldwin	5627	1881	4-4-0	10×16	42		ex-HN&P 1, "Edward M. Burns." to CV 9, Sc. 1899
2	Mason		1874	2-4-4T	12×16	36		ex-HN&P 2, "Henry W. Dexter." was ex-New Brunswick Ry. Final disp. unknown
3	Baldwin	4286	1878	2-6-0	14×18	42		ex-HN&P 3, "William Smith." was ex-Georgia Land & Lbr. Co. "J. C. Anderson." to CV 12-4
1	Schenectady	3510	1891	0-4-0	16×24	51	1891	CV 211; Rut 80; NCYL 50; Rut 50
2	Schenectady	3515	1891	0-4-0	16×24	51	1891	CV 20-49
4	Rh. Island	710	1878	2-4-4	11×16	42		ex-N.Y. Elevated Ry. 45. To 99
6	Schenectady	828	1872	4-4-0	16×24	63		ex-NYC 224; ex-361; To CV 13-42
7	No data						1897	Scrapped W. Albany
11	Schenectady	3511	1891	4-4-0	18×24	69	1891	CV 232; Rut 182; NYCL 862; Rut 82-67
11	Schenectady	3593	1892	4-4-0	17×24	63	1892	CV 30-50
12	Schenectady	3512	1891	4-4-0	18×24	69	1891	CV 233; Rut 183; NYCL 863; Rut 83
12	Schenectady	3594	1892	4-4-0	17×24	63	1892	CV 31-51
13	Schenectady	3513	1891	4-4-0	18×24	69	1891	CV 107-102
14	Schenectady	3514	1891	4-4-0	18×24	69	1891	CV 108-103
15	Schenectady	3754	1892	4-6-0	20/30×26	70		NYC 993-2025
16	Schenectady	3755	1892	4-6-0	20/30×26	70		NYC 994-2026
17	Schenectady	3825	1892	4-6-0	20/30×26	70		NYC 995-2027
30	Schenectady	3706	1892	4-6-0	19×24	62	2/94	LV 707-1125
31	Schenectady	3506	1891	4-6-0	18×24	56	1892	VC 234; Rut 480; NYCL 2061; Rut 61
31	Schenectady	3707	1892	4-6-0	19×24	64	2/94	LV 706-1124
32	Schenectady	3505	1891	4-6-0	18×24	56	1892	CV 235; Rut 481; NYCL 2062; Rut 62
32	Schenectady	3722	1892	4-6-0	19×24	63	1892	CV 116-209
33	Schenectady	3723	1892	4-6-0	19×24	63	1892	CV 117-210
34	Rh. Island	2730	1892	4-6-0	19×24	56		Ren. 113. 1892, to CV 113-206
35	Rh. Island	2727	1892	4-6-0	19×24	56		Ren. 114. 1892, to CV 114-207
38	Rh. Island	2726	1892	4-6-0	19×24	56		Ren. 112. 1892, to CV 112-205
39	Rh. Island	2762	1892	4-6-0	19×24	56		Ren. 115. 1892, to CV 115-208
50	Schenectady	3686	1892	2-6-0	20/30×26	57		NYC 842-1813
51	Schenectady	3687	1892	2-6-0	20/30×26	57		NYC 843-1814
52	Schenectady	3826	1892	2-6-0	20/30×26	57		NYC 844-1815
60	Schenectady	4055	1893	2-8-0	22/33×26	51		NYC 996-2210
61	Schenectady	4056	1893	2-8-0	22/32×26	51		NYC 997-2211
80	Schenectady	3879	1892	4-6-0	19/28×24	69		NYC 998-2186
81	Schenectady	3880	1892	4-6-0	19/28×24	69		NYC 1000-2187
82	Schenectady	3883	1892	4-6-0	19/28×24	69		NYC 1001-2188
83	Schenectady	3884	1892	4-6-0	19/28×24	69		NYC 1002-2189
84	Schenectady	3885	1892	4-6-0	19/28×24	69		NYC 1003-2190
99	Schenectady	3639	1892	2-4-6	16×22	61		"St. Lawrence" to CV 109
99	Rh. Island	710	1878	2-4-4	11×16	42		From #4. Inspection engine
101	Schenectady	3878	1892	4-4-0	19×24	69	1892	CV 129-106
110	Rh. Island	2760	1892	4-6-0	19×24	56	1892	CV 110-203
111	Rh. Island	2761	1892	4-6-0	19×24	56	1892	CV 111-204
112	Rh. Island	2726	1892	4-6-0	19×24	56	1892	From 38. To CV 112-205
113	Rh. Island	2730	1892	4-6-0	19×24	56	1892	From 34. To CV 113-206
114	Rh. Island	2727	1892	4-6-0	19×24	56	1892	From 35. To CV 114-207

115	Rhl Island	2762	1892	4-6-0	19×24	56	1892 From 39. To CV 115-208
116	Schenectady	4114	1893	2-6-0	19×26	57	1893 CV 130-336
117	Schenectady	4115	1893	2-6-0	19×26	57	1893 CV 131-337
118	Schenectady	4116	1893	2-6-0	19×26	57	1893 CV 132-338
119	Schenectady	4117	1893	2-6-0	19×26	57	1893 CV 133-339
120	Schenectady	4118	1893	2-6-0	19×26	57	1893 CV 134-340
—	Schenectady	4144	1893	4-4-0	18×24	74	11/93 Sold to C. R. R. of Pa. #6. Named "Ne-Ha-Sa-Ne." No A&StL number.

Note: #99, Schenectady #3639, was sold to the Central Vermont, where it was rebuilt to a 4-4-0, an inspection engine, retaining its name "St. Lawrence." #99, Rhode Island #710, was rebuilt from a former N.Y. Elevated Railway locomotive.
The above record, showing Schenectady Nos. 3706 and 3707 as going to L. V. Nos. 707 and 706, respectively, concurs with the L. V. records. Schenectady records show that Nos. 3706 and 3707 became L. V. Nos. 706 and 707, respectively.
Nos. 116 through 120 were probably ordered by the A. & St. L., but were probably delivered to the C. V., without ever seeing service on the A. & St. L.

LOCOMOTIVES OF THE ST. LAWRENCE & ADIRONDACK R. R.

(Names shown at end of roster)

No.	Builder	C/N	Date	Type	Cyls.	DD	Date Disposition	To
1	Schenectady	4130	1893	2-6-0	19×26	57		NYC 784-1687
1	Schenectady	4437	1896	4-4-0	18×24	67	1897	CAR 24-628; GTR 1331-2240; CN 311
1	Manchester	445	1872	4-4-0	15×22	66	1898	ex-CV 170; ex-NLN 20. To Rut 238-79
1	Schenectady	1655	1882	4-4-0	17×24	64		From #11; ex-NYC 452, ex-256. Received 12-1898
2	Schenectady	4393	1895	2-6-0	19×26	64		NYC 785-1688
2	Brooks	2677	1896	4-6-0	20×26	57		Ren'd 4
2	Schenectady	4438	1896	4-4-0	20×24	67		CCC&StL 203; NYCL 7143
2	Schenectady	2221	1886	4-4-0	17×24	64		From #12; ex-NYC 494, ex-267, ex-489, ex-276. Rec'd 4-1900
3	Brooks	2678	1896	4-6-0	20×26	57		NYC 2028
3	Schenectady	4394	1895	4-4-0	20×24	73		From #13; to CCC&StL 202; NYCL 7142
3	Schenectady	5591	1900	2-6-0	20×28	57	1900	Rut 320; NYCL 1884; Rut 144
4	Schenectady	4439	1896	4-6-0	20×26	57	1896	MC 452-8180
4	Brooks	2677	1896	4-6-0	20×26	57		From #2; To NYCL 2029
4	Schenectady	5592	1900	2-6-0	20×28	57	1900	Rut 321; NYCL 1885; Rut 145
5	Schenectady	4334	1895	4-6-0	20×26	64	1896	MC 453-8181
5	Brooks	2772	1897	4-4-0	18×26	64	1900	Rut 249-190; NYCL 1000; Rut 80-65
6	Brooks	2668	1896	4-6-0	18×26	69	1896	LS&MS 602-544-5019
6	Brooks	2773	1897	4-4-0	18×26	64		NYCL 1002 (1903–4)
7	Brooks	2669	1896	4-6-0	18×26	69	1896	LS&MS 603-545-5017
7	Brooks	2774	1897	4-4-0	18×26	64	1900	Rut 250-191; NYCL 1001; Rut 81-66
8	Brooks	2670	1896	4-6-0	18×26	69	1896	LS&MS 604-546-5018
8	Schenectady	4932	1898	4-6-0	20×28	61	1900	Rut 251-420; NYCL 2153-2063; Rut 63
9	Schenectady	4933	1898	4-6-0	20×28	61	1900	Rut 252-421; NYCL 2154-2064; Rut 64
10	Schenectady	4401	1896	4-4-0	14×22	63	1900	NYC&HR 49; Rut 100; NYCL 33; Rut 99
10	Schenectady	6128	1901	4-4-2	19×26	69	1901	NYCL 2900-2800-3800-800

10	Schenectady	5181	1899	4-6-0	20×28	70		ex-NYCL 2002; ex-2028; ex-NYC 950. To NYCL 2002 again, 1903–4
11	Schenectady	1655	1882	4-4-0	17×24	64		ex-NYC 452; ex-256; To 4th #1
11	Schenectady	6136	1901	4-4-2	19×26	69	1901	NYCL 2901-2801-3801-801
11	Schenectady	5182	1899	4-6-0	20×28	70		ex-NYCL 2003; ex-2029; ex-NYCL 951. Back to NYCL 2003, 1903–4
12	Schenectady	2221	1886	4-4-0	17×24	64		ex-NYC 494; ex-267; ex-489; ex-276. To 4th #2
12	Schenectady	6137	1901	4-4-2	19×26	69	1901	NYCL 2902-2802-3802-802
12	Schenectady	5184	1899	4-6-0	20×28	70		ex-NYCL 2005; ex-2031; ex-NYC 953. Back to NYCL 2005, 1903–4
13	Schenectady	4394	1896	4-4-0	20×24	73		To 2nd #3, etc.
15	Brooks	2667	1896	4-8-0	21×26	55	1896	BR&P 139. To Cumberland & Manchester #56.

Locomotive Names

Road No.	C/N	Name
1	4437	Beauharnois
2 (4)	2677	Kushaqua
3	2678	Cascapedia
4 (2)	2677	Kushaqua
6	2668	Mattawa
7	2669	Mirimichi
8	2670	Madawaska
10	4401	Ne-Ha-Sa-Ne
15	2667	Manitou

BIBLIOGRAPHY

Alco Historical Locomotives. Schenectady, New York; Mohawk and Hudson Chapter, Inc., National Railway Historical Society. Second Edition. 1979.

Beebe, Lucius. *The Big Spenders.* New York; Doubleday & Company. 1966.

————, *Mixed Train Daily, A Book of Short Line Railroads.* New York; E. P. Dutton & Company, Inc. 1953.

Beetle, David H. *Up Old Forge Way.* Rochester, New York; Louis Heindl & Son. 1948.

————, *West Canada Creek.* Rochester, New York; Louis Heindl & Son. 1946.

Burnett, Charles H. *Conquering the Wilderness;* Privately Printed. 1932.

Carson, Robert B. *Main Line to Oblivion.* Port Washington, New York; National University Publications, Kenniket Press. New York/London. 1971.

Cookinham, Henry J. *History of Oneida County, New York.* Chicago; S. J. Clarke Publishing Company. 1912. Vol. 1.

Davis, Margaret P. *Honey out of the Rafters.* Boonville, New York; Boonville Graphics, Inc. Printers. 1976.

DeSormo, Maitland C. *The Heydays of the Adirondacks.* Saranac Lake, New York; Adirondack Yesteryears, Inc. 1974.

Donaldson, Alfred L. *A History of the Adirondacks.* New York; The Century Co. 1921. Vols. 1 and 2.

Donnelly, William B. *A Short History of Beaver River.* Beaver River, New York; Mimeographed. 1979.

Fleming, Howard. *Narrow Gauge Railways in America.* Salinas, California; El Camino Press. 1949.

Franklin Historical Review. Malone, New York; Franklin County Historical and Museum Society. Vol. 6, 1969. Vol. 8, 1971. Vol. 10, 1973. Vol. 13, 1976.

Freight Department Rules and Regulations. Malone, New York; Mohawk and Malone Railway and St. Lawrence & Adirondack Railway. 1896.

Fynmore, Jim. *The Central Adirondacks, A Picture Story.* Prospect, New York; Prospect Books. 1955.

Gardner, Ed. *Adirondack Vistas.* Harrison, New York. Harbor Hill Books. 1975.

Gove, William and Others. *Rails in the North Woods. Grasse River Railroad.* Lakemont, New York; North Country Books. 1973.

Grady, Joseph F. *The Adirondacks, Fulton Chain-Big Moose Region. The Story of a Wilderness.* Old Forge, New York; North Country Books, 1933. Second Edition. 1966.

Hardin, George A. *History of Herkimer County.* Syracuse, New York; D. Mason & Son. 1893.

Harlow, Alvin F. *Road of the Century.* New York; Creative Age Press, Inc. 1947.

Health and Pleasure on America's Greatest Railroad. New York; New York Central and Hudson River Railroad. 1894.

Herkimer's Flood. Herkimer, New York; Telegram Print. 1910. Pamphlet.

Higby, Roy C. *A Man from the Past.* Big Moose, New York; Big Moose Press. 1974.

Hill, Dewey D. & Hughes, Elliott R. *Ice Harvesting in Early America.* New Hartford, New York; New Hartford Historical Society. 1977. Pamphlet.

Hilton, George W. & Due, John F. *The Electric Interurban Railways in America.* Stanford, California; Stanford University Press. 1960.

Hochschild, Harold K. *Township 34,* New York; Printers George Grody Press, New York. 1952. Including separately printed extracts by Adirondack Museum, Blue Mountain Lake, N.Y.

Hungerford, Edward. *Men and Iron.* New York; Thomas Y. Crowell Co. 1938.

———, *The Story of the Rome, Watertown and Ogdensburg Railroad.* New York; Robert McBride & Company. 1922.

Hyde, Floy S. *Adirondack Forests, Fields and Mines.* Lakemont, New York; North Country Books. 1974.

———, *Water Over the Dam, at Mountain View in the Adirondacks.* Mountain View, New York; Vail-Ballou Press, Binghamton, N.Y., Printers. 1970.

LaBastille, Anne. *Woodswoman.* New York; E. P. Dutton & Co., Inc. 1976.

MacKenzie, Mary. *Newman.* Lake Placid, New York; Lake Placid-North Elba Historical Society. Undated. Pamphlet.

May, Edward L. & Edson, William D. *Locomotives of the New York Central Lines.* Irvington-on-Hudson, New York; Edson-May Publications. 1966.

Newport Bicentennial History 1776–1976. Newport, New York; Newport Bicentennial Committee. 1976.

Palmer, Richard F. and Others. *Rails in the North Woods. The "Peg-Leg" Railroad.* Lakemont, New York; North Country Books, 1973.

Paul Smith's College Catalog for 1973–74. Paul Smiths, New York.

Pitcher, Charlotte A. *The Golden Era of Trenton Falls.* Utica, New York; Firestine Printing House. 1950.

Press Summer Resort Guide. Utica, New York; Utica Daily Press. 1925.

Reed, Frank A. *Lumber-Jack Sky Pilot.* Old Forge, New York; North Country Books. 1965.

Seaver, Frederick J. *Historical Sketches of Franklin County and its Several Towns.* Malone, New York; J. B. Lyon Company, Albany, N.Y., Printers. 1916.

Shaughnessy, Jim. *The Rutland Road.* Berkeley, California. Howell-North Books. 1964.

Simmons, Louis J. *Mostly Spruce and Hemlock.* Tupper Lake, New York; Vail-Ballou Press, Inc., Binghamton, N.Y., Printers. 1976.

Stauffer, Alvin F. *New York Central's Early Power, Volume II.* Carrollton, Ohio; Carrollton Printing Company, Printers. 1967.

—————, *Steam Power of the New York Central System. Volume I.* Author. 1967.

Stoddard, Seneca Ray. *The Adirondacks.* Glens Falls, New York; Privately published. 40th Edition. 1910.

Thomas, Howard. *The Life of a Village, The Story of Prospect, New York.* Prospect, New York; Prospect Books. 1950.

—————, *Trenton Falls, Yesterday & Today.* Prospect, New York; Prospect Books. 1951.

Transportation in America. Washington; Association of American Railroads. 1947.

Wallace, E. R. *Descriptive Guide of the Adirondacks.* Syracuse, New York. 1894.

Wessels, William L. *Adirondack Profiles.* Lake George, New York; Adirondack Resorts Press Inc. 1961.

Whipple, Gurth. *Fifty Years of Conservation in New York State;* Conservation Department and New York State College of Forestry. 1935.

OTHER SOURCES CONSULTED

ANNUAL REPORTS

Annual Reports of the Forest Commission of the State of New York. 1891, 1893, 1894.

Annual Reports of the Forest, Fish and Game Commission of the State of New York. 1899, 1901.

Annual Reports of the Board of Railroad Commissioners of the State of New York. Passim.

Annual Reports of the Public Service Commission, Second District, of the State of New York. Passim.

Annual Reports of the State Engineer and Surveyor on Railroads of the State of New York. Passim.

Moody's Transportation Manual. Moody's Investors Service, Inc. Passim.

Poor's Manual of Railroads. Passim.

GUIDES

Official Guide of the Railways, New York; National Railway Publication Company. Passim.

Rand-McNally Official Railway Guide. Passim.

INDIVIDUAL COLLECTIONS

Adirondack Railroads Files of Howard Thomas.

Katherine Burnop Drury Scrapbook.

Linus Ford Scrapbook.

Mrs. Adelaide Grace Folts Palmer Scrapbook.

BULLETIN
> Bulletin No. 90. Boston, Massachusetts; The Railway and Locomotive Historical Society, Inc. May 1954.

PERIODICALS
> Adirondack Life. Spring 1975.
> Conservationist. Oct–Nov 1956, Apr–May 1961, June–July 1965.
> New York Central Lines Magazine. May 1928, March 1929, May 1929.
> The Northern Logger. June 1970, September 1970, December 1970, April 1971.
> Railroad Magazine. May 1940.
> Tower Topics. Utica & Mohawk Valley Chapter of the National Railway Historical Society. Passim.
> Trains. September 1950.
> York State Tradition. Winter 1965.

NEWSPAPERS
> Adirondack Echo. Passim.
> Boonville Herald. Passim.
> Herkimer Evening Telegram. Passim.
> Lake Placid News. Passim.
> Little Falls Journal & Courier. Passim.
> Malone Evening Telegram. Passim.
> Newport Journal. Passim.
> Newport Weekly Advertiser. Passim.
> New York Times. Passim.
> Syracuse Herald-American. Passim.
> Syracuse Herald-Journal. Passim.
> Syracuse Post Standard. Passim.
> Tupper Lake Free Press and/or Herald. Passim.
> Utica Daily Press. Passim.
> Utica Herald-Dispatch. Passim.
> Utica Observer-Dispatch. Passim.
> Utica Saturday Globe. Passim.

MAPS
> Adirondack Map. Conservation Department, State of New York. 1964.
> Adirondack Forest and Adjoining Territory. New York State. Forest, Fish and Game Commission. 1911.
> Franklin County Highway Department. 1976.
> Grant's Bankers and Brokers Railroad Atlas. 1891.
> Herkimer County Highway Department. 1973.
> New Century Atlas of Oneida County. 1907.
> New York Central Lines/New York Central & Hudson River Railroad Employee's Time Tables. Passim.

Oneida County Highway Department Map. Circa 1973.
Railroads in New York State. Board of Railroad Commissioners of the
  State of New York. Passim.
United States Geological Topographic Maps. Passim.